THE WORKING WOMAN'S HANDBOOK

How to Organize Your Life

Edited by Audrey Slaughter

CENTURY

LONDON MELBOURNE AUCKLAND JOHANNESBURG

First published in 1986 by Century Hutchinson Ltd,
Brookmount House, 62–65 Chandos Place, Covent Garden,
London WC2N 4NW

Century Hutchinson Publishing Group (Australia) Pty Ltd,
16–22 Church Street, Hawthorn, Melbourne, Victoria 3122

Century Hutchinson Group (NZ) Ltd,
32–34 View Road, PO Box 40-086, Glenfield, Auckland 10

Century Hutchinson Group (SA) Pty Ltd,
PO Box 337, Bergvlei 2012, South Africa

Set in 11/12 Times Roman
Printed in Great Britain by
Redwood Burn Ltd, Trowbridge, Wiltshire

British Library Cataloguing in Publication Data

The working woman's handbook.
 1. Success   2. Women——Employment   3. Women
 ——Life skills guides   I. Slaughter, Audrey
 158'.1'088042   BF637.S8

ISBN 0-7126-1213-0

Contents

List of contributors

Maggie Allen trained as a primary school teacher, and then spent three years running the *Observer* Picture Library. She found her way into journalism via IPC and for the past few years has been working as a freelance journalist for *Money Observer*, *What Investment*, *Working Woman* and *Your Retirement*.

Serena Allott has worked as a research assistant on the *Daily Telegraph* and for *Vogue*, including a spell as Shophound. She spent a year in the Far East and Kenya, working in Hong Kong as Assistant Editor for an American magazine and freelancing for the *Tatler*. She is currently assistant editor of *Working Woman*.

Carolyn Faulder started her journalistic career on *Nova* of which she became Assistant Editor. She has since specialized in health and career development subjects – she ran a Careers Guidance Service for *Nova* and then *Cosmopolitan*. Carolyn is the author of several books including *Cosmopolitan's Career Guide*, *Treat Yourself to Sex* (Penguin, co-author with Dr Paul Brown), *Breast Cancer, a guide to its early detection* and *Whose Body is it?* (both Virago).

Felicity Green has had a long and illustrious career on Fleet Street working chiefly for the national titles in the Mirror Group where she had overall responsibility for women's news and features. In 1970 she was named as Woman's Page Journalist of the Year. In 1973 she was appointed to the main Board of Mirror Group Newspapers as Publicity Director for all titles – the first woman in Fleet Street to reach board level.

More recently, her career has included a spell as Managing Director to the Vidal Sassoon Corporation in Europe, Associate Editor of the *Daily Express*, co-authoring a book with Mary Quant, teaching journalism at St Martin's School of Art and contributing editor of *Working Woman*.

Kathryn Samuel has worked on *Now* magazine, the *Evening Standard*, *Daily Mail* and *Flair* magazine as Fashion Editor. Since 1981 she has been working as a freelance fashion journalist and senior lecturer in Fashion Communication at St Martin's School of Art. She has edited a shopping guide to London and written *Dress For Your Lifestyle* for Marks and Spencer. She is Fashion Editor of *Working Woman*.

Audrey Slaughter (editor) Along with her husband Charles Wintour, she founded Wintour Publications which publishes *Working Woman* magazine, of which she is also editor and director. Previously, she helped to launch the *Sunday Express Magazine* as Associate Editor, was Assistant Editor of the *Sunday Times*, editing the *Look* pages, and launched and edited her own magazine *Over 21*. Audrey Slaughter has also edited *Vanity Fair*, worked as a columnist with the *Evening News* and as Editor of *Honey* magazine tripled its circulation.

Working Woman Magazine, 40 Fleet Street, London EC4Y 1BT. Tel: 01 583 2990.

Introduction

What does it take to get on in this tough old, competitive largely male-dominated world? Guts, brains, stamina. All of them, of course, plus the ability to seize an opportunity when it's up for grabs. Confidence, too, and a belief that just about *anything* is possible.

Those women who have made it in their careers are essential role models for those of us still scratching away wondering perhaps how to get started, how to get off the middle plateau. A small climb out of the ranks gives a slight sense of achievement but there's a disquieting feeling that we're underused, firing on three cylinders when we'd like to bring in the fourth. We feel our potential isn't being fulfilled. But these women are realising that today, a job has to be considered for *life*. Women are creeping up – not as fast as one would wish, but *moving*. There are more women in the work-force every year; more women entering the professions, industry, management and their impact will be immense.

Let's consider, for a moment, what has brought about these far-sweeping changes. It is currently estimated that by the year 1990 well over 60 per cent of married women will work and most women over forty will have to work whether they like it or not.

The last world war saw women being taken out of their pre-ordained domestic scene, dusted down, and told their patriotic duty was to keep the wheels of industry turning whilst the men were away fighting. Though many of the jobs were repetitive and dull, women enjoyed the companionship of other women. War work gave them a feeling of being needed too, but there was the added bonus of sharing a commitment with other women; work wasn't purely a pay

1

packet. After the war, they weren't so keen to be herded back into the kitchen. Besides, there was virtually full employment and the job world still beckoned.

At the same time, universities were losing their elitism to a certain extent. There were many first-generation under-graduates on grants. And teenagers found jobs were easier to find and comparatively well paid. They had economic in-dependence thrust upon them – and enjoyed the heady excite-ment of flat-sharing, disco-dancing, boutique-owning without parents breathing heavily down their necks. In addition, the birth control pill gave them control over their own bodies.

All these were far-reaching sociological changes. And as a result of breaking down the barrier which kept women at home, the opportunity to work outside the home and have economic independence, and the freedom to choose to have a family or not, meant that women began to toy with the idea of *careers*, as opposed to jobs.

Recession has reinforced social change, and now women are in the work-force in larger, more vociferous numbers. We *are* going to move onwards and upwards, but how fast? Have we shaken off completely our early conditioning? We still need to encourage women to aim higher, and believe they *could* achieve.

Too many women get on the bottom rung of the executive ladder and then plateau. Men, on the other hand, are invariably planning their next step. Women still want to be liked because they've been taught to please. They believe with ready smile and hard work, virtue will be rewarded and someone will tap them on the shoulder with the offer of a nice senior managerial job and matching salary cheque. But it doesn't happen like that. We have to join in the office politics, find out where the power lies (and it isn't necessarily with whoever has the major title) and make sure we 'sign our work' – in other words, ensure our efforts and achievements aren't hijacked by someone else. We have to be noticed in our own right though this doesn't mean being pushy or aggressive.

A young woman came to me because she was doing a study on women in business for her MBA. I asked her why she'd taken an MBA when she was, apparently, doing very well in her bank. 'Well, I was still one of the few females in banking and all the interesting work kept going to the men. I was working in Kenya for a spell, and a project was mooted around. It was so dull, none of the men wanted to do it, but I discovered it was the Chairman's pet project, so I volunteered. For the first time when I completed the project, I was noticed. And then I realized if I wanted to go further, I needed an edge – and I feel the MBA will put me one up on most men. At the very least, it will show I'm serious about my career and no training is ever wasted.'

She was clear-eyed about the hierarchy in which she worked. She played politics in that she knew the project she undertook would bring her the Chairman's attention, and she cast about for the next step. The next advantage.

Women suffer too because we shrink from the pejorative labels pinned on ambitious women. A man is called 'dominant', a woman is 'domineering'; a man is ambitious, a woman grasping. 'Ruthless bitch', 'hard-faced castrator' are some of the things women are called if they have their eye on the next promotion, whereas a man is admired for his whizz-kid tactics and confident assumption of superiority. 'Sticks and stones may break my bones but names will never hurt me' was a childhood chant, but names, or labels, *do* hurt. Having swum in the warm pool of peer group companionship and approval, many women are hesitant about taking a dive into the icy waters of senior management. It is lonely there – or lonelier. In fact it doesn't take very long to establish a new kind of rapport with a group on your level, though often it has to be outside the company – with customers or opposite numbers in other companies.

We aren't used, yet, to losing our diffidence, shaking off our childhood conditioning, or believing in ourselves and our own abilities.

Another big stumbling block to progress is, of course, maternity. Most women want a family, and unless they are on salaries high enough to pay for help or have a willing parent ready and anxious to look after the children, there's bound to be a career break which can be crucial in some cases. If you're a scientist or in information technology change is swift and it can be difficult to keep up, though at least as far as IT is concerned, Steve Shirley has proved it can be done. Founding a company called F-International, she plugged into all the trained women computer programmers who had left to have a family. It was a simple matter of working from computer terminals at home, and fitted in so well with family life that her company grew at a rate of knots. Funnily enough, the young mothers missed the companionship of working with people, so it was organized that a couple of days a week they'd work from a central office. Most women can find help to cover at least two days and Steve Shirley proved that with willingness, most obstacles can be overcome.

Despite the problems many more firms are enlightened now about the financial loss of valuable trained or experienced women employees and are making it possible for them to keep their hand in during the time they have to care for their small children, but there is a distinct lack of government initiative. There is the erroneous belief that if women stayed at home to look after their families unemployment would fall. Since most female jobs are in areas like shop assistants, catering and clerical work, there is hardly likely to be a male rush to fill posts such as these.

As women lose their diffidence, become more confident of their commercial value, and not quite so grateful for being employed at all, they will become more vociferous about the

4

need for good state nurseries. Facilities were created quickly and readily during the war when every town of any size had two or three 'day nurseries' and there is no good reason why a similar project couldn't be undertaken today. Britain needs every scrap of talent and skill going, and it can hardly afford to lose 50 per cent of that talent.

Surely the best way to get women to believe in themselves is for them to see how other women have managed it. Trail blazers are essential for the more apprehensive of us. You need, of course, the wish to get out of a rut; a woman who thinks like a typist, who is forever complaining about her lack of opportunity, her lack of education, the male attitudes that prevent her from getting on, is merely lazy and short on energy and initiative. She will always remain on the typist's chair. Setting oneself a goal means that even though you may not reach it, you get a lot further than you would if you'd never aimed at all.

Looking Good All Day Everyday

The organization of every aspect of your life – from how you dress and look to how you run a home and family, and even your finances – is surely the crucial key to success at work, at home and at play. Time spent considering how to make the most of yourself, analysing your strengths and weaknesses in all aspects, and planning ahead will help you to meet a challenge with energy and enthusiasm and enjoy your busy life to the full.

Planning a Working Wardrobe

Your clothes and you

No woman can afford to underestimate the important role clothes play in self-presentation. They may be superficial but they are deadly silent communicators that inform on you, sending out all kinds of clues about your personality, your taste, your life-style and even your capabilities. Does that sound too serious? Well, dressing *is* a serious business, and it's something we British have a very unsophisticated approach to. We tend to link clothes with 'fashion' rather than style. We think of fashion as a never ending string of gimmicks that demand we revamp our wardrobes every season at vast expense. We are not encouraged from an early age, as many other European girls are, to discover simple personal style, learn about colour, and distinguish between clothes that flatter our basic figure faults and those that enhance our good points. Of course, many women do eventually find their own parameters to being well-dressed, while others own a hotch-

7

potch wardrobe of clothes that turn dressing into a trying hit and miss affair. Some decide that a preoccupation with dress is frivolous nonsense and that what matters is the job itself, not appreciating that presenting an attractive, stylish image will help rather than hinder a career.

The phrase 'anything goes' is used endlessly when describing the current state of fashion. It is usually spoken with an air of satisfaction to sum up a situation where we have all been liberated from the dictates of arbitrary 'in or out' fashion, where we can, should we wish, dress like a gypsy one day and a cricketer the next. It's true. You can, should you have the time, the money, the confidence and the life-style. However, if you need a collection of clothes that can be relied upon to suit your working life and that make being well-dressed an effortless exercise each morning, it's time to re-instate some rules. Rules that will help you to plan a perfect wardrobe, guide your choice of clothes to suit your job, your shape and your colouring and help you to spend your budget where the returns will be highest. There are laws that shouldn't be broken if you are to live a sartorially blameless life!

Understanding fashion

The basic philosophy of your approach to dress should be to understand what is happening in fashion, appreciate the trends but never become a fashion victim.

Avoiding victim status, however, doesn't provide you with a carte blanche for a lapse into dowdy dress. It means rejecting the obviously short-lived fads, the fussy trims, the extremes of cut, the acting cupboard looks and the jokey, if not the witty, accessories. The vital aspect of fashion to appreciate is the changing proportions of clothes. Ignoring those proportions is the surest route to looking out-of-touch. Think back and remember how dated women looked who wore the mini skirt long after it was dead and buried. Recall the horror that greeted the Japanese designers' 'bag lady' look. It was extreme, but it altered everyone's attitude to proportion and attuned our eyes to a much looser and more comfortable silhouette.

Take a look at your own wardrobe and you may well

discover that the reason why you no longer feel enthusiastic about a perfectly good suit is that the armhole is too skimpy, the sleeve too tight and the shoulder line too narrow. These changes in proportion are rarely an overnight occurrence but a slow and gradual evolution – keep in touch with fashion and these changes will begin to infiltrate your wardrobe naturally season by season.

RULE NUMBER 1: WATCH FASHION FOR THE CHANGES IN THE PROPORTIONS OF CLOTHES
Don't get too hung up on new colours, fabrics or looks. Analyse a picture or an outfit in a shop window. Observe the overall silhouette:
- Are the shoulders the widest point?
- Is the emphasis on waist or hips?
- Where does the jacket finish in relation to the length of the skirt?
- What heel height balances the overall look?

Try it and you'll be surprised how simple it is to pin-point the essence of fashionable shape. Apply this knowledge to new purchases, to revamping existing separates, or simply to the decision of whether or not to eject some item permanently from your wardrobe.

Finding your style

These days to be called fashionable is almost an insult but to earn the label of being a stylish dresser is the greatest compliment. Style has become the watch word of the '80s.

It's virtually impossible to define style. It is an intensely personal quality which relates specifically to an individual and what looks good on one woman may well look disastrous on another. Style can sometimes be simply a case of dressing with 'good taste' and wearing well-cut clothes in good fabrics in a simple, uncluttered way. Style can be dressing adventurously to suit your personality, especially the extrovert type, and going against the tide of accepted fashion. Equally it can describe someone who dresses very classically with idiosyncratic touches like always wearing eye-catching glasses or marvellous ear-rings. Style is certainly something that belongs to women who dress with consistency. They understand the look that suits them best and they stick with it.

It is sometimes inferred that a grasp of style is a quality that is bestowed at birth to a select few and that those of us not blessed will have to endure a lifetime muddling along without this advantage. But like most qualities it is perfectly possible to acquire style – if you want it badly enough.

The very first step to discovering style is to pin-point your own personal look. Trust your own instinctive taste about clothes. If you have an outfit you always feel your best in and that wins you compliments, analyse its shape and mood. Perhaps you should base your style on that very specific look.

It may be a clean-cut, crisp and classic style of sharp tailoring or perhaps a softer, more obviously feminine mood where dresses or fluid knit separates provide the key. It may be a sophisticated style with elegantly sexy overtones, a sporty way of dressing with the emphasis on comfort and ease of movement or a romantic traditionalist approach where Fair-Isle knits and tweeds mix happily with lace collared shirts and suede skirts. It could be any of these or many more.

Don't ignore your personality when pin-pointing your look.

The wolf in sheep's clothing may have certain tactical advantages but the ideal is to match clothes and character. The shy girl, while she does not want to look mousey, can find herself in all kinds of uncomfortable situations if she dresses the part of the punchy extrovert. The extrovert, while she wishes to be taken seriously, can confound if she dresses with no eye for colour or excitement in her clothes. Clothes are an advertisement of personality and can be used to reinforce or disguise it if you wish.

Physical characteristics also affect that decision about style. There is little point in striving to be a willowy sophisticate if your body refuses to be anything other than short and curvy. Just as it's hard to turn a tall, big-boned girl into a someone who looks good in lace-trimmed chintz.

So mull over the style that not only suits your personal ideas and tastes in clothes but also compliments your physical attributes and your personality. How much of your wardrobe already measures up to that style? Perhaps approaching your clothes in this way explains why you have never felt entirely at ease or at your best in certain little numbers hanging there. Or it explains why you never have the right accessories for a certain dress or the right skirt to wear with a certain shirt – they don't fit in with the overall way you dress, or they simply don't do a lot for you. Once you have convinced yourself of this fact, be ruthless and get rid of the interlopers, the clothes that don't conform to your style, and send them off to a deserving cause.

RULE NUMBER 2: ESTABLISH YOUR PERSONAL STYLE
This is your first step to winning the ultimate acolade of stylish dresser.·But you must follow it through consistently. Don't lurch from shapely suit and high heels one day to baggy sweater dress and striped stockings the next. Don't confuse yourself by being Laura Ashley one minute and *Dynasty* the next.

Once you are at home with your look you can polish it to a truly stylish point with a confident hand. So often this is achieved by the way you accessorize your clothes. Keeping accessories to a minimum, with the emphasis on quality rather than quantity, is the classic course to style. Discard unnecessary jewellery, let one strong piece make the impact. Don't wear patterned or textured tights with anything but the plainest coloured clothes and shoes. Don't appear to be trying too hard with perfectly matched bag, shoes and belt, choose them to tone with what you are wearing.

But, above all, be comfortable in your clothes in both a mental and a physical sense. It's difficult, if not impossible, to look good if your shoes are giving you hell,' your middle shirt-button keeps popping undone or you wish you hadn't decided to wear that tartan beret with the pom-pom.

It's all in the colour plan

It must be the dream of every busy working woman to own a perfectly organized collection of clothes: one that is ideally suited to the life you lead and makes getting dressed in the morning a speedy and effortless action, one where your clothes form a co-ordinated circle so that no matter how many shirts are in the laundry basket there is still an ideal one to wear with that Prince of Wales check suit.

There is one very simple key to the perfect wardrobe, it's so straightforward a solution that many of us overlook it. The key is colour and preferably just one rather than a bunch. Choose just one colour, it should be favourite and one that suits your own colouring, and stick with that colour for all your major buys, making sure you have all your basic every-day clothes in that shade. By basic I mean a coat or jacket, a suit, a simple skirt, a good pair of trousers, several shirts and sweaters plus the essential accessories of shoes, bag, belt and tights. This way you will never waste time worrying about what can be worn with what because it will all work together in every possible combination.

When you choose your colour pick one that is literally a basic like black, navy, brown or grey. This scheme is a long-term plan that you will be adding to year after year and you will need to be certain that your chosen colour will never be out of fashion and out of the shops as might well be the case should you pick a certain shade of red or green for example.

Perhaps an undiluted diet of grey sounds a little dull and might need some variety from time to time if you are going to stick to it. It must of course. But when you branch away from your base colour make sure you pick a shade that will work well with it. Remember you are complementing the coordination plan rather than complicating it. Remember that as with all diets temptation will strike time and time again, but you must be firm with yourself if you are to achieve a collection of clothes that will all work effectively together.

RULE NUMBER 3: CHOOSE A BASIC COLOUR
This must run through all your clothes and you should remain faithful to that choice through thick and thin.

Finding your colours

Another element to discovering how to dress successfully is isolating which colours or which shades of a colour you should or should not wear. Often we are drawn instinctively towards those that flatter our own particular hair and skin tones, the deciding factors in whether a colour 'does' anything for you. But instincts can become fuddled sometimes by a particular shade being currently in fashion or by seeing someone else looking marvellous in a certain colour and wishing to gain the same effect when your own physical colouring is drastically opposed.

The science of colour is a precise one. All colours are either warm or cold, meaning that they are either yellow-based shades or blue-based shades. For example, all hues of brown and most greens are yellow-based colours, while pinks and reds, excepting the orange-reds are all blue-based colours. Working your way through the colour spectrum it is possible to judge in most instances which is a warm colour and which is a cold.

Now apply this to yourself. If you are a redhead with a golden or freckled skin or a deep blonde with honey-toned skin stick with all the warm, yellow-based shades. If you are blonde with a pinkish skin tone or a brunette with skin that ranges from porcelain pale to a true blue-black it is the cold, blue-based colours that will bring your skin and hair to life. Blondes obviously look better in the more delicate, powdery shades while darker-toned girls can wear the brighter stronger colours well.

That, very briefly, is the way to approach choosing colours to make the most of each individual. If you wish to delve further into the theory there are now many colour consultancy organizations which will assess your own shade spectrum more minutely, deciding whether you fall into their Winter or Summer categories (cold) or their Autumn or Spring categories (warm). They will then send you off with a wallet containing fabric swatches of your colours to be used as a guide to future choice.

RULE NUMBER 4: DISCOVER THE COLOURS THAT SUIT YOUR HAIR AND SKIN TONES

You can then make your clothes selection from within that spectrum. It will help prevent costly mistakes and prove invaluable at sale time when an undoubted bargain in terms of price, style and cut may turn out to be a personal dud simply because the colour doesn't suit you. Make sure your make-up shades correspond and bear in mind that if you change the colour of your hair you may well have to change the colour of your wardrobe. Allowing hair to go grey, however, usually only requires a softened approach to colour.

Now where did I put that. . . .

You can have the most beautifully planned selection of clothes but if they are not readily visible in your cupboards and drawers you will not get maximum mileage from them. It's surprisingly easy to forget you own a certain item if it is buried too deeply and you simply can't see it. So organize your storage space clearly, allotting specific areas or drawers for sweaters, shirts, undies and scarves etc, stacking or hanging clothes according to colour.

Don't cram drawers too tightly or squash clothes on top of each other in a wardrobe. They need space to breathe and will only crease if jam packed, undoing all that time saving work that has gone into careful colour planning by requiring attention from the iron every morning. It's a variation of Parkinson's Law that however much cupboard space you have your clothes will expand to fill it – so do have a weeding session from time to time. If you haven't once worn an item for over a year the chances are you never will. If it's too precious to jettison, pack it away. If it's still in a good state try selling it at one of the secondhand shops or sales that seem to be popping up everywhere and recycle the proceeds into something you will wear.

RULE NUMBER 5: ORGANIZE YOUR CUPBOARDS
CLEARLY AND SPACIOUSLY
Invest in some good hangers and always hang clothes immediately after you take them off so that the remains of any body heat will help any small creases to drop out. Never put clothes away that are in need of attention be that washing, dry cleaning or mending – it's too easy to forget the fact and infuriating to find them unwearable on their next proposed outing.

Proportional representation

What is a well-proportioned body? Most of us think in terms of bust, waist and hip measurement – the familiar old 34-24-36 syndrome – but these isolated measurements don't neccessarily mean perfect proportions. It's your height and build that are the key factors in deciding whether your body is a well balanced shape.

A good way of discovering whether your proportions are roughly ideal is to strip off and stand bare-foot in front of a full-length mirror. Arm yourself with a wipeable crayon and mark your height, the outside edge of your shoulder bone, waist and hips plus the position of your armpit. With a tape measure note the distances. Your shoulders should be 1 inch (2·5 cm) wider than your hips. Your waist should fall halfway between your armpit and your crotch. Your crotch should be equidistant from your height mark and the ground.

You can also measure your arm and if your elbow marks the middle and is also parallel to your waist, your proportions are perfect. The same applies to legs – your knee should mark the centre point.

It's a fairly arbitrary guide but if these measurements roughly tally your proportional problems are non-existent, even if in your heart of hearts you know your shape could be improved by more regular exercise or the loss of a few extra pounds. If, however, the measurements don't match up then you can pin-point in a positive way where your proportional difficulties lie and act to disguise or minimize the problems.

The two most common problems are the pear-shaped and

the top-heavy figures. Here colour can serve both shapes. Light colours 'advance' towards the eye while dark colours 'retreat' into the background. So a large busted girl can use this principle, wearing a dark top and a lighter bottom half. Conversely a big hipped girl can wear a light coloured shirt and a dark coloured skirt, to deflect the eye and balance the disproportionate halves. Bright, highly visible primary colours are also quickly registered by the eye and have much the same effect as a light colour.

Another useful trick to deceive the eye is the clever positioning of horizontal lines. Your eyes are trained to move slowly along the horizontal while quickly absorbing the vertical. A small person can make the most of their stature by wearing a lean, slim dress in one colour plus tights and shoes in the same shade – the look provides an unbroken line of shape and colour. Whereas a tall girl in the same outfit will look a veritable bean-pole. It's also the reason why horizontal stripes are usually fattening and vertical are slimming. Anyone with a pear-shaped or a top-heavy figure should take great care never to let a band of contrasting colour or the hem of a jacket or sweater finish at their widest point for this is where the eye will linger and digest its dreaded information.

RULE NUMBER 6: UNDERSTAND YOUR BODILY PROPORTIONS
Then you can learn to use the line and colour of your clothes to advantage.

The ingredients of a basic wardrobe

By now you should have a realistic approach as to how you can make more of yourself in terms of the colours you wear, the proportions you pick and your own personal style. Now it's time to consider exactly what are the key garments, based on the one colour plan of course, that go to make the perfect basic wardrobe.

1. COAT OR JACKET
Remember when choosing your coat or jacket to make sure that its style will work over the clothes in your wardrobe. If you wear a lot of differing lengths a jacket rather than a coat

16

eliminates proportion problems. If you are fond of wearing trousers be cautious about the style of coat you buy. Loosely structured mannish tailoring works best over trousers.

2. A SUIT
If your job requires that degree of formality you will probably need more than just one suit. Buy the best quality you can possibly afford in terms of fabric and make, if your investment is to last. Never wear a suit two days running – clothes need time to recover and regain their shape. Never buy a suit in a strongly fashionable cut, and avoid fussy trimmings; this way the suit will not have become dated long before the fabric wears out. Current fashion is now moving away from the baggy, mannish style for women's suits towards a more shapely, feminine look.

3. THREE SHIRTS OR LIGHTWEIGHT SWEATERS
It's difficult to beat a soft, fresh white shirt and everyone should own at least one. Lambswool or cashmere sweaters, either crew-necked, polo or with a small flat collar and three buttons, are currently a good look with suits and, being soft and knitted, extremely comfortable to wear.

4. A DRESS
Pick a style and fabric that with different accessorizing can work equally well for both day and evening wear. Wool crepe is an excellent example of a fabric that can bridge the gap.

5. A KNITTED TWO-PIECE OR A CLASSIC SWEATER DRESS
A sweater with its own matching slim skirt or a sweater dress can prove one of the most successfully smart ways of dressing for work. You win points on fashion terms and also for ease of movement and comfort. It's essential to buy good quality knits if skirts are not to bag.

6. EVENING SEPARATES
It is so much easier to cope with evening dressing if you stick to separates rather than a selection of dresses. Choose a basic black pleated crepe skirt or a pair of really well cut black velvet or satin trousers which can be worn with a bright silk shirt one evening, a beaded sweater the next, or a brocade

jacket on another occasion. Few evening functions are very formal these days so this approach should prevent you from feeling either under or over dressed.

7. TWO PAIRS OF SHOES
One pair of low/flat pumps and one pair with mid to high heels will cover your needs.

8. ONE BAG
This should be large enough to carry vital necessities without looking over stuffed. A bag with compartments helps.

9. JEWELLERY
This is obviously a matter of taste, but remember that often you can convincingly turn an outfit from day to night simply by substituting a stunning pair of ear-rings.

10. TIGHTS
You can give a much more fashion conscious look to your clothes by wearing opaque or patterned tights with a suit rather than flesh tones.

This is very much a skeleton capsule wardrobe, but as the experts say, everyone thinks they need many more clothes than they really do.

RULE NUMBER 7: DON'T CONFUSE YOUR LIFE BY OWNING TOO MANY CLOTHES
Ruthlessly weed out your wardrobe from time to time. Make sure the clothes you do own are working for you and that there are no missing links.

Getting to grips with shopping

It's all too easy to come back from a shopping trip having made some pretty useless purchases. The golden rule on how to beat the impulse buy is to know more or less what it is you need before you go shopping.

Shop early at the beginning of a season when the shops have the biggest and best selection of clothes. For summer this is in March and for winter in early September.

Discover the shops you know you can rely on to stock the style of clothes you like, where the assistants are not only pleasantly helpful but also well informed on what is happening in fashion and are capable of guiding your choice of clothes and the accessories you might wear with them. There is no quick route to making this discovery but time initially spent finding a favourite outlet will save time the next season.

Also get into the habit of looking at the labels of clothes so that you recognize the names of designers or companies whose clothes suit you. All designers have not only a handwriting that is distinctive but also tend to cut in a consistent way that makes their clothes either particularly suitable for a small person or a taller woman, for someone who has smaller shoulders or another with larger hips. For example, once you recognize that a certain designer's trousers are right for your shape they are likely to go on being so.

RULE NUMBER 8: GET TO KNOW YOUR SHOPS AND THEIR DESIGNERS

Planning the Way You Look

The idea that brains and efficiency are synonymous with a stark exterior died the death in the old movie where the hero removes the anonymous secretary's glasses, releases a tumble of hair from her scraped-back bun and breathes 'Why, Miss Smith – you're *beautiful*.' The message has got home because working women now spend three times as much on cosmetics and hairdressing as do full-time housewives. They know that in this competitive world, you must capitalize on every asset and that means putting your best face forward every day. Everyone can have well-kept hair and good make-up.

Finding your image

An argument isn't less strong because it has been made by a trim, well-groomed blonde – and she's less likely to be overlooked at a meeting than someone bulging in all directions with nondescript hair and a face entirely as Nature gave her. Nature makes so many mistakes it is legitimate to fight back with all that's available. Obviously no one wants to look

19

overdone, but even company accountants present their figures in the best possible light – short of cooking the books – so why shouldn't it be good business practice to present yourself as someone with sufficient brains to know how to handle her own packaging?

It's important, though, to preserve your own individuality, your own look. Plum eyelids and little-boy haircuts may be in one season, but if all they do is draw attention to piggy eyes and a heavy jawline, then opt for another variation that says 'now' but is more personally flattering. Even if you find a look with which you feel comfortable, review it every now and then. There are too many middle-aged women fluttering around who look like a faded snapshot of themselves when young instead of evolving a more confident, positive style as they get older, looking contemporary instead of believing they're holding on to their *jeunesse dorée*. If you have a good eye, can look at a large nose and thin, difficult hair dispassionately, and stage manage your good points, then you will probably be able to evolve your own look. Don't become so familiar with your looks that you don't even notice them.

Make-up changes every season, not entirely for frivolous reasons but as part of the total fashion look. And fashion isn't something happening in a vacuum but as a response to social change. Students of fashion can pinpoint the reactions to the world at large – nipped waists and full swirling skirts after the military precision of the war; fear of the future resulting in nostalgia, a clinging to the tried and true; the reality of space travel which spawned the white moon boots and pared-down mini dresses of Courrèges; it is all there and fashion is another way of expressing a view, of showing you know what is going on. Being stuck in old tweed skirts and dreary twinsets is not an indication that your mind is on higher things but that you simply aren't *aware*. Awareness is surely a key attribute in any valuable executive.

SEEK ADVICE . . .

Acknowledging you could do with some help is half way to solving your problems. Magazines love make-overs and they can sometimes help you achieve objectivity, but just as you need a solicitor or an accountant from time to time, so too can a beauty professional help with getting your looks under control. Look at the cover credits of the magazines you admire and see which hair and make-up artists continually crop up. Sometimes the make-up artist will give professional consultations, but the absolute cream are usually too busy to fit in many private clients. There are professionals who specialize in advice to the rest of us, and it is worth investing in at least one consultation if only to learn the right way to apply your make-up.

The big department stores throughout the country sometimes hold beauty seminars whilst some of the cosmetic houses train their sales assistants in make-up advice, but don't

put too much reliance on an objective assessment of your own features. You need someone with the time to do that, and time costs money. A 90-minute consultation with a professional will allow you to watch how make-up is applied, find out which colours suit you, and what little tricks to adopt to make eyes look larger, noses look smaller and generally balance up minus points with pluses. If you hesitate over the initial cost, think of how much beauty products cost today and how you will recoup the outlay by avoiding some of the more expensive mistakes.

... AND EXPERIMENT

If you live out of reach of expert help then you just have to learn to do it yourself. Boldness, a willingness to experiment, and keeping an eye on good magazines will all help your own expertise. The important thing to do is to be scrupulously clean with fingers, brushes and puffs. Don't dip grubby fingers into a pot of cream and then expect to blend magic over your skin. Apply with a barely-damp make-up sponge and wash after use. Use brushes to apply eyeshadows and blusher, and rinse them in a small bottle of carbon tetrachloride every two or three days. (Let them dry naturally in an open, airy place not in a drawer or cupboard.) Use puffs of cotton wool for powder and throw them away. Adopt the hygiene practices of a surgical operating theatre and you can't go far wrong.

Your maintenance plan

Once you are comfortable with your look, you need a maintenance plan. Most of us are too busy to spend hours in front of the mirror; anything that takes over 10 minutes is too long. This is where knowing your face and its shortcomings helps; you can slip into an automatic routine where cleaning is done almost unthinkingly, a film of cleansing cream or lotion followed by a swab of tonic-moist cotton wool to sweep away the last of grease and grime. You're ready for a moisturizer and foundation when your skin is greaseless and tingling slightly from the stimulus of thorough cleansing.

Cleansing is best done at the end of the day, naturally – probably two goes with a cleansing cream or lotion, or until the cotton wool looks clean. Then, a whisk with tonic – a mild one, whatever your skin type, or use cold water – and if you're going to bed, a quick massage with a nourishing cream just to counteract the effects of make-up, weather and pollution. Spend a minute or two stroking it in, with light upward movements (don't drag and stretch the muscles), until it is absorbed and the skin looks moist but doesn't feel tacky, and you can go to sleep without leaving the surplus on your pillowcases.

In the morning, splash your face with cold water, pat with a pad of cotton wool moistened in tonic lotion, and slide on moisturizer. At this point, bath or have breakfast to give your skin time to absorb the moisturiser.

Applying make-up

When you are ready you can apply foundation. Tip a little on a barely damp sponge and press it evenly over the skin. Take a little time to blend it smoothly and evenly – time spent on this stage means make-up lasts all day. Don't let a tide mark show at the edges of hair and jawline. Keep blending until skin and foundation are indistinguishable. Under eyes, in those dark sockets either side of the bridge of the nose, and perhaps round the nostrils, which often look pinker than the rest of the skin, use a slightly heavier touch-up stick a degree or two lighter than your skin tone. Most make-up houses do one, the best having a sponge-tipped wand for delicate application. The purpose of this is to light up the uneven colour and the dark patches of skin so that the whole facial 'canvas' is primed ready for the colour palette.

At this point you have to decide what you need. Someone with a high colour may need a little toning down, whereas the rest of us may merely look anaemic without carefully placed blusher. Again, blending is important. You don't want round blobs of colour on your cheeks, rather a subtle colour shading. Try smiling into the mirror and where the cheek bunches place a dot of colour and then blend upwards and outwards.

Apply eyeshadow next, preferably on a brush or sponge-tipped wand. For daytime keep to soft shades of grey or brown, irrespective of your eye colour and leave the more technicolour effects for later on. People with strong colouring can probably get away with deeper shades, but during the day it is safer on the whole to stick to soft enhancement. It used to be said that you keyed your eyeshadow to your eye colour until it was discovered that this had the effect of draining the natural eye colour, not enhancing it. Eyeshadow should be exactly that – shadow. Thin eyelashes look thicker if a soft line is drawn just behind the lashes – blur it with another streak of shadow over it. You don't want hard lines anywhere. Then, brush mascara through your lashes – again stick to brown or grey unless you have very dark colouring, in which case you can probably dispense with mascara altogether during the day. Just gloss your lashes with a little oil or Vaseline to dispel any clinging shadow or powder and leave mascara for evening.

Fair eyebrows may need a little pencil, but use short, slanting feather strokes simulating hairs rather than the ageing affect of a straight horizontal line. If you have well-defined brows just see that they're plucked into a tidy arc, groomed into submission with a little gloss, and leave them alone. There is no sense in wasting time on unnecessary jobs.

Lipstick can curve a mouth more prettily but the colour you choose is a matter of taste. Some people key their lipstick to their dress, toning or giving a flagrant flash of contrast. Others like understated lips, barely coloured and softly moist. Yet more prefer a darkish, flat liver colour which needs a certain sophistication to carry off. You must experiment yourself to find your own preference.

Finally, fluff on a film of light, translucent powder with soft cotton wool. Press it in with light tapping movements all over the face and neck, and then brush off the surplus with a fat, soft brush – a man's shaving brush will do. This sets the colour, and will postpone touching-up sessions, and keep you shine free. You may have to go over lips and eyeshadow again, just to bring the colour up, but it won't be necessary to re-apply. If you dislike a powdered finish, press a slightly damp tissue over the make-up again or spray with a fine mist of water. The whole operation from start to finish should take under ten minutes, once you've become deft and automatic.

SOMETHING MORE EXOTIC
Of course, in the evening you may want to achieve a more dramatic effect. You can get away with the glitters and golds and silvers. You can deepen the eyeshadows or go mad with daring colour schemes. You can thicken your lashes with mascara and heighten the flush on your cheeks, but be warned – the effect you want is exotic and glamorous not bizarre and pitiful. Strong make-up needs a confident hand and the style to carry it off. If you feel you're not centre stage material be content with merely emphasizing your normal make-up with deeper intensity – remember you're wearing make-up, it isn't wearing you.

Caring for your skin

Looking after your skin is vitally important, though it's not as much fun as playing with cosmetics. It means respecting your skin as a living, breathing organ. Skin is a marvellous substance, soft yet tough and resilient. It's thermostatically controlled, cooling you with sweat and warming you with shivers in the cold. Though it is so hardworking, it shows up neglect. Poor diet, extremes of heat, pollution, indifferent cleansing will all show eventually, in a lumpy, bumpy, scaly – even greyish – complexion that can't be hidden under a ton of make-up. Yet looking after it is another simple routine taking but minutes a day.

Diet will obviously affect the skin, as it will other parts of the body, but a well balanced diet with a good proportion of fresh fruit and vegetables, no sugars, little fat and only moderate alcohol is all that is needed.

SKIN CARE PRODUCTS
Thorough cleansing will take care of the pollution if you back up deep cleansing with a protective moisturizer and foundation. It is the extremes of heat that are the hardest to combat. In the desperate scramble for a tan, the skin is offered up to the relentless rays of the sun like a sausage to a grill, and roughly the same result is achieved. The skin toughens, darkens and dries up and whereas a sausage looks appetizing when it's brown and bursting, a complexion never quite regains its resilience and moisture. Gradually, over the years, a tough carapace is built up until in middle age people who have pursued the sun religiously look like battered alligator suitcases and at least ten years older than they are. If you believe a tan is the most desirable thing in the world do it gently, put back all the moisture you can, and don't bake away until you're done to a crisp. Colour gently, or take your tan from a bottle.

Cosmetic houses which used to be known for their colour ranges have all moved gradually into skin care products today because women have come to realize that a good, clear, healthy skin is probably more alluring – and certainly longer-lasting – than the latest paint job. It's good news for us because the manufacturers are so keen to compete for our custom that they maintain research laboratories with top chemists looking into ways of caring for the skin which will give them an edge over their competitors.

Do regenerative creams and lotions really work and delay ageing? Well, yes, they all work up to a point. They *won't* remove wrinkles; they *won't* restore elasticity to the skin; they *won't* take away the damaging effects of alcohol, an over-fatty or acid diet. Used regularly they will keep your skin protected from the drying effects of weather, central heating and low-humidity. It will be more difficult for the skin to pleat into tiny wrinkles, and those that have an exfoliating effect do seem to encourage a faster natural cell renewal, with the dead surface cells being removed leaving the skin baby soft and more translucent.

It is a good idea to use all the help you can get – or at least afford because these creams are not cheap. Thanks to more stringent legislation it is not possible for manufacturers to make wild claims that they can't support with evidence, so make sure you have read the labels on the jars and not just the advertising.

EXERCISE

The best beauty care of all, however, is affordable by everyone: exercise in the fresh air (and a daily walk to work or at least to the station or round a handy park at lunch time). Swimming, of course, if you can cope with all that changing out of wet swimsuits, wet hair, and crowded swimming pools, or running. Anything that whips up the circulation, increases your heart beat and your breathing is a complete beauty treatment. Glance into a mirror after a bout of exercise and you'll see what we mean.

Exercise is a way to combat stress and depression too – both bad for the skin. If you feel blue or worried about problems at work, go for a run or a brisk walk. Don't overdo it – you're not in training for the marathon – just walk briskly without stopping for a good half an hour *by your watch*, and you will be surprised at how much better you will begin to feel both physically and mentally.

The importance of exercise is more fully discussed in the following chapter.

DIET

It's amazing that people still don't eat properly when television programmes, newspapers and magazines are full of dietary advice. Watch people in the streets, in snack bars, in your workplace and you will be horrified at the way teeth are being sunk into fat sandwiches made from white bread filled with sweaty-looking ham or calorie-laden cheddar cheese, hamburgers and chips, chicken in batter, chocolate bars and doughnuts. Bakers' shops first thing in the morning are filled with cakes and pastries and by lunch time they're invariably sold out. All this stodge is responsible for the stolid bodies squashing you in tube trains in the rush hours, the suet-pudding complexions, the spots and bad breath that make rush hour travel so nauseating.

Eating sensibly is not the slightest bit difficult, though like everything else worthwhile it needs a little planning. If you haven't shopped in advance to have enough fresh fruit, salads, wholemeal bread available, then you can't help it if you have to send out for a useless sandwich just to fill a hungry void.

Once you've trained yourself in good eating rules, you become automatically selective and should not need to diet again, as long as calorie input is balanced by energy output. Tea, coffee and alcohol are the baddies, but life would be altogether too dull and worthy if we didn't do anything that was bad for us. The point is to have plenty of water – tap or mineral – on the lunch or dinner table and liberally space your wine with quaffs of water. So much office coffee is virtually undrinkable anyway that it shouldn't be difficult to substitute a herb tea – there are many to choose from and once you get used to the more delicate taste after the assault of caffeine or tannin, you will find them even more refreshing.

Learn which foods to avoid – the fatty meats like pork and beef. Substitute fish and poultry (except goose and duck) and offal like liver, kidneys, sweetbreads. Step up grains and pulses to give protein and fibre.

Don't bother about puddings. Raw fruit, a little yoghurt, or a low-fat cheese like Edam are much better for you. Make a big fresh fruit salad of citrus fruits and keep it sealed in a fridge so that you can breakfast on it or finish the evening meal with it.

Make your own muesli – it takes minutes to tip bran, porridge oats, and other fibrous cereals into a lidded plastic box, sweeten with chopped dried fruit like apricots and raisins, and add chopped almonds. It makes a good daily starter with yoghurt and some fresh orange or grapefruit juice.

Also see *Healthy Eating*, p. 44.

We know so much more about being fit and healthy today, that merely by following a sensible regime at the food table, regarding daily exercise as much part of your routine as bathing and teeth-cleaning, and keeping to basic hygiene rules, you needn't do anything else. Cosmetics are merely the products with which we highlight up our looks – they're not camouflage. With these rules, spots shouldn't appear and your skin condition – too dry or too oily – should gradually normalize. Persistent skin conditions like dermatitis or psoriasis are medical, not beauty, problems and so need a doctor.

Drip Dry Hair

As a new haircut will probably have the greatest effect on your 'look' you should consider getting an objective appraisal of your looks, and find a good hairdresser who will prune and re-shape your hair like a good gardener training a tree. Be brave enough to take his/her advice, decide whether you can afford the time and money to change your colouring, and then monitor new trends and your own evolving style just to keep up to date.

HAIRDRESSER – FRIEND OR FOE?
Making friends with your hairdresser is one of the very best professional moves you can make. Too many women are terrified of putting their looks so totally in the hands of another that they never make an appointment for anything but an occasional trim. Still others submit to whatever the stylist suggests, with regret. So if you want a new look, make a note of your best and worst features and your lifestyle before you make your next hair appointment, then discuss your requirements before the scissors get to work. Initially, your face shape is probably your most reliable guide to what is likely to suit:

- **Big nose?** Fullness around the face will help disguise it. Avoid swept-back styles and full fringes.
- **Short neck?** Keep hair clear of your shoulders. Consider a swept-up style or hair shaped neatly into the nape.
- **Receding chin?** Take the eye away from it via a short, wavy style.
- **Square jaw?** Avoid centre partings. Direct hair towards the face and don't keep hair too short.
- **Long jaw?** Keep hair above jaw length to avoid that horsey look. Aim for softness, perhaps via a perm.
- **Round face?** Avoid width at the sides. Try for some height on top or perhaps a short, straight bob. Waves around the face help break up the chubbiness.

And if you're not happy with the result of your cut, complain. Hairdressers, like most service industries, do actually want and need customer satisfaction. If you just walk out never to return you will suffer continual disappointment and could spend a fortune trying out new places. It's better to explain your disappointment, and give the stylist at least one more chance. To find a good hairdresser, personal recommendation can't be beaten. And keep your eye on the 'credits' given to hairstyles in magazines – you can always try the salon mentioned if you like their work.

HAIR CARE

But once you've done all that, you still have the upkeep. In any busy life, you adopt or adapt a style that fits in with the time you have available. Unless you have naturally curly hair or are prepared to spend time with heated rollers, the quickest, slickest way with hair is a good, straight bob.

If that sounds like something out of the 'twenties, think again. Those dramatic sculptured shapes adopted by Mary Quant and Twiggy in the 'sixties were simple to keep that way as long as the hair was clean and shiny. A trim every two or three weeks was enough to keep it shapely. It was so practical that we've kept a variation of it ever since.

Today we're moving away from the shaved necks and curly fronts of the schoolboy look into something more feminine and adaptable. Styling gels and lotions can help you achieve curls one minute, and pop under a shower and straighten it all out the next. But so much depends on the basic style – and the condition of your hair, its thickness and its quality.

Thin, fine hair is always difficult. You need a good cut and basic shape to make as much of it as possible, and probably a few rollers popped in before your bath in the morning so that you can lift the crown and give it a little bulk.

Coarse hair can be easy to handle, but it usually takes a curl too quickly and rolls into a muddle. Adopt a clubbed cut, where the underneath hair is slightly shorter, and the top smooths down with the ends rolling slightly under. Avoid perms because the hair tends to frizz unmanageably.

Shampooing can be done under the shower if you prefer a shower to a bath. Towel the hair dry by patting rather than vigorous rubbing, and when it is just damp, drop your head forward and brush up all the way round from the hairline. This helps the hair dry with a lift at the roots and gives it bulk.

Frequent washing can strip the oil off the hair shaft, so smooth it down again by rubbing a little conditioner into your palms and sleeking it over the hair. The hair shaft, the visible bit, is actually dead hair, covered in tiny scales rather like minute fish scales. Unless these are smoothed down with a soft bristle brush and the conditioner, they curl up like stale sandwiches – which is why hair can sometimes looks dry and lifeless.

KEEN TO COLOUR?

Dyeing, tinting, highlighting all can help nondescript hair but only if you can spare the time and money to keep it up. The DIY jobs rarely have the subtlety of professional colouring although if you're apprehensive you can experiment first of all with temporary colour rinses to gauge the effect. Until you feel confident about doing it yourself, however, put yourself in a hairdresser's hands. Dry, permed or sun-bleached hair all need special care if you are to avoid a too colourful result. The main colouring systems are:

- **Temporary rinse** – it washes out with your next shampoo so you can afford to experiment, whatever your hair type or colour may be.
- **Semi-permanent colour** – good on dark hair but cannot lighten fair hair. It lasts around six washes.
- **Permanent colour tinting** – as its name suggests, this is a fairly radical method of colour change. It uses hydrogen peroxide to strip out some natural colour, and a tint to deposit a new pigment; the result grows out over several months. This is best carried out by a professional; expect to need your 'roots done' every four weeks or so.
- **Bleaching** – uses ammonia with hydrogen peroxide to strip colour totally. An old-fashioned idea, not recommended by most good stylists and certainly not an idea for the home-grown amateur.
- **Highlights, streaks etc.** – this normally involves bleaching strands of hair to give life, movement and a rejuvenating lift to dull hair. There are various good DIY products on the market and there are no re-growth problems if the technique is done subtly.

PERMS

Today's perming systems are gentle, sophisticated and a blessing for hair that is fine, greasy or fly-away. On longer hair a perm may be less successful. For a busy working woman, a perm's wake-up-and-shake-it-out ability is a real bonus and many modern styles don't need anything like rollers or blow-drying to keep them in shape. But perming is a drastic treatment for hair. It breaks down the hair's molecular structure then 're-sets' it in a different form. So do ask a reputable hairdresser to tackle the job. Home perms are best left to those who can afford the odd disaster to their looks.

DIFFICULT HAIR

Dandruff is one of life's most taxing problems. It can betray you if you're the anxious type by trying to conceal your worries. But it can also be caused by excess grease in the scalp or your diet, sweating, poor scalp circulation or a dozen different disorders. Apart from eating properly, using a gentle shampoo and rinsing it out well, the best external control is a shampoo containing zinc pyrothione. Expect some slight greasiness afterwards, and revert to a normal shampoo when the problem has cleared.

Split ends are unmendable. Have them trimmed off, then watch the habits that could have caused them. Too vigorous brushing, broken combs, too much sun or bleach, over-heated rollers can all cause the trouble.

Any run-down condition and poor diet (there we go again) shows in the hair. Sometimes severe bouts of stress or emotional shock can bring about frightening hair loss. Treat it as a warning signal and try to face up to whatever you think is causing the problem, and do something about it. Once the problem is solved, you can return to emotional serenity, and the hair will grow again of its own accord. There is no need to rush to an expensive trichologist, though a visit to your doctor to make quite sure there is nothing fundamental wrong is a good idea.

Hair and nails are of the same basic material, surprisingly enough, and if your hair is out of condition you usually find nails are playing up too – flaking and breaking and ridging. Take these signals as the body's protest at its treatment. Check you're getting sufficient rest and relaxation. Are you worrying about your job, your family, a relationship? Are you badly in need of a holiday? Emotional and mental stress can pull you down perhaps more quickly than a physical illness if it goes on too long. If you have been eating badly, or skipping meals, try taking a course of multi-vitamin tablets or some B_{12} tablets.

Don't neglect the look of your hair. It can have a profound effect upon your general appearance and is worth a little time and trouble from you. You are busy, we know, but every woman deserves a little time and attention spent on herself.

Useful Addresses

London

COLOUR CONSULTANCIES

Colour Me Beautiful
35 Webbs Road, London SW11
Tel: 01 228 4103

Colours
289b King's Road, London SW3
Tel: 01 351 6754

MAKE-UP CONSULTANTS

Cosmetics à la Carte
16 Motcomb Street, London SW1 8LB
Tel: 01 235 0596
Lets you sample make-up, watch an expert and practise yourself.

Face Facts (Stephen Glass)
75 George Street, London W1
Tel: 01 486 8287

Face Place (Joan Price)
33 Cadogan Street, London SW3
Tel: 01 589 9062
Will also let you sample products and practice, and watch an expert
demonstration.

Harrods Beauty School
Harrods Ltd, Knightsbridge, London SW1
Tel: 01 730 1234

BEAUTY SALONS

Bath
Partners (Hair Salon)
10 Upper Borough Walls, Bath, Avon
Tel: 0225 66045

Two Flights to Beauty (Beauty Salon)
10 Upper Borough Walls, Bath, Avon
Tel: 0225 66045

Birmingham
Beauty at Charles Russell
56 St Marys Row, Moseley, Birmingham
Tel: 021 449 6051

She
12 Ethel Street, Birmingham
Tel: 021 632 6631

West End Beauty Clinic
415 Hagley Road West, Birmingham
Tel: 021 422 0568

Brighton
Steiner's Salon
Hannington's Department Store, North Street, Brighton
Tel: 0273 24774

Bristol
John Bristow Hair and Beauty
72 Whiteladies Road, Clifton, Bristol
Tel: 0272 738228

Nailsuns Beauty Salon Consultants (specialists in Nail Care)
68 Alma Road, Clifton, Bristol
Tel: 0272 732790

Edinburgh
Tau Skincare
14 Melville Street, Edinburgh
Tel: 031 225 2642

West End Beauty Salon and Slimming Clinic
26 Stafford Street, Edinburgh
Tel: 031 225 3337

Glasgow
Face Facts Beauty Clinic
49 Marywood Square, Glasgow
Tel: 041 423 6921

Dawn McClure
Taylor Ferguson Salon, 106 Bath Street, Glasgow
Tel: 041 331 1728

Manchester
Essanelle
Kendal Milne & Co, Deansgate, Manchester
Tel: 061 832 3414

Razor's Edge
24–26 Fountain Street, Manchester
Tel: 061 832 7747
and
12 Royal Exchange, Manchester
Tel: 061 832 7798

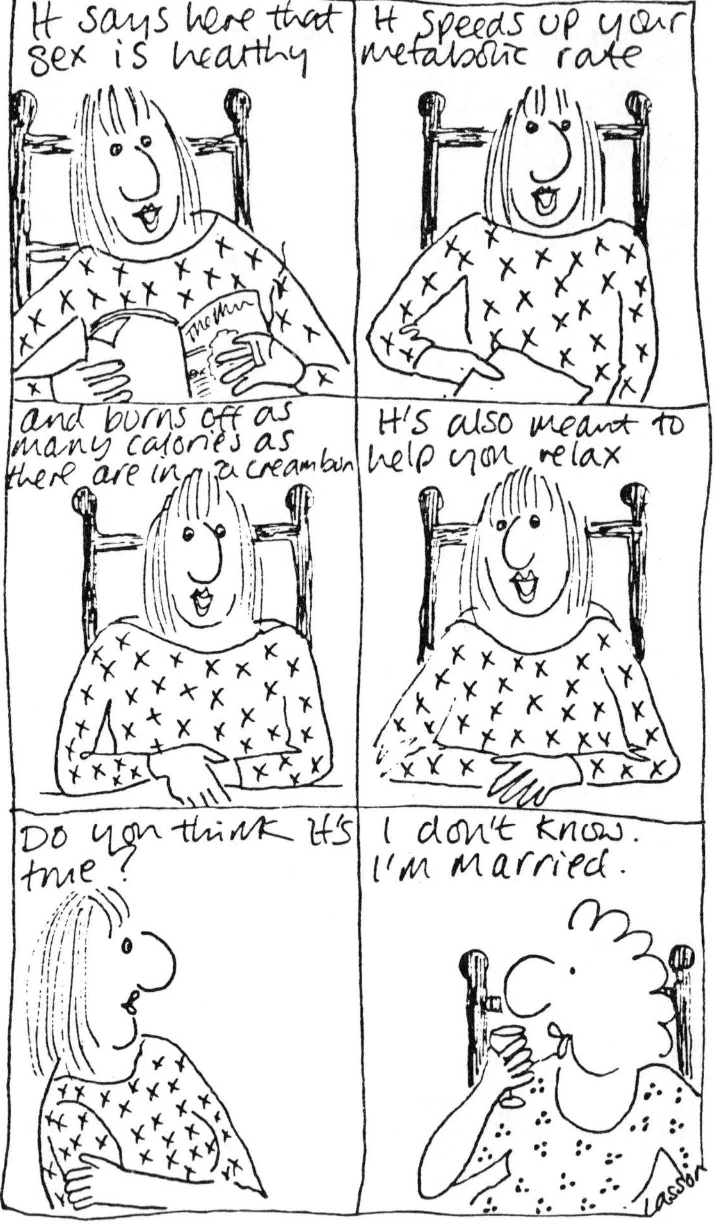
It says here that sex is healthy
It speeds up your metabolic rate
and burns off as many calories as there are in a cream bun
It's also meant to help you relax
Do you think it's true?
I don't know. I'm married.
Lasson

Your Health and You

You know when you are on top form. You feel good, look great, and enthuse all around you with your energy and optimism. Generally, you feel glowingly confident that you can meet any challenge. Work is an exciting adventure and you can't wait to get to grips with it each day. Your mind is agile and brimming with ideas and plans, your body feels so light and nimble it's almost airborne. Nothing is too hard for you. No one is too difficult.

To be in that kind of condition is to enjoy positive good health. It's an ideal state of physical and mental well-being, but how often does it happen for you? Most of the time, once or twice a month, a few times a year, or only occasionally after a long holiday or a spell at a health farm?

Positive good health is a state of being that not enough people enjoy enough of the time. It's surprising how unaware so many of us are about the way we live inside our skins. We allow ourselves to become out of touch with our bodies and then complain when they let us down. Women especially are far too adept at putting up with mild malaise, ascribing it to time of the month, time of life or too much to do, when maybe they should be asking themselves whether there is a recurring pattern or a link between certain situations and a specific complaint. Often it's only when a conscious effort is made to modify our lifestyle, taking more exercise for instance, or changing our eating habits, that we realize how wonderful it is to feel really well all of the time.

And even if, hand on heart, you can honestly swear you usually feel pretty marvellous, that doesn't mean you can afford to be complacent about your health. You may be lucky and be blessed with a sound genetic inheritance which has given you a strong constitution and a vigorous immune defence system. All the less reason for tempting fate by abusing your body with pollutants like cigarettes or over-indulgence in alcohol or driving yourself to the edge of a nervous breakdown because you're convinced you've got to be Superwoman.

Make a Personal Health Plan

As a working woman you're used to organizing your time to the best advantage. You probably know down to the last five minutes how you spend your working day, but have you carved out any private time for yourself in that busy schedule? To be at your best, strong and resilient, more than able to cope with the pressures of a demanding career and with energy to spare to enjoy a fulfilling private life, you need to work out a realistic physical and mental health plan which suits you and fits comfortably into your crowded programme.

Don't say you're too busy or that you can't be bothered with faddy ideas. Your good health is probably your most precious personal asset. You can't afford to lose it, so making a health plan is just as sensible as taking out a life assurance policy or investing in a pension plan. It's also more fun and costs a great deal less.

Look on it as you would any other project, something requiring careful thought and be prepared to do a spot of self-analysis. You are going to concentrate your mind on the *why* rather than the *what* you do and you may be in for some shocks. For example, you could find that with a little ingenuity you can dispense with or certainly reduce some work activities you had previously thought to be quite essential, replacing them by others that you enjoy more and still find yourself functioning more efficiently.

Preparing a Personal Health Plan

Work	Hours per week (average)	
Travel	9	
Office	45	
Home	12	
Out of hours (meetings etc.)	9	
	75	75.00

Pleasure/Leisure

Exercise routine	30 min.	
Organized exercise	1.30 min.	
Craft class	2	
Social life	8	
Concert/theatre/cinema	4	
Reading for pleasure	3.30	
Television	5	
	_____	
	20.30	20.30
	_____	

Chores/Duties

Cleaning/laundry (mostly over weekend)	5	
Household shopping	1	
Cooking	5	
Ironing	1.30	
	_____	
	12.30	12.30
	_____	

Sleep   49.00

Private time   11.00

                                                                        _____

                                                                        168.00

                                                                        _____

Charting your time

Start by looking back at your diary over the past three, preferably six months. Look at the illustration above and then take a
piece of paper, head it *Work* and note under separate
headings the average number of hours a week you spend:
- at work
- travelling
- at meetings
- giving talks or presentations
- entertaining clients
- doing other work related activities.

   Now, on another piece of paper headed *Pleasure*, jot down
the hours you spend a week on anything which could be
termed a leisure activity, for example:

- reading
- exercise
- gardening
- playing the piano
- watching television
- visiting friends.

Do the same with what can be classified as *Chores*:
- cleaning
- ironing
- shopping
- cooking, etc.

Add all these up and total the average number of hours you sleep in a week and how much time you spend eating meals.

There are 168 hours in the seven-day week. For a balanced and healthy lifestyle no more than 70 of those should be spent working and doing chores. If you allow work, however enjoyable it may be, to creep towards the 100 hour mark then you are putting yourself at risk. Should this be happening to you then you must ask yourself how far you have allowed your work life to take over your private life. Have you lost contact with old friends? Do you only socialize with people who might be useful to you in a work context? And what about your partner or spouse, your friends, your family? How much of your time do *they* get? Have you recently dropped a sport or a hobby?

Examine the details of your daily life. Draw a line down the centre of yet another large sheet of paper and head one column *Negatives* and the other *Positives*. Under *Negatives* write down anything you do or allow to happen to you which you know is detrimental to your good health. Here are some examples:

Negatives
- Are most midday meals a sandwich either snatched on the wing or munched, hunched over your desk?
- Is all the exercise you get walking in and out of other people's offices and jumping into taxis?

Positives
- How often do you read a novel or biography, see a film, dine with friends or follow a hobby – purely for your own pleasure
- How's your sex life – good, middling or practically non-existent?

40

- Are you cramming yourself with artificial stimulants like cigarettes, alcohol and coffee and then wondering why first you feel more stressed and then you end up feeling depressed and lethargic?
- Do you often go to bed with your brain spinning like a top and wake up feeling jaded and more exhausted than ever?
- Do you feel a bit like Sisyphus – always pushing the stone upwards only to have it rolling back on you?

- Are you doing at least one form of exercise or sport on a regular basis?

These are merely guideline questions, designed to jolt you into asking your own personal ones about yourself. And more will probably occur to you as you start filling in the columns, though you may be shocked to see which one turns out to be so much longer than the other. This, of course, is why it's so important to write everything down. Once you have committed the facts to paper, you won't find it so easy to go on fooling yourself. And it's only when you have got this information about yourself that you can start to create your own Personal Health Plan.

Your life is beginning to unfold before you. On another piece of paper write across it the following headings: *Diet*, *Exercise*, *Sleep*, *Personal Time*, *Relationships*. These are the five essential factors that have to be included into your Personal Health Plan. You don't need to be told how to recognize what's good, bad or lacking under each heading. For instance, if you have to write 'nil' under Exercise and 'not enough' under Personal Time you know you have a problem. That is all that's needed for this page – just brief comments about each of these areas of your life indicating what you feel about them.

On another page do the same under columns headed Physical Problems, Psychological Difficulties, Addictions, Bad Habits, Illness. These are the factors which prevent you

41

achieving positive good health and part of your plan will be to find ways of eliminating them.

When you have finished this inquest into your lifestyle – and be prepared for it to take a bit of time – put the whole thing on one side and sleep on it. Go back to it when you have had time to think about it and alter anything that seems wrong to you or add in whatever you may have forgotten.

Your Personal Health Plan

Now you are ready for the fun part of the exercise, actually devising your own custom-made Personal Health Plan. Rule off two pages marked up with the days of the week as if preparing a weekly diary and run off some photocopies because you are going to be doing a lot of re-ordering and re-writing before your Plan is exactly as you want it. (See example below.)

Begin by marking up all the current 'bespoke' time you have to spend at work, travelling, doing domestic chores etc. Now see where you can fit in some 'free' time for yourself either before, during or after the working day. You may not yet be very certain what you want to do with this time. It could be a vigorous lunch-time workout in a gym, a short break for relaxation, or learning a new skill like a language or a special kind of cooking, so at this stage just ring round the amount of time available *each day*.

During the week you may only be able to give yourself half an hour, say early in the morning or before you eat your evening meal, but at weekends you will surely be able to find more time, even if you do have to spend some of the time catching up on the chores. Be firm with yourself and find that quiet time for yourself in your daily schedule. Even a walk through the park on your way home from work is better than nothing at all.

If you are self-employed or mainly work from home you may find it quite hard to exert this self-discipline because working outside the ordered framework of an office life tempts you to think that if the time is there, then it should be filled 'productively'. You can overcome this problem by working strict office hours, 9 to 6 weekdays with short breaks through the day, but if there's a deadline to meet then you

The Working Woman's Personal Health Plan

Monday	Tuesday	Wednesday	Thursday	Friday	Saturday	Sunday
7.00 Wake up Drink glass hot water with lemon tea	7.00 As usual	7.00 As usual	6.00 Wake and read reports	7.00 As usual	Indulge yourself	Walk/run in country or park
7.15 Exercise routine for 15 min	7.45 Swim	7.15 Exercise routine for 15 min	7.30 Swim in hotel pool	7.30 Exercise routine for 15 min	Cook a super meal	Play tennis
Dress	9.00 Arrive at office	Dress	9.00 Day spent with clients	8.30 Walk through park to station	Entertain friends	Visit an exhibition
8.00 Breakfast		8.00 Breakfast		9.30 Arrive at office	See a film	
8.30 10 min walk to station		9.00 Catch train to North Company visit				
1.30 Wholemeal sandwich lunch, with apple and mineral water. Read newspaper Relax in chair for 10 min	1.00 Business lunch	1.00 Business lunch	1.00 Business lunch	12.30 Lunch meeting	Read a novel right through	Telephone neglected friends
6.30 Meeting with clients 1 glass white wine	5.30 Spanish lesson	6.30 Arrive in hotel	5.30 Train back to London	6.00 Meeting		
8.00 Dinner out with work associates. Choose light meal and drink sparingly	8.00 Dinner out with friends	6.40 Read reports for 30 min	Spend evening relaxing	7.30 Turkish bath and massage		
		7.10 Relax for 10 min		Supper at home		
		7.30 Dinner with clients		Watch TV		

43

could work the waking hours, including weekends, and give yourself time off in lieu when the rush is over.

Working mothers undoubtedly have more problems in this area than anyone else. Forget about that polite euphemism 'dual role'; a mother with a career and young children has two full-time jobs to cope with and she needs all the help she can get, if she is not to be torn apart by worry and guilt. Pay for as much reliable, responsible assistance as you can afford and see that your partner or husband takes his fair share of parental responsibility. You did, after all, decide together to have children, so bringing them up should also be a mutual activity as far as possible.

The single working mother is even more burdened and her problems are likely to be exacerbated by financial worries. Join a group (like Gingerbread) which organizes special rate holidays and other facilities for single parents and will put you in touch with your local group.

Whatever your personal situation, beware of falling into the trap of thinking that once you have worked out the time-table for your Personal Health Plan that's how it must stay for ever. Inflexibility and obsessiveness are the enemies of good health because they prevent you from being able to relax. Longterm, if you allow yourself to be dominated by the demands they create, they could eventually cause you serious ill health. If you know you are prone to suffer from these personality traits, the sections dealing with stress and relaxation will give you some useful pointers for keeping them under control.

Now read on for some ideas and ways to improve your health care.

Healthy Eating

'You are what you eat' is a truism always worth repeating. Quite simply, if you eat the right foods, you will feel well, you *are* well and everything benefits – skin, hair, nails, eyesight and teeth. You will also feel much more alert mentally. Food is the essential fuel which builds your body, keeps it in good running order and energizes you. A healthy diet must include a balanced intake of the following elements: proteins, fats, unrefined carbohydrate, salt, fibre and water, plus vitamins and minerals.

Adult human beings consume approximately one pound of food in dry weight per day, that is about 500 grammes. A reasonable average daily calorie intake for a healthy and energetic woman is about 2000 calories. What nutritionists call the *prudent diet* contains these elements in the following proportions:

Protein 10–12% of total daily calorie intake – 220 calories, 50 grammes.

Fat 30% of total calorie intake of which not more than 10% should be saturated fat (butter, lard etc) – 600 calories, 67 grammes. The remainder can be divided between poly-unsaturated (sunflower and similar light cooking oils) and monounsaturated (olive oil).

Carbohydrates 60% of total calorie intake – 1,180 calories, 295 grammes. *Simple* carbohydrates consist of refined sugar (sucrose), fructose (fruit sugar) and lactose (milk sugar) and single-sugars such as glucose and fructose (in fruit and honey). *Complex* carbohydrates include the starches to be found in grains, cereals, vegetables and some fruits. At least half our carbohydrate calorie intake should come from the complex form.

Fibre Between 25 to 50 grammes.

Water At least two pints daily.

Minerals The major ones are calcium, phosphorus, potassium, magnesium and sodium. They are stored in the body and amount to at least 5 grammes. Trace minerals such as zinc, sulphur, chromium and iodine are found only in minute quantities but any deficiency will cause problems.

Unless women make sure they drink enough milk or consume sufficient dairy products (yogurt, cheese) and eat sardines and certain green vegetables, they are liable to become deficient in calcium. A recommended minimum daily intake of calcium is 800 mg, which in pregnant and post-menopausal women should be increased to at least 1000 mg.

Vitamins Vitamins A, D, E and K are fat soluble, stored in the body and measured in international units (IUs). The B complex and C are water soluble, excreted daily and measured in milligrammes.

Recommended daily vitamin allowance for women

Vitamin	Allowance
A	4500–5000 IU
D	400 IU
E	20–25 IU
B₁	(Thiamine) 1.0–1.1 mg
B₂	(Riboflavin) 1.3–1.5 mg
B₃	(Nicotinic acid) 12–16 mg
B₁₂	(Cyanocobalamin) 5 mg
C	40–50 mg

(All these amounts need to be increased for pregnant and lactating women.)

Vitamin and mineral requirements vary with each individual and depend on your age, your sex, the climate you live in and how efficiently your body metabolizes its input and the stresses to which it is being subjected. For a fascinating description of what vitamins do and where they can be found, read Patrick Holford's book *Vitamin Vitality* (*see* Books to Read). Before spending extravagantly on food supplements, do his health check in chapter 9 to see what, if anything, extra you need. Then follow his guidelines for deciding how much extra that ought to be.

Translated into eatable reality all this means plenty of fresh wholefoods including cereals (avoid the processed breakfast variety), pulses (lentils, peas and beans of all types), nuts, fruit and vegetables. Eat as much raw food as you can – a wholemeal sandwich with lettuce, and fresh prawns or cottage cheese washed down with a glass of mineral water at lunchtime is far tastier as well as being better for you than warmed-up pub grub with a glass of beer or acid white wine. Red meats and animal fats in the form of dairy products or fried foods should be eaten sparingly, and refined, sugary foods like cakes, sweet drinks and most tinned and packaged foods should be avoided at all costs. Quite apart from being full of useless weight-gaining calories, these convenience foods also contain toxic additives like chemical preservatives, colourings and drugs which actually deplete your body of its stored nutrients. Too much tea, coffee, and alcohol have the same effect. Try some of the delicious blends of herb teas now available and drink plenty of bottled water to flush out the toxins from your kidneys.

Be aware that even the apparently fresh fruit and vegetables you buy from your local greengrocer may have lost a good deal of their goodness by the time they reach your shopping basket. They will have been sprayed with pesticide in the growing stage and may have lain around too long picking up lead pollution from the passing traffic and losing their vitamin content. Buy organically grown produce whenever you can and thoroughly wash the fruit you eat raw.

We have no way of knowing how much of the meat we consume has been injected with growth hormones and anti-biotics. Instead, eat more fish which is a good source of protein, rich in essential minerals, feeds the brain and, according to recent research from Holland, plays a significant part in reducing heart disease because it contains a certain polyunsaturated fat which reduces the amount of cholesterol made in the liver.

The United Kingdom has the world's highest annual death rate from heart disease (1 in 20) and the proportion of women in that toll is increasing. A recent report on 'Diet and Cardiovascular Disease' produced by the Committee on Medical Aspects of Food and Health Policy (COMA) has estimated that the British diet includes an animal fat intake which is *25 per cent* in excess of our dietary needs. A high fat diet is also suspected as a cause of many cancers (including breast). Too much refined sugar and flour is a contributory factor in many other degenerative diseases like arthritis, respiratory problems, mental illness and various digestive complaints like ulcers and diverticulitis.

Don't think you have to turn yourself into a nut cutlet cum fibre freak to eat healthily. And don't imagine that it's going to take you hours you haven't got to shop and cook for such food. All it needs from you is a little determination to change bad habits and an investment in one or two good vegetarian cookery books to give you some new ideas. Turn to the 'Cop-Out Cook' section (p. 103) for ideas for delicious recipes which are quick and easy to prepare, and healthy as well.

The great advantage of improving your diet is that you, and those around you, will swiftly notice the changes. The years will drop away as your skin clears, your eyes brighten and your hair shines. You may not have realized how chronically run down you were until the lethargy and listlessness lift. You will find yourself less prone to mood changes, irritability, headaches and colds. Even severe premenstrual tension can be relieved by overhauling your diet.

Unfortunately, doctors receive minimal training in nutrition so when patients, especially women, present themselves with symptoms such as these they tend to assume depression and hand out the tranquillizers. If you think you need more specific dietary information to cope with PMT or a suspected food or chemical allergy turn to page 77 for useful addresses and recommended reading.

A second advantage of balanced healthy eating is that it enables you to maintain whatever is the right weight for you in the most enjoyable way. If you eat enough fibrous fruits and vegetables and whole grains you won't need to sprinkle wheat bran on your soups and stews, too much of which can cause flatulence and irritation to the bowel. Fibre has no nutrient value but it's important because of what it does. It makes food pass quickly through your system thus eliminating dangerous toxins and reducing the risk of potentially harmful bacteria; it's also useful as an appetite appeaser.

Don't be fooled by the latest low calorie diet or miracle weight reducing plan. Certainly you will initially lose weight (mainly water) by cutting down your calorie intake, but since you are putting your body onto starvation alert you will also lower your basic metabolic rate which means that food converts much less quickly and your organs will function less efficiently, resulting in loss of energy and concentration. Other side effects of a crash diet, particularly the kind which allows you to eat only one or two foods, can be dizziness, fainting, a sense of weakness and an increased vulnerability to various infections.

Faddy diets of this kind basically don't work because ultimately they either make you feel so ravenously hungry that you go on a binge and put everything on again, overloading your digestive system at the same time, or your metabolic rate slows down so much that even the little you have trained yourself to eat is too much for your body to convert into energy and body building so it gets laid down as fat. Meanwhile you are depriving your body of many essential nutrients. A doleful cycle indeed.

If you really need to lose weight for health reasons, and it appears that one woman in four in this country is overweight, then there is only one way to set about it. Cut out salt and the refined carbohydrates – all sugar and white flour products – reduce the animal fats, and give up alcohol.

And do some regular exercise!

Get Moving

You may think it's pounds you need to lose but take a good look at yourself in the mirror. If what faces you is a saggy tummy, flabby arms and heavy thighs (one, all or more) then you're obviously not in peak condition. Your new improved diet needs to be supplemented by regular exercise of some sort which will firm up your muscles, tone up your circulation and make you look slimmer and more shapely, even if your weight stays much the same. It doesn't really matter what the scales say and certainly not what your friends *say* they weigh. It's how you feel that counts.

Exercise does more than improve your appearance. Using your body to its full capacity, making forgotten muscles work again and discovering how pleasurable it is to move lightly and

be so much more in touch with yourself enhances your sense of well-being, mentally as much as physically.

Exercise is a marvellous stress-reliever because it uses up the substances which our body mobilizes to deal with any threatening situation but is not always able to disperse naturally. For example, if you have to take what you consider to be an unfair rebuke from your boss you may outwardly meekly accept the blame while inwardly seething at the injustice. You have been obliged to suppress your anger and with it, all those energizing elements which in less 'civilized' circumstances would have enabled you to hit out or yell at him, or her. Unused, these compounds silt up our system, making us feel tired, anxious or even quite severely depressed. If this type of situation is repeated too often it can lead to serious illness. Heart disease and, it is now thought, even some cancers may be caused by excessive stress.

Exercise is important throughout your life. For post-menopausal women it can help to prevent the onset of osteo-porosis. Insufficient calcium in the diet aggravated by a diminished supply of oestrogen causes the bones to become porous and weakened. If neglected, this ultimately leads to loss of inches, the 'dowager's hump' and those distressing fractures of hip, wrist and spine, so common to old ladies. Exercise has the effect of aiding calcium retention and it stimulates the reproduction of bone cells.

Regular exercise also helps some people to reduce or stop their smoking altogether. Once your heart, lungs and blood have been thoroughly oxygenated, the idea of clogging them up with nicotine and tar becomes less appealing.

So what exercise should you do?

Posture and Body Awareness

Standing Orders
There are many permutations of bad posture, here are two of the most common ones.

The tensed-up sergeant major stance with chest thrust forward and knees pushed back. The weight cannot fall evenly through the legs and feet so posture and movement are very badly effected.

Just as harmful, the pelvic droop with lax abdominal muscles and a hollow back.

Standing Tall
The correct stance.

Feet: stand with the feet hip width apart. Sway forwards onto the balls of your feet, then back onto your heels. Now stand at the mid-point between the two where your weight falls just in front of your ankles and spreads out evenly through the pads of your feet. Keep your arches lifted and your toes long. *Knees:* very slightly bent. *Pelvis:* centre your pelvis. For most people this means doing a very small pelvic tilt (see below) so that your pubic bone in front lifts a little and your back lengthens. However, if you are one of the few people who hold your pelvis in an exaggerated tilt all the time then you will need to move your pubic bone downwards and create more of a hollow in your back. *Ribs:* lift your ribcage upwards away from your hips to flatten out your tummy and to allow space for easy breathing. *Shoulders, neck and head:* make sure your shoulders are directly above your hips then pull your shoulders down away from your ears. At the same time, keep the puppet on a string image in your mind an imagine that the top string in the middle of the crown of your head is being pulled upwards. The result will be that you will feel a lengthening in the back of your neck. Think of this movement as the Three Point Pull – i.e. crown of the head upwards and both shoulders down. Repeat the Three Point Pull regularly throughout your day, it is a very useful postural adjustment.

The Pelvic Tilt
The correct tilt of your pelvis is the basis of good, balanced posture and movement. This is because the pelvis is our centre of gravity and the heaviest part of our bodies. So if the pelvis is correctly balanced there is a very good chance that the rest will follow, particularly if you remember to do the Three Point Pull regularly also.

The Pelvic Tilt is also the basis of all effective tummy strengthening exercises – if you don't do it you will be practising a paunch during tummy work instead. Of course, you can tilt your pelvis in several directions but the movement where you lift your pubic bone upwards is usually referred to as *the* Pelvic Tilt because it is such a useful postural adjustment (see above Standing Tall). Practise it on the floor first to get the feel of it.

Lie on your back with your knees bent and feet on the floor hip-width apart. Place your hands on your tummy. Breathe in. As you breathe out press your back into the floor and press your tummy in gently with your hands to get the feel of how it should sink into the pelvis during this movement. Breathe in and release. Repeat a few times. Don't worry if you feel you want to breathe in the opposite way at first. The correct breathing will come naturally with practice. Just remember that it makes sense to breathe out when you pull your tummy in tightly so it is completely deflated of air and can flatten as much as possible. Develop the Pelvic Tilt into an exercise to strengthen your abdominal muscles as this will help to correct posture further.

N.B. If you normally hold your pelvis in this exaggerated tilt the don't practise it. Instead practise lifting your back off the floor a little and hollowing it.

Curl Ups
Use the same starting position as for Pelvic Tilt exercises but place your arms by your sides. If this exercise strains your neck put one or even two pillows under your head. Breathe in. As you breathe out tuck your chin in towards your chest, do a pelvic tilt and curl upwards sliding your hands up your thighs. Eventually, try to touch your knees. Breathe in and rest. Repeat 4 times at first and work up to 12 slow repetitions. When this gets easy cross your arms over your chest when you curl up to make the exercise stronger.

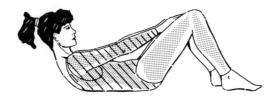

You can also use the Pelvic Tilt as part of an exercise to strengthen your buttocks – another essential aid to good posture.

Buttock Squeezes

The same starting position. Breathe in. As you breathe out do a pelvic tilt, squeezing your buttocks tightly together and lifting your hips off the floor. Lift your head tucking your chin in at the same time. Breathe in and rest. Repeat 4 times working up to 12 repeats gradually.

Support system 1

Sitting pretty means sitting up straight. Slump at your desk and your muscles slump with you. Standing tall is only half the battle. Sitting tall can be equally important. Good posture starts off with getting the right chair. Beg, borrow, steal, demand or even buy a chair that supports your lower back.

Support system 2
Below. Even when you're driving, posture is paramount. If your driving seat offers less than total comfort, supplement its support with a firm cushion to bolster the lower spine and help to alleviate the strain on your neck and shoulders while driving.

A minimum home workout

Try to do it three or four times a week or use the first three exercises as a warm up before stronger exercise.

STRETCHING
To energize you and to get rid of tension and stiffness in your neck and shoulders.
   Start with your feet comfortably apart. Do a pelvic tilt to ensure that you don't tighten your back, and raise your arms above your head, stretching upwards for all you're worth. Then think of climbing up a rope so you lift one arm higher and then the other, several times. Breathe well as you do this. You should feel the stretch right down to your hips.

Now brush your arms past your ears, push them on backwards, lower them and bring them forwards. Repeat the arm circles several times, breathing in as you lift the arms and out as you lower them.

Stretch regularly in your daily life:
- In bed
- Sitting at your desk
- Reaching up to the lintel of a doorway and swinging your body gently through (remember to do a pelvic tilt)
- After relaxation
- After driving

CURLING AND UNCURLING
To mobilize your back.

Round your spine, bend your knees and lower your head forwards as though you were buckling having been punched in the tummy. Go on lowering your body forwards until your hands touch the floor. Uncurl slowly straightening the knees last of all, then look up. Repeat several times.

When you are used to the movement, try breathing out on the way down and in as you come up if this feels comfortable.

You can also do this movement sitting.

KNEE BENDS AND RISES
To strengthen your thighs, calves and balance.

Take your legs further apart and turn them outwards so your knees and feet face outwards. Bend your knees (checking that they are over your feet and not in front of them). Straighten your legs. Rise up on your toes then lower your heels. Repeat the sequence several times until your legs begin to tire. Finish by balancing up on your toes for a few moments. Pull your shoulders down and lift the crown of your head as you do this. Also, correct the tilt of your pelvis. Breathe easily.

If your thighs are weak and flabby always try to walk up stairs two at a time (and don't hold on to the bannister, make your thighs do all the work). Also, when you walk wear sensible shoes so that you can stride out parting your thighs and making them work.

TWISTS AND SIDE BENDS
For your waist and to mobilize your spine.
Kneel with your thighs hip width apart. Fold your arms and lift them to shoulder level. Do a small pelvic tilt and hold your abdomen in tightly throughout the exercise. Twist round to one side, looking behind you, and continue twisting round in small further movements three times. Return to centre.

Check your pelvic tilt and tight tummy muscles then repeat to the other side. Repeat from side to side several times.

Still on your knees, lower your arms to your sides and bend from side to side touching the floor with your fingertips if possible.

'THE CAT' AND 'THE DOG'
To mobilize your pelvis and use your tummy muscles.
'The Cat'
Go onto all-fours. Position yourself well – wrists under shoulder and knees under hips. Hump the back of your waist up towards the ceiling allowing your head to curl in. Breathe out as you do this and pull in your tummy as tightly as you can. Clench your buttocks too. Breathe in as you flatten your back and look up to the ceiling. Repeat slowly several times.

'The Dog'
In the same position, waggle your hips from side to side turning to look at each hip as you waggle it.

LEG RAISING LYING ON YOUR FRONT
To strengthen back, buttocks and thighs.

Lie on your tummy. Put one hand flat on top of the other and place your forehead on your hands. Do a small pelvic tilt and maintain it throughout the exercise. Raise one leg keeping it straight. Aim to lift the front of your thigh off the floor a little way, but do not lift your hip. Lower and repeat with the other leg. Repeat several times checking that you are maintaining your pelvic tilt in between each lift.

Curl up into a ball to stretch out your back when you have finished. When you are in this comfortable foetal position, take the opportunity to relax and breathe easily.

N.B. No woman's exercise programme is complete without giving attention to your pelvic floor muscles. If you don't know where these muscles are, next time you pass urine try to stop the flow midstream. It is the pelvic floor muscles that you use to do this. You should be able to cut off the flow without any dribbling. If you can't, then your pelvic floor needs attention. The exercise you do is just hauling up the muscles inside you regularly (as you did when stopping the flow of urine), at least 20 times a day. You can do it anytime, anywhere, so there is no excuse. The ultimate test of a strong pelvic floor is if you can jump up and down with your legs apart, coughing at the same time, and not a trace of a leak appears. You need a strong, sensitive pelvic floor:

- To avoid stress incontinence
- To avoid prolapse of the womb
- To improve lovemaking
- During childbirth
  You can exercise your pelvic floor:
- Walking
- Sitting
- Lying
- Waiting
- When brushing your teeth

Go for the fun . . .

And forget about the burn! But don't push yourself *beyond* your limits. Advice to do precisely this has been responsible for sending a lot of unfit and badly taught people limping out of their aerobic classes, some injured for life.

A good exercise programme will give you strength, stamina and suppleness. Swimming is excellent because it wraps this all up for you in one session, and without danger of injury as the water supports your muscles, but to get the benefit you must do it continuously and as fast as you can for at least 20 minutes. Most people find it easier to do a combined programme; for example, a run twice a week, wearing good shoes, to built up stamina, plus some exercises at home or in a gym or with a Yoga teacher for suppleness and strength.

Tips for choosing a good class or gym

- Ask how long the teacher has been teaching and where he or she has been trained. An untrained amateur can do a lot of damage.

- If you are a beginner say so. A good teacher will keep an eye on you and not make you do unnecessary repetitions.
- The teacher should ask you whether you have any history of back trouble, illness or joint problems.
- Make sure that the class starts with warm-up exercises (bending, stretching and rolling) to loosen your limbs and get your body thoroughly oxygenated. These exercises are also essential before starting any strenuous sport, a game of tennis or squash for instance.
- Don't join a class which is obviously overcrowded. There will not be enough supervision – or enough room to move.
- Make sure the routine is varied and flexible, adjusting to students' needs.
- Ask to be shown how to take your pulse.
- Aerobics done barefoot jars your spine and can cause a lot of problems – you should be asked to bring a pair of running shoes.
- *Always* stop before the strain, otherwise you run the risk of damaging your muscles.

I joined a gym. I must go there sometime.

Whatever exercise you choose, do it because you enjoy it and not because you're reminding yourself all the time through gritted teeth, 'this is doing me good'. It won't actually be much use to you if you're punishing yourself mentally and you certainly won't stick at it for long. So if you find jogging a bore or aerobics embarrassing or cycling to work through the traffic terrifying, *don't do it*. Find something you do like enough to persevere through the aches and pains which you must expect at the beginning until you get fit.

If you are one of those people who are put off by all forms of organized exercise because it reminds you of beastly cold winter days running round the hockey pitch in an Aertex shirt and gymslip, then try to find some alternative activity, preferably outdoor, which you can do with gusto. Gardening or walking the dog both count. And here are a few suggestions for getting more movement into your everyday life.

- Walk up tube escalators
- Take the stairs instead of the lift at your office
- Walk to the shops
- Walk two shops beyond your nearest bus stop
- Get off those high heels and stride instead of trip

Stand Tall

Most of us carry heavy briefcases and have adopted shoulder bags that get stuffed with ever more unnecessary things – a full make-up kit, a wallet bulging with credit cards, diary, notebook, and a purse which, thanks to the pound coin, is weightier than ever. As a result, most of us have one shoulder hunched somewhere near our ear to counterbalance the other weighed down with trappings.

A bad posture has a serious as well as unattractive side – it can lead to all sorts of orthopaedic abnormalities which in time produce discomfort and pain and even permanent disablement. The alternative isn't to try to achieve a stiff, military stance as though you've been put through your paces by a Sandhurst sergeant major, but to visualize your body as a puppet on a string. Pull the head string, pull your shoulders down away from your ears and centre your hips and your body falls naturally and easily into place, a long fluid line as one bone supports the next. 'Biomechanics' the specialists call it, and basically it means the analysis of body movement in mechanical terms, with medicine, physics, and engineering all behind the theory.

No amount of exercise will be of benefit if the body is out of balance. 'Straight leg lifting can be particularly bad,' says Jo Pickin, resident physiotherapist at the Pineapple Dance Studios. 'Lying flat on the floor, lifting the legs straight up, is designed to strengthen the abdominal muscles. But because these are initially weak, the movement tilts the pelvis instead, causing a hollow back and hyper-tensing the lower spine. Sit-ups with straight legs hooked under a bar can also strain weak abdominal muscles.

So what is the correct way to work out, biomechanically speaking? The simple answer in both cases is to bend the knees, release the pull on the back and put more strain on the abdominal muscles (see diagrams).

Even standing still has its posture pitfalls. There is a definite difference between the biomechanical idea of good posture and that of the standard 'military' definition. The famous Alexander technique encourages posture improvement by making you aware of your bad body habits before teaching you the good ones. Instead of thinking of yourself as a pile of crumbling vertebrae with the head on top, try instead to visualize the body suspended by a thread from the crown.

Good body movement is never a static business. Rather it involves having an easy sense of equilibrium. 'One of the greatest problems of sedentary workers is the amount of time they spend immobilized,' says Jo Pickin. 'The body isn't well designed as a static unit. When they're not working, muscles relax and thus gradually put a strain on the ligaments.'

The answer to long hours of deskwork, he suggests, is to get into a routine and repeatedly sit upright, then relax. 'Constantly adjust yourself,' he says. 'Adjusting your seat to the right height and having a chair with a mid-back rest is not enough. You need to bring the body into a standing position even when sitting down.'

It sounds awkward, but nowadays there are chairs designed to do just this. The Balans chair, designed in Norway, inclines the body forward, bending the knees and thus bringing the pelvis into the proper position. You can simulate the action by sitting with your chest close to your desk, moving your body forward to the front edge of the chair and bending your knees while keeping your back straight.

Young children often adopt this position naturally when they first learn to sit on chairs. Sadly they're often dissuaded by anxious parents saying, 'Don't rock forward like that, you'll fall off.' Little do the parents know that infant wisdom is simply searching for the most natural and comfortable position it can find.

Posture points

- If you're deskbound, or on a long plane journey, take frequent breaks to go for short walkabouts.
- Sitting puts twice as much strain on the back as standing, so if you are driving for long periods, constantly shift your position.
- Whether you're standing or sitting, try to work at a height that means you don't have to bend the lower back.
- When you're doing the chores, bend from the knees or hips and keep your spine as straight as if you were standing. According to the experts, bending from the lower back is a major cause of strained, aching muscles.
- Kneel down to lift heavy weights – including children.
- Wear flat or low-heeled shoes when constantly on the move. We've all seen that undignified Disneyland waddle stilettoing its way down the street.
- If you jog, don't use a backpack or hand weights. These only transmit their load through the body and result in unnecessary strain. And try not to run on hard surfaces. Long-term degenerative damage can result from jogging on concrete.
- Taking a course of supervised exercise, tailored specifically to your needs, is still the best way of exercising the body biomechanically. In a good gym you can learn how to strengthen the body without strain and, most important, you can observe when you are misinterpreting an exercise.

Sleep Easy

People vary in the amount of sleep they need but it's thought that probably five-and-a-half hours is the minimum that people can get by on without feeling exhausted and deprived. Many people find it impossible to function with less than eight. You may be one of those lucky people who can sleep short for several nights on the trot providing eventually you are able to have a good long lie-in. The more relaxed you are the less sleep you will need. It is the worriers and those who are under some kind of severe emotional strain or having to meet intense intellectual demands who need more, yet it is of course precisely these people who are not able to get enough good quality sleep because they are too tense and over stimulated.

Sound sleep is absolutely crucial to good health. It is the time when babies and children do their growing and when adults rest their bodies and refresh their minds. It remains a largely mysterious function although we know that it is cyclical and that these 90-minute cycles consist of distinct and distinct phases. First, there is the deep sleep stage when our heart rate slows down and our breathing becomes deep and even. It is followed by the REM (rapid eye movement) stage which lasts for about 15 minutes and this is the time when the body systems are on alert and we do most of our dreaming. We then sink back again into the deep sleep and so on through the night. We need about one-and-a-half to two hours of the light REM sleep each night in order to keep us mentally alert.

Food and exercise both have an effect on the quality of our sleep. A heavy meal late at night followed by tea or coffee full of stimulating caffeine is unwise for anyone; if you have a tendency to insomnia you should make a point of eating a light protein-based meal early in the evening and drink a calming cup of camomile tea just before you go to bed. Some people find that strenuous exercise late in the day disturbs their sleep. There are others who swear that a run round the block last thing at night is the ideal prelude to a good night. And we shouldn't forget the virtues of sex – whether it's what Mrs Patrick Campbell called 'the deep peace of the marriage bed' or 'the hurly burly of the chaise longue'.

Tips for insomniacs

- First find out why you can't sleep. Noise – traffic or a snoring partner? Buy earplugs. Too hot? Too cold? Adjust the bed coverings but try to sleep with an open window as you will wake feeling much fresher.
- An uncomfortable bed? Buy a well-sprung new one and if you have a sleeping partner choose a bed which is independently sprung. If you have any back problems get one with an orthopaedic mattress. Alternatively be really daring and get a waterbed. Addicts swear by them.
- Try not to worry if you are going through an insomniac phase. Read a book, drink a cup of warm milk, write that letter which is hanging over you. A temporary period of wakefulness is not going to damage your health. It's better to try and solve the problem naturally rather than resort to sleeping pills which tend to deprive you of your essential REM sleep and therefore make you feel dozy and un-refreshed the next day. They can also be habit-forming.

If the problem is more deep-seated, then it may be because you have allowed yourself to get into a state of chronic exhaustion. Feeling tired at the end of a long hard day is healthy when you know there's a comfortable bed inviting you to drop into a deep undisturbed sleep for all the hours you need. It's your body's signal warning you that you've passed the peak of efficient functioning – your system has had enough and now it needs to be switched off and given a chance to recuperate and recharge its batteries.

But once you start ignoring the signals of natural fatigue by driving yourself over the top and into the downward curve of exhaustion you are running yourself into danger with ill-health round the corner and eventually, if you go on for too long, a breakdown. Your body uses fatigue as an in-built device to control your arousal response to the tensions and conflicts you cannot avoid meeting. If you override your 'fatigue check', which is rather like the thermostat on a central heating system, this means you will physically have to expend much more energy to stay in the same place, thus depleting valuable reserves. You will also be pushing up your arousal response to an artificially high level from which it becomes progressively more difficult to descend to normal.

The Gentle Art of Relaxation

Some people are never off the boil. In their waking hours they are hyper alert, hyper tense, and hyper impatient. Small setbacks are seen as major frustrations, encounters with colleagues swiftly turn into confrontations, and they drive themselves and their subordinates through punishing schedules and then look for more. They cut down their sleeping hours and because they are operating on a perpetual 'high' of adrenalin such sleep as they have is fitful and unrestorative. They have become addicted to stress and so have totally lost the precious health-giving ability to unwind and relax. If, as is so often the case, the addiction is compounded by an unhealthy lifestyle (drinking too much, smoking, and bad eating habits), then they are turning themselves into prime candidates for all manner of stress-related ills.

This is a thumbnail sketch of the type A personality which two Americans, Dr M. Friedman and Dr R. H. Rosenman, first defined when they were studying the behaviour patterns of patients with coronary heart disease. If you recognize yourself in this description then it's high time you took yourself in hand. There are now alarming indications from other research studies to show that high-flying working women who exhibit these characteristics – especially those who combine family responsibilities with their career – may be *twice* as prone to coronary heart disease as their male colleagues.

Bad habits can be unlearned and replaced by good ones but it's not enough to change your behaviour; you have to change your attitudes and to do that successfully the type A person must be convinced that relaxation is not a waste of time. It will enable her to function more efficiently.

It is important to make people understand what is going wrong with their body and then learn how to integrate that knowledge into their lifestyle. Relaxation is not something you do once a week in a class and then forget for the rest of the time. It has to be something you do all the time, at odd moments at home and at work, in fact whenever you find yourself in a stress-producing situation.

Obviously you can't immediately lie on the ground, kick off your shoes and sink into a self-induced trance every time you feel threatened by stress. This kind of deep relaxation is a skill which is best learnt under personal guidance but, once acquired and you have made it a daily habit, you can then train yourself to take snatches of relaxation whenever you feel yourself becoming tense. All it takes is a deep slow breath in and out to the count of ten – *before* you pick up the telephone or *as* you see the traffic lights changing through orange to red. It sounds a simple enough technique but it does need quite a lot of practice before it becomes an automatic reaction and it also requires a fair degree of self-analysis to recognize the situations which cause you particular stress.

Unless you are very skilled, deep relaxation is probably best done listening to a tape, either of dreamy music or someone talking you through it.

Deep relaxation method

Here is a simple description of the deep relaxation method. Lie down on the floor in a darkened room where you know you will not be disturbed for half-an-hour. Cover yourself with a blanket and make sure you are warm and comfortable. Lie with your feet 18 inches apart and your arms resting quietly by your side, palms upwards. In yoga this is called the *Savasana*, corpse position. Take a deep breath, hold it for a count of three, and let it out slowly. Continue breathing this way throughout your relaxation.

Start by thinking of your feet, your toes, the soles of your feet and all the tiny bones in your feet. As you picture them with your mind feel the tension draining out of them. Now move to your ankles, then your shins, calves and knees, all the time thinking of what each part looks like and enjoy the heavy warm sensation creeping over you as your muscles relax. Move slowly up your body to your shoulders, then slowly down your arms to the tips of your fingers. By now you will be feeling drowsy and very relaxed. Consider your neck, your chin, your cheeks, eyes and forehead. Feel the tension ooze away, soothing out the lines. Let your lips drop apart and your tongue rest gently behind your teeth. Think of nothing but your delicious state of relaxation. You may even drop off to sleep so have a gentle alarm clock to wake you. When you are ready, give a big yawn, roll slowly over to one side and get up quite gently.

An alternative method is to do the autogenic training which is, in essence, a westernized adaptation of eastern meditation techniques. It involves learning some relatively simple mental exercises which enable you to focus your mind on various bodily sensations. It is particularly effective for anyone suffering from mild anxiety states but you don't have to be ill to enjoy the benefit of this method and it can be done very quickly (ten minutes only) at odd moments of the day. (See 'Useful addresses' for details of training centre).

Relaxation techniques, including transcendental meditation and biofeedback, can work as energizers for healthy people working at full stretch, as much as they can be therapeutic for those who are already suffering from stress-induced illness. They are not, however, advisable for someone whose chronic exhaustion is a symptom of *clinical* depression as opposed to the ordinary 'fit of the blues' we all feel from time to time. Clinical depression is an illness which needs specialized treatment. If you have any doubts about which particular category you fall into, you should consult your doctor first.

Managing Stress

Stress has potential for both good and ill. If you can learn to harness stress to your energies instead of allowing it to consume them, you can then make stress work to your positive advantage. The point where stress turns into *dis*-stress is different for each one of us; as with pain, we have our own individual stress endurance thresholds. To cope with stress you have to learn to recognize when you are approaching that threshold and what it is that triggers *dis*-stress for you. Otherwise stress will become a negative and corroding factor in your life; unchecked, it will ultimately make you seriously ill.

The Stress Triangle

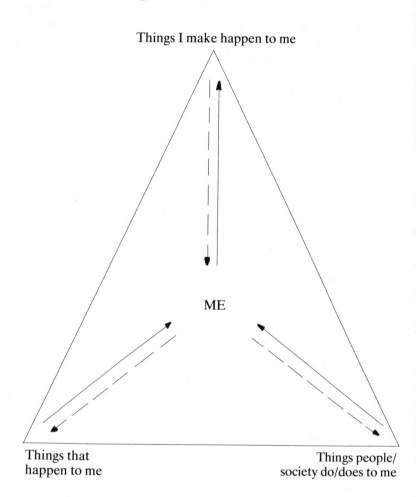

Things I make happen to me

ME

Things that
happen to me

Things people/
society do/does to me

Looking at this triangle you might think that you can only do
something about the statement at its apex – 'Things I make
happen to me'. Is it really possible to change the way other
people behave to you (right), especially where you have no
personal relationship with them? And what about 'things that
happen to you' (left) which again are mostly beyond your

1. **The things I make happen to me**
   e.g. Take on too much work
   Choose the wrong job
   Marry the wrong person
   Set myself impossible goals
   Relate badly to other people therefore cause a bad/ hostile reaction

2. **The things other people/society do/does to me**
   e.g. Make demands on my time, attention and emotions which I find difficult to meet
   Frustrate, bully or exploit me at work
   Make me unemployed
   Oblige me to live in bad housing, over-crowded environment
   Mugging/burglary/rape

3. **The things that happen to me**
   (a) My life cycle – birth, childhood, adolescence, maturity, ageing, sickness.
   (b) Life events – school, choice of a career, travel, marriage, parenthood etc.
   (c) Life events over which I have no control
   Major
   e.g. Accidents
   Bereavement
   Minor
   e.g. Getting onto a slow train
   Not finding what I want in a shop

---

control? (The dotted line in the illustration indicates the rebound effect of stress.)

Not feeling in control is a significant cause of stress for many people; for others, who are in controlling positions, the stress comes from fearing that they are not up to the responsibilities they hold. This simple triangle illustrates the dilemmas we

71

face when we try to manage our stressful situations. The way to approach the problem is to put the stressee before the stress-inducing factors; in other words, the 'me' at the centre of the triangle. Were it not for that central dot – the unique 'me' at the heart of my own life – the triangle wouldn't exist.

To manage stress you must start by trying to understand the kind of person you are. Look again at the list you made of positive and negative factors about your lifestyle when you were preparing your Personal Health Plan. Consider your 'problem' page and ask yourself why it is you have those particular problems. If you want a more detailed psychological profile of yourself consult the books on stress management listed on page 81 which are full of helpful quizzes and check-lists.

Rating the stress in your life

Now consider some recent or forthcoming events in your life. Every life event is a life changer to some degree. And change is always stressful to some extent because it forces us to change ourselves, and try to adapt and adjust to the new situation. Some people thrive on change and may take on more than they can handle; others are scared of fairly minimal changes in their daily schedule because they feel they won't be able to cope with the upheaval. The lucky ones are those who enjoy change but also know when to blow the whistle and can stop.

There's no good or bad about this, it's just a question of personality, but it is sensible to learn to pace yourself. If you have done your homework properly you should have a fairly clear idea of your stress-endurance threshold. Now look at this list of life events and tot up your own personal score for things which have happened to you in the last 12 months. The mean value figure stands for the number of life change units calculated per event and indicates the degree of stress that accompanies it.

Use your score as a guide only but if it frequently tips over 150 do be careful. You may be putting yourself over your stress-endurance threshold. Try to anticipate future stressful situations and, where possible, space them out. And do give yourself a bit of leeway for the unexpected bolt from the blue.

The Social Readjustment Rating Scale (Holmes & Rahe, 1967)

Mean value	Life event
100	Death of spouse
73	Divorce
65	Marital separation
63	Imprisonment
63	Death of a close family member
53	Personal injury or illness
50	Marriage
47	Being fired at work
45	Marital reconciliation
45	Retirement
44	Change in behaviour or health of family member
40	Pregnancy
39	Sexual difficulties
39	Gaining new family member
39	Major business readjustment
38	Major change in financial state
37	Death of a close friend
36	Changing to a different line of work
35	Change in number of arguments with spouse
31	Taking out major mortgage or loan
30	Foreclosure on a loan or mortgage
29	Major change in work responsibilities
29	Son or daughter leaving home
29	Trouble with in-laws
28	Outstanding personal achievement
26	Wife begins or stops work outside home
26	Beginning or ending school
25	Major change in living conditions
24	Revision of personal habits
23	Troubles with the boss
20	Major change in working hours or conditions
20	Change in residence
20	Change to a new school
19	Major change in recreation
18	Major change in social activities
17	Taking out small mortgage or loan
16	Major change in sleeping habits
15	Major change in number of family get-togethers
15	Major change in eating habits
13	Holiday
12	Christmas
11	Minor violations of the law

73

Stress and the working woman

There is no doubt that working women encounter additional stress for some or all of the following reasons:

- Sex discrimination – either in job recruitment or when seeking a promotion.
- Being a token woman which means that tremendous pressure is put on them to perform outstandingly.
- Work relationships may be difficult to establish because of prejudiced attitudes. Older men, specially those who have non-career wives, may find it difficult to accept a woman as a colleague; younger men may not enjoy having a woman in a position of authority. Other women, particularly clerical and secretarial staff, may object to working for a female boss.
- Sexual harassment.
- The dual role and all the problems it brings of combining a career with a family life.

No doubt you can think of other stressful situations from your own personal experience but don't regard them as insuperable. Instead, think of ways of handling them. Join a woman's group or network. Seek out a mentor at work to give you advice and encouragement. Learn a new skill.

For example, if you have trouble saying what you want, you might consider doing a course in assertiveness training. Being assertive is not the same as being aggressive. The assertive person is someone who knows her rights and is prepared to stand up for them, yet is prepared to concede that others have them too. Assertiveness means being cool, calm and persistent about stating those needs. It means being able to deflect aggressive responses from others without either wilting or becoming defensive.

Changing your behavioural patterns gives you a chance to grow within yourself and once you have acquired certain basic techniques of assertiveness and plucked up the courage to practise them in real life, you immediately feel that you are a better, more competent and self-confident person. Problem-solving and decision-making no longer hold the same terrors (and therefore stresses) for you. If the trainer is good you will acquire valuable insights about yourself which will stand you in good stead always.

How to meet the challenge of stress

- Identify your areas of particular vulnerability.
- Know who you are and accept yourself for what you are. Willingly take on responsibility for yourself.
- Resolve to correct your thinking and attitudes. Modify your behaviour and, if necessary, learn skills to manage your stress.

Keeping a Health Check

It's a good idea to keep your own medical record. Use it to remind yourself when you had certain injections; your re-actions, if any, to antibiotics; your history of illnesses – major and minor; the types of contraception you have used and for how long: the date of your last cervical smear; your menstrual record; any unusual changes in your health. Should these last persist, see your doctor.

Remember to examine your breasts every month. The best time is immediately after your period. Either stand or sit in front of a mirror so that you can see whether there are any changes in skin texture or shape of your breasts. Another good place is in the bath when you can feel your breasts with soapy hands. If you do find anything unusual, *don't delay*. Go to your doctor at once. Nine out of ten breast lumps are harmless but if yours should prove cancerous you have a very good chance of being cured if it is caught early. Early de-tection also makes it more possible to save the breast. A small lump can usually be cut out, together with some surrounding tissue, and leave practically no scar or change in the appear-ance of the breast.

Ask your doctor to check your blood pressure annually, particularly if you smoke, are on the pill or there is a history of high blood pressure in your family. Some companies offer their executives an annual health screen and it's well worth while accepting if the offer comes your way. You will get a full range of function tests – eyes, hearing, lungs, heart etc. Women are additionally offered a gynaecological examin-ation. However, don't imagine that because you have been given a clean bill of health once that means you will be all right for ever. To be effective, screening once started must be kept up and you must be psychologically prepared that one day something may reveal itself which will need further treatment.

Purely for Pleasure

Don't forget that life is for living and laughing as well as for working hard, making money, and getting to the top – if those are your aims. You love your job, you are ambitious, you are determined to be successful – that's all wonderful – but don't be so single-minded about your career that you crowd everything else out of your life to accommodate it. Be generous to yourself and guard jealously the time you keep for yourself, your private life and the people you care for. Cultivate other interests which are right outside your working life. Otherwise, quite frankly, you will become that most boring of creatures, a workaholic who can only talk shop.

This is the moment, in making your Personal Health Plan, when you sit down and do a bit of quiet thinking about your personal priorities. Maybe everything is not as good as you would like it. You feel you have got yourself into a bit of a rut; you are so busy coping with the everyday demands of your work that you have lost sight of what you really want to do with your life. Perhaps you feel trapped in the career you have chosen or dissatisfied with the direction it has taken but are afraid to make a move or consider something else for financial or other reasons. This reluctance to change is affecting other parts of your life as well. You have been smoking for years so . . . 'I could never give up now'. You are fed up with your present relationship but . . . 'I don't want to be on my own'.

Take things slowly and do the easier things first. Introduce one or two relatively minor changes into your lifestyle along the lines we have suggested like going to an exercise class or cutting down on your alcohol intake. Whatever you plan to do, *don't* talk about it to other people because their concern will make you feel nervous and uneasy, specially if you fall down on yourself. Wait until someone says, 'You're looking wonderful' and then tell them why. Their recognition will make you feel even better and encourage you to make other, more major changes if that's what you feel you need.

If you are facing some sort of crisis in either your working or private life which you despair of resolving, for instance a

76

relationship which is causing you a good deal of unhappiness, then don't be ashamed to seek professional advice. Counselling has become a well developed industry and there are many well qualified, experienced people around to give you specialized advice on a one-to-one basis. It will cost you something but you must measure the value of what you get for that money against what you may have been spending on fake comforters like fags and booze. (See Appendix for useful addresses.)

The Whole Woman

As we said at the beginning, positive good health is about more than just being able to rub along through everyday living, managing somehow but never feeling on top form. It's about being energetic, vibrant and enthusiastic. It means that you are living harmoniously within your environment; that you are at ease with your body and that your mind and spirit are strong enough to meet most problems and cope with setbacks. This is the holistic concept of health and it must be worth working for; it is part of every working woman's business. You surely owe yourself this investment.

Useful addresses

The British Holistic Medical Association
179 Gloucester Place, London NW1
Tel: 01 262 5299
Membership open to orthodox doctors who believe in a holistic approach to healing, practitioners of complementary medicine and members of the lay public. Annual membership is £10 and entitles you to quarterly magazine, access to library and reduced rate for workshops and tapes on stress reduction, exercise, healthy eating etc.

The Positive Health Centre
Centre for Autogenic Training
101 Harley St., London W1N 1DF
Tel: 935 1811

The College of Health
18 Victoria Park Square, London E2
Tel: 01 980 6263
For medical consumers. Annual membership is £10 for quarterly magazine and access to information service.

CCAM (Council for Complementary and Alternative Medicine)
10 Belgrave Square, London SW1X 8PH
Tel: 01 235 9512
Umbrella organization representing acupuncture, chiropractic, homeopathy, medical herbalism, naturopathy and osteopathy. Will put enquirers in touch with individual organizations.

Gingerbread Association for One Parent Families
35 Wellington Street, London WC2 E7BN
Tel: 01 240 0953

The Body Workshop School of Fitness and Health
Lambton Place, London W11 2SH
Tel: 01 221 7989
Runs classes and training courses. Specialists in body alignment with gentle exercise and relaxation.

The Institute for Optimum Nutrition
15–17 South End Road, London NW3 2PT
Tel: 01 794 4971
Runs seminars, workshops and training courses. Annual membership fee of £6 entitles you to quarterly magazine and a reduced rate on all services offered including a detailed analysis of your dietary needs.

The Maisner Centre for Eating Disorders
41 Preston Street, Brighton, East Sussex
Tel: 0273 29334

The Patients Association
Room 33, 18 Charing Cross Road, London WC2
Tel: 01 240 0671

Pre-Menstrual Tension Advisory Service
PO Box 268, Hove, East Sussex BN13 1RW
Tel: 0273 771366

Women's Health Concern
17 Earls Terrace, London W8 6LP

Tel: 01 602 6669
Specializes in advising women on all gynaecological problems

Women's National Cancer Control Campaign
1 South Audley Street, London W1
Tel: 01 499 7532
Supplies leaflets and information on breast self examination, cervical
smears and offers help to women undergoing treatment for various
forms of cancer.

Women's Therapy Centre
6 Manor Gardens, London N7 6LA
Tel: 01 263 6200

HEALTH CLUBS
Bath
The Bath House
2 Edgar Buildings, George Street, Bath
Tel: 0225 65797

Springs of Bath
7 Hasfield Park, Bath
Tel: 0225 337030

Birmingham

Corinthians Health Club
41 Smallbrook
Queensway, Birmingham
Tel: 021 643 8712

Midlands Arts Centre
Cannon Hill Park, Birmingham
Tel: 021 440 4221

Pat Roach Health Club
1st Floor, Piccadilly Arcade, New Street, Birmingham
Tel: 021 643 8888

Brighton

Metropole Hotel Health Club
Kings Road, Brighton
Tel: 0273 775432

Shape Health Club
38 Devonshire Place, Kemptown, Brighton
Tel: 0273 608617

Bristol

The Body Work Health Studio
The Berkeley Shopping Centre, 15/19 Queens Road, Clifton, Bristol
Tel: 0272 294800

The Downs Fitness and Health Centre
213 Whiteladies Road, Clifton, Bristol
Tel: 0272 739787

Grafton Health/Fitness Centre
The Pithay (off Fairfax Street), Broadmead, Bristol
Tel: 0272 297311

Cardiff

Ffisical
17 High Street, Llanbradach
Tel: 0222 886657

Secrets
5–7 West Gate Street, Cardiff
Tel: 0222 382411

Edinburgh

Champneys
Stobo Castle, Stobo
Tel: 072 16 204

George Kerr's Health Club
2 Hillside Crescent, Edinburgh
Tel: 031 556 8845

Manchester

Herriots Leisure Ltd
Sunlight House, Quay Street, Manchester M3 3JU

Leisure Spa
Portland Hotel, Portland Street, Manchester
Tel: 061 228 3400

Spindles Health Club
Britannia Hotel, Portland Street, Manchester
Tel: 061 228 2288

Books to read

Birth Right, the Parents' Choice Peter Huntingford (BBC Publications 1985, £3.25)

The Body Electric Anne Hooper (Unwin £2.50)

Breast Cancer – a guide to its early detection and treatment Carolyn Faulder (Virago 1982, £3.50)

Coping and Adapting – how you can learn to cope with stress Dr Robert W. Howard (Angus & Robertson 1984, £5.95)

Curing PMT the Drug-Free Way Moira Carpenter (Century 1985, £2.95)

How to Beat Fatigue – put more zest in your life naturally Louis Proto (Century Arrow 1986, £2.95)

The Mirror Within – a new look at sexuality Anne Dickson (Quartet 1985, £3.95)

The New Guide to Women's Health Dr Norma Williams and Hetty Einzig (Macdonald 1985, £12.95)

Stressmanship Dr Audrey Livingston Booth (Severn House 1985, £9.95)

The Tranquillizer Trap and how to get out of it Joy Melville (Fontana 1984, £1.95)

Understanding Cystitis, a complete self-help guide Angela Kilmartin (Arrow Books 1985, £2.95)

Vitamin Vitality Patrick Holford (Collins 1985, £3.95)

Cop-Out Cook

What precisely does it mean – to cop out? Regular readers of *Working Woman* magazine know that it means to plead guilty in order to receive a lighter sentence than if you plead innocent and are subsequently found guilty. So the sensible cop-out cook pleads guilty to having no time for slaving over a hot stove. She refuses to compromise on quality and veers towards good food that is not only fast but full of flavour, won't make you fat and will help keep you fit. What more could any working woman ask?

Every cop-out cook worth her sea salt knows that more time spent in the kitchen does not automatically mean more delicious results. If speed and simplicity are your watchwords you're on the right track – provided you pick your recipes with care and try to develop a palate that is as sensitive and receptive to flavour as your eyes and ears are to good sights and sounds.

Let Your Cooking Fit Your Life-Style

Whether cooking is a pleasure or a chore, as a busy working woman with a fast lane life style your watchword must be *simplify*. Discard all the over-exotic recipes that need endless ingredients, hours of preparation and are guaranteed to give you indigestion or make you fat, or both. You don't want to feel uncomfortable or unable to sleep at night having eaten food that is too rich, too heavy, or too much. The cop-out cook gravitates towards healthy eating, cutting down on, if not cutting out altogether, the megabaddies that make us fat/ill/feel guilty.

The optimistic cop-out cook is constantly on the lookout, in magazines, newspapers and on TV, ever hopeful of discovering fresh and even more simple dishes to add to her repertoire. Some have more appeal than others. In one glossy magazine devoted solely to food and drink they were recently advocating stuffing a mangetout! These are precisely the kind of twiddly-fiddly recipes to be avoided at all costs by the busy working woman. Into the same category go most recipes that have more than eight ingredients, two of which ought to be salt and pepper. And beware of anything that has to be served *at once*. There's quite enough stress during the day, thank you very much. So, to begin at the beginning, start with a system that will make your kitchen life as simple and smooth running as possible.

Get Organized

Wherever a working woman works the key to enjoyable and trouble-free cooking, whether for family, friends or a formal dinner for ten, starts and finishes with being organized.

Start with the basics

A word about microwave cookers – they may or not be an essential feature of the cop-out cook's kitchen. Undoubtedly, they can be a boon when used in conjunction with a freezer to defrost or heat-up dishes in seconds. Properly used they're a good friend to the cop-out cook who is in a hurry or just plain tired. The end result, until now, has too often tasted bland, looked boiled and been beige all over rather than brown – in other words, a grill or a blast of traditional heat has been needed to 'finish off' the cooking process. The newest machines, however, are designed to make everything look as brown and/or crisp as any expert cook would wish.

Your kitchen may be the size of a boat's galley. Into a less than infinite space you can put those essential items however much copping out goes on: a refrigerator, a freezer, double oven, double sink, dishwasher, and washing machine. It can be done, I've done it. Make sure there is ample storage space, that no square inch is unspoken for and you learn to be tidy out of sheer necessity. There's a place for everything and everything had better be in its place because there may be nowhere else for it to go. If you don't have all the room in the world off-load the gadgets which look good but are seldom used.

Here is a list of essentials which is in no way gospel but is a good way to begin. Add to it as space, money, personal preferences and culinary experiments dictate.

CUTTING, SLICING, PEELING ETC.
- A good heavy wooden chopping board
- At least four good quality steel knives, from small to large – one with serrated edge. And, as no one can cook properly with cheap, blunt knives, a knife sharpener. Optional extra: a curved grapefruit knife
- A pair of good quality kitchen scissors for cutting, trimming and chopping herbs
- A vegetable peeler with swivel blade, apple corer, and a good stand-up four-sided grater. (If you have an electric mixer you can be sure that one day there'll be an electricity failure.)
- A first quality carving knife and fork
- A bread knife

BOILING, STEAMING, FRYING
- A set of good quality heavy saucepans with lids – at least four. (Cheap ones turn out very quickly to be dear.)
- A steamer – the metal folding 'strainer' which drops into any size saucepan is best
- Three frying pans, preperably with lids
- A ridged iron pan for searing steaks as no domestic grill is hot enough and frying rump or fillet is a sin
- One fish kettle
- One omelette pan, to be used for *nothing* else!

ROASTING, CASSEROLING, BAKING
- At least three roasting dishes of varying sizes. Iron Le Creusets can be used on the stove top or in the oven and go straight to the table
- Casseroles, one small and one large, and at least one in earthenware rather than iron because it produces quite a different, less boiled, effect

- At least four pie dishes ranging in size from very small to large enough to cater for a dinner for ten
- One rolling pin
- One funnel
- Two flan cases, one small, one large
- Cake tins – two or more if you're an enthusiastic cake-maker

MISCELLANEOUS
- Two fine sieves, one large and one small
- One colander
- A selection of mixing bowls and basins (six is a minimum)
- A measuring jug
- Garlic press
- Selection of wooden spoons, a spatula, tongs and draining spoon, fish slice
- Egg whisk, rotary or 'spring'
- Six skewers
- A battery-powered 'pinger' timer
- Scales
- Pastry brush
- Two Napoletana coffee pots, one large, one medium
- Two pepper mills, two salt dispensers
- Two soufflé dishes
- Two or more ovenproof serving dishes for vegetables
- Storage jars, with well fitting lids
- Plastic containers with lids for fridge and freezer
- One carving dish
- Fruit squeezer – electric or manual, depending on your preference or the strength of your wrist. An electric mixer and/or blender – essential for every working woman

Don't be a hoarder

If your kitchen space is limited limit your food store to only the most basic requirements. If you live near the shops there's no need to have dozens of cans on the shelves or half a sheep in the freezer. Buy as and when you need it and remember that planning ahead is a good idea but not a religion. Spontaneity has its place too and one woman's batch baking is another woman's self-inflicted punishment. A gesture to longterm culinary commitments is to cook twice as much boeuf bourguinon or navarin of lamb as you need for a dinner party and then freeze the remainder in a plastic container clearly marked with the date as well as the contents. When you fancy one or the other, out it comes and you're half way to another dinner party.

Suggestions for essential stored staples:

IN PACKETS

Two of white sauce
Two of cheese sauce
Two of bread sauce
Two sage and onion stuffing
Rice
Spaghetti

Vermicelli
Black peppercorns
Cornflour
Matzo meal
Sea salt
Brown and white sugar

IN CANS

Peeled tomatoes
Tomato purée (or paste in a tube)
Sardines
Anchovies
Tuna fish
Red, green and white beans
Petit pois with lettuce and baby onions
Fish soups (crab, lobster, prawn)
Consommé
Rollmops
Baked beans

IN BOTTLES OR JARS

Gherkins
Black and green olives
Mayonnaise
A screw top bottle of home-made French dressing
Dijon mustard
Capers
Sweet red peppers
Ginger in syrup
Red and white horseradish
Tomato ketchup
Worcester sauce
Tabasco

Olive oil
Corn oil
Soy sauce
Red and white wine vinegar
And some sultanas which you can leave to soak in the dregs of whatever liqueur you have just finished (Cointreau, Kirsch, Grand Marnier, brandy etc.)

IN THE FREEZER
Leaf spinach
Sweet corn
Wholemeal, short and puff pastry in 1lb (or 500g) packets which are big enough for party-sized pies with only one roll-out
Garlicky pâté from your favourite Italian delicatessen
Fresh raspberries
Blueberries, blackberries and loganberries, all of which freeze and thaw ready for use, month in, month out until the next season's crop comes around
Frozen mashed potato
One home-made tub of taramasalata
One tub of smoked salmon (your local fishmonger may sell packets of 'pieces')
Two packets of fresh pasta, although the dried kind is probably every bit as good, provided you buy it from a shop where they sell a lot and use it before it dies of old age at the back of the cupboard

HERBS
If your jars of herbs have been with you through thick and thin for as long as you can remember . . . throw them out and start again. You will merely be flavouring casseroles with elderly, tasteless dust. Thyme, oregano and rosemary straight from the garden (or window box), dried and then mixed are delicious. Remember that too many mixed herbs used too lavishly make most foods taste strongly of mixed herbs.

PLAN AHEAD
Many working women may find it difficult to get to the shops so it clearly pays to buy in as much as possible in advance. After all, everything keeps nowadays and grabbing groceries on the way home is hardly conducive to a relaxing evening.

Persuade yourself to think ahead, planning your family menus for the week (see pp. 93–98 for a selection). If you live alone or à deux, forget it.

BE FLEXIBLE
Don't feel, however, that your decisions are inviolable. You may have decided on ratatouille, but supposing there are no aubergines? There are some lovely carrots . . . or fresh spinach. Don't let your list become a fixation. Keep your mind and your options open and adjust your shopping accordingly.

Be prepared

Is it possible at the end of a long, hard day to dash home and conjure up a delectable meal for family – or, even more daunting, a dinner party for eight – without being flustered beforehand and exhausted after?

Yes, it is, provided you learn the rules of the copping-out game. Which includes doing as much as is sensible and possible in advance. So, if you're feeling energetic at the weekend cook a dish or two which you can freeze for future eating.

When giving a dinner party it pays to do as much as possible the night before – or pre-departure in the morning if you're an early riser. Unless you do the kind of work where you can be sure of getting off at 4.30 on the day, crises can and do arise. Why not lay the table the night before – cloth or mats, cutlery, glasses and napkins? Paper napkins are perfectly acceptable, though fabric ones are nicer. Just tuck them casually into the glasses – waterlilies are definitely out!

Panic stations

One of the most useful tips is **how to resurrect a pie that ought to have been crisp and golden but stayed too long in an unreliable oven and is now dark brown and frankly burnt**. Remove the crust entirely. Cut some thick slices of bread, brown or white whichever you fancy. Remove the crusts and butter generously. Lay them on top of the pie, butter side up and pop back in the oven for at least 10 minutes or until the top is once again crisp and golden. If it's a fruit pie rather than a savoury one you can use slices of plain cake or scones if you have them to hand.

We do know, of course, that **all vegetables with the exception of potatoes should be served all nutty and al dente. They're now soggy and overdone?** Get out your faithful blender and make them into a purée. There's practically no vegetable that doesn't look and taste delicious served up in this way, specially if you add a large knob of butter and egg, grated cheese or some cream and to hell with the extra calorific contents at such fraught moments.

There are excellent alternatives which are less loaded with calories. I am a great advocate of Greek yoghurt or you might like to try out some silken tofu which is one of the staples of Japanese cuisine. Put through the blender and used as a thickening agent for puréed vegetables it's invaluable and it keeps unopened for up to six months. So you can store it.

Two-veg purées are often more interesting than one – especially when they are not at their prime – so at panic station time remember carrot-and-parsnip, carrot-and-potatoes, swede-and-parsnip, swede-and-celery, sprouts-and-peas, spinach-and-courgettes. Come to think of it, spinach is probably the one vegetable you can't overcook since the longer it cooks the more butter it can absorb and the more butter it absorbs the better it tastes, puréed or not.

You either misjudged the quantity or there's an extra guest and the stewed rhubarb/apple/plums you planned for the pudding won't make enough to go round? There's always whipped egg white to be folded in, ditto yoghurt mixed with runny honey, ditto whipped cream, ditto blended tofu and how about adding some ground almonds which give a lovely subtle bite to most fruit as well as extra 'body'? Taste to see if it's sweet enough. This kind of mousse looks good served in individual wine glasses topped off with some toasted flaked almonds on the top. Serve with tiny ratafia biscuits for an extra treat.

The casserole of beef/chicken/lamb you made with such loving care has a surfeit of fat floating around on the top? No time to chill so it can be lifted off? Simply fold several layers of kitchen paper on the top and you'll find it will absorb the lot.

You've overdone the salt? By changing to sea salt, perhaps, which is twice as salty as well as twice as healthy as the chemically assisted kind? Peel a large potato, cut it into chunks and drop it in to your casserole. Heat up for 20 minutes or so, remove the potato and be surprised by the more delicate taste and be a bit more careful next time. If the saltiness is still there, add a few drops of wine vinegar or a scant teaspoon of sugar.

The soup/stew/sauce is too liquid? (You *have* been careless, haven't you?) There are several ways to rectify the damage. First with cornflour. Pour off a little of the liquid, allow to cool and add a half of it to a tablespoon of cornflour. Mix to a paste, add the rest of the poured-off liquid and bring to the boil. Let it bubble away until it thickens. Add back to the erring dish and mix gently in. Let it heat through thoroughly so the flavours blend and there is no taste of uncooked flour. If the dish is a spicy one thicken it with tomato purée added to either the creamy yoghurt or blended with tofu.

A real lifesaver for thickening is *beurre manié* – equal parts of plain flour and softened butter mixed together. In order to save time and agony when panic stations are called, it's wise to keep a supply on hand. Make a small quantity to store, using 4 oz butter and 4 oz flour. Drop half teaspoons on to a baking tray or a flat dish and freeze. Tip these tiny 'nuggets' into a plastic container and keep at the frozen ready. Penultimate thickening thought: use some instant mashed potato reconstituted with some of the excess liquid. Final thought: use less liquid next time.

Wilted salad greens used to be a major hazard but less and less now that the iceberg lettuce and Chinese leaves are with us. However, if **fatigue has overtaken your lettuce for the salad and you need to crisp it up**, tear the leaves apart and put them to soak in a bowl of iced water for about 10 or 15 minutes. Shake off the excess water, wrap in a clean dish towel and leave in the refrigerator for about half an hour. If they're too far gone, make some lovely lettuce soup. Peel and chop an onion and soften in butter. Stir in the wilted leaves. Add a dessert spoon of cornflour and mix well. Cook gently for a couple of minutes and then add about a pint of the stock you happen to have handy and if you don't, use a chicken or, preferably, a vegetable cube. Or milk. Cook for another five minutes and then liquidize or blend. Reheat and season. A pinch of sugar is nice or a couple of drops of the concentrated apple juice that you can buy at the health food shops. (The ordinary kind won't do, not sweet enough.) Serve with a swirl of cream (fattening) or a sprinkling of fresh mint, chives or parsley. If summer is a cumin' in, serve the soup cold in which case you will need a slightly heavier hand with the seasoning.

And talking of seasoning and summer, **what about that meat which is, shall we say, a little 'high'**. Not off exactly, but in a condition which would be fine if it were game which it isn't. Wash the meat under the cold tap, dry thoroughly and leave to marinate in a mixture of red wine vinegar, olive oil, slices of onion and a few crushed peppercorns. Other possible fragrant additives: a bay leaf, crushed coriander seeds, fresh or dried thyme or rosemary. Do *not* in any circumstances add salt which will merely make it tough. The offending meat should be allowed to sit in its remedial bath for a minimum of an hour and no harm will come to it if left there all day, turned once or twice. Remove, part dry with kitchen paper, cook in the usual way and then stand by for compliments about the subtle flavour.

Resurrecting curdled mayonaise is a well-known pushover if you start again with a fresh egg yolk, dropping in the curdled stuff drop by tiny drop at the beginning and then increasing as the new mixture thickens.

The poached fish has fallen to bits? Flake it up, mix gently with boiled rice, chopped hard boiled eggs, a packet of de-frosted sweetcorn and season well, cover with grated cheese and pop it in an ovenproof dish for about 45 minutes or until the top is crisp and golden. (If you don't care about the calories it's nice topped with mashed potato before you add the cheese.)

The hollowed-out-filled-with-dried-fruit baked apples have burst out of their skins? Scoop out all the flesh, mix in an egg yolk or two, taste, sweeten with brown sugar or honey if necessary, pile back into a buttered ovenproof dish. Crush a packet of digestive biscuits, mix with softened butter and scatter on top. Bake until the top is crisp. Serve with cream or creamy yoghurt flavoured with a little brandy or with some calvados.

Few disasters that befall the cop-out cook are ever on a truly megascale and most can be coped with if you stay cool and philosophical. It's not the end of the world.

"two prawn bhagis, one fried rice, one vegetable curry and two tandoori chicken..."

Feeding a Family

If there's more than two in your family a degree of planning ahead will save your sanity. Planning every single meal is a madness but try for at least four or five 'fixtures'. Here are some ideas to spark you off.

Spaghetti alla ceca (Serves 4)

1 lb spaghetti
2 lbs tomatoes
Best olive oil
24 black olives
Fresh basil, salt and black pepper

Roughly chop the tomatoes. Halve the olives and remove the stones. Cover the tomatoes and olives with olive oil, add lots of chopped basil, salt and freshly ground black pepper. Leave for half an hour.

Boil the spaghetti until *al dente* (about 12 minutes or 3 minutes if fresh). Drain and put into a hot dish and pour the sauce over. Toss. Add more olive oil if necessary.

N.B. This dish is good only if there is plenty of sauce. Avocados make a nice – and unexpected – change from tomatoes.

JUST ADD . . .

The wonderful thing about pasta is that you can add almost anything to it and come up with lovely appetizing meals. My standbys are as follows:

Herbs: dill, tarragon, basil, parsley
Fish: cooked prawns, strips of smoked salmon, anchovy fillets
Nuts: walnuts, pinoli (pine kernels)
Meats: bacon, ham, cooked chicken
Vegetables: peas, mushrooms, courgettes, artichokes
Or a combination: cream, ham and peas, cream, peas and mushrooms, cream, smoked salmon and dill, cream, cheese and walnuts.

Incidentally, pasta may be reheated the next day in a covered casserole in the oven. Just add a little butter.

Green salad

Iceberg lettuce
Watercress
Avocado pear
Sunflower seeds
Vinaigrette dressing (made with walnut oil)

Remove the outside leaves of the lettuce and discard. Break the lettuce into thick chunks and add the watercress. Roast the sunflower seeds for three minutes until crisp and add. Remove the skin from the avocado pear, and discard. Slice thickly and add to the salad. Toss in a tart vinaigrette dressing.

N.B. The avocado must be added just before serving or it will go brown.

Poulet basquaise (Serves 4)

2 lb chicken cut into pieces	2 red peppers, sliced
3 tablespoons of oil	2 medium onions, finely sliced
2 tins tomatoes	Salt, pepper, 1 clove garlic,
2 green peppers, sliced	crushed

In a pan deep enough to hold all the ingredients, sauté chicken pieces until golden brown. Remove and in the same oil sauté the onions until translucent. Add peppers, tomatoes, garlic and cook for a further 10 minutes. Taste for seasoning – and a glass of white wine works wonders for this dish – cover and cook over a low heat for about 20 minutes.

Cop-out cheese soufflé (Serves 6)

12 slices white bread, crusts removed
½ lb grated cheddar cheese
4 eggs
1 quart of milk

Preheat oven to 375°F (190°C, gas 5). Using an oblong or square oven dish about 9 inches across, layer in alternately first bread and then cheese for about 4 layers. Mix eggs with milk and pour over making sure all the surface is covered. Bake in a hot oven for about an hour or until a knife comes out clean.

Spicy lamb chops (Serves 2)

2 large lamb chops	4 fl oz recurrant jelly (use a good
1 onion	one otherwise it will be too sweet)
1 carrot	½ pint red wine
¼ teaspoon peppercorns	1 sprig fresh rosemary
¼ teaspoon cloves	4 tablespoons orange juice
1 teaspoon tomato purée	A little oil and butter for browning
	and for frying the vegetables

Gently fry chopped onion and carrot, peppercorns and cloves for eight minutes. In a blender put tomato purée, redcurrant jelly, wine, rosemary and orange juice. Pour over the vegetables. Simmer for one hour. (This can be done the night before.) Brown chops gently in oil or butter, pour sauce over and heat in a pre-heated oven (350°F (180°C, gas 4) for one hour.

Five spice rice

Pre-cooked rice　　　　　　*¼ teaspoon poppy seeds*
1 onion　　　　　　　　　　*¼ teaspoon mustard seeds*
¼ teaspoon fennel seeds　　*½ teaspoon turmeric*
¼ teaspoon cumin seeds　　*1 oz butter*
¼ teaspoon fenugreek seeds

Fry onion in butter until soft. Add seeds and turmeric. Fry until mustard seeds 'jump'. Stir in rice until it is yellow. Can be made the night before and heated, covered, in the oven. Enough for two.

Baked courgettes with rice (Serves 4–6 people)

4 courgettes　　　　　　　*Olive oil*
1 onion　　　　　　　　　 *1 large tomato, skinned*
5 heaped tablespoons　　　*1 glass white wine*
cooked rice　　　　　　　 *Grated cheese*
1 clove garlic

Peel and slice courgettes. Peel and chop onion and gently fry both in olive oil in which garlic has been crushed. Add rice and tomato. Simmer for about 5 minutes. Turn the mixture into a fireproof dish, moisten with wine, cover with grated cheese and brown in the oven.

Cold avocado soup (Serves 4)

3 soft avocados　　　　　　*Small onion*
1 tin chicken noodle soup　*1 clove garlic*
Juice of ½ lemon　　　　　*Pinch of paprika*

An hour before serving, blend all ingredients, except for paprika and ½ avocado, which should be left with the stone in it to stop discolouration. Leave the mixture to stand until required. If too thick, it can be thinned down with cold milk. Garnish with slices of avocado and sprinkle with paprika.

Audie's whopping mushrooms

3–4 large mushrooms per person
Butter
Garlic to taste
Dash soy sauce
Black pepper

Butter a large ovenproof dish very thickly. Put in mushrooms, smooth side up, and dot heavily with finely chopped garlic and a dash of soy sauce on each one. Add a big dot of butter on top of each – and a really good go with black pepper. Cover with foil and put in middle shelf of moderate oven. After 20 minutes toss them about and cover for approximately another 15 minutes. You should now have lots of evil-looking black gravy. Serve with some good dunking bread. A good starter and also a good veg dish with lamb chops.

Egg and lemon sweet and sour fish (Serves 4)

This is a classic Jewish dish and is eaten either hot or cold. It also works with turbot, cod, haddock or large slices of thick plaice. (The frozen kind does perfectly well.)

2 tablespoons oil
2 small onions, sliced into rings
4 slices halibut
Salt and pepper

For the sauce:
2 teaspoons cornflour or arrowroot
Strained juice of 2 lemons
1 dessertspoon caster sugar
Stock from fish
2 eggs lightly beaten

Gently heat the oil in a large shallow pan. Add the onions and fry until soft but not brown. Lay the slices of fish on top, season and cover with warm water. Bring to the boil and simmer very gently until cooked – for thin slices, just 7–10 minutes, for thick ones 20 minutes. Using a fish slice, arrange the pieces on a serving dish, cover with the onions and keep warm in the oven.

To make the sauce, mix the cornflour or arrowroot with the strained lemon juice and sugar, add about half of the liquid the fish was cooked in, bring to the boil and stir over a gentle heat for 2 or 3 minutes until it is the consistency of cream. Remove from the heat, and allow to cool slightly. Now pour onto the 2 beaten eggs. Heat this over a pan of boiling water until it thickens. Pour over the fish and keep warm in the oven.

Good accompaniments are tiny boiled potatoes, rice or fine green beans. It is even more delicious if allowed to get cold and served straight from the refrigerator with a sliced cucumber salad. But go easy on the dressing, because the fish has a wonderful piquant taste that needs little else to titillate your palate.

The most time- and health-conscious cop-out Cooks serve desserts based on fruits and yoghurt. These can either be served separately, or blended together to make a lovely creamy purée.

Entertaining at Home

Know your limitations

When entertaining always know your limitations and work within them. Plan your menu with care and do not attempt to show off. A very difficult piece of advice to define and even more difficult to take until you reach the age and stage where you realize that the best things in life are not necessarily five-star gastronomic binges, but simple meals served to appreciative guests.

If you are thrown into a nervous frenzy by the thought of making complicated sauces at the last minute in one room while guests are waiting in the other – don't. This fear may well be irrational and unjustified but why fight it? On more fraught occasions choose dishes that (a) are sauce-free, (b) you have made before – at least twice and (c) require no last-minute sleights of hand – you can't beat dishes that are left to cook quietly on their own until ready to serve. They help you create an atmosphere of relaxation, which in its turn results in all round pleasure. A strained, anxious hostess, with one eye on the clock in case the soufflé is collapsing or the Baked Alaska isn't browning, results in strained, anxious guests. For the best of copping-out suggestions – starters, middles and ends and sympathetic combinations thereof – see pp. 103–19.

Organize yourself

Organization is your key to a relaxed and enjoyable evening or Sunday lunch when you're entertaining. As we discussed earlier, plan your menu but be flexible. Unless everything required is in your store cupboard – which would be a pity since fresh and seasonal foods tickle and tantalize our palates in a way that unrelieved, unrelenting frozen or canned ones never could – you may well face disappointment, even panic at dinner party time. When you go shopping, take an open mind as well as your list or you'll give yourself a hard time. No crab soup in the supermarket? How are the avocados? No baby chickens? The ducks look even better. The strawberries have all gone? Make a chocolate mousse.

STAY COOL . . .
Unless it's soup, do not attempt to serve a hot first course since the strain on your nerves communicates itself to the guests. If you have a large-ish table and there are more than six guests, it helps to have two separate dishes from which the guests can help themselves. Two pots of pâté, two plates of crudités, two little dishes of butter, two racks of hot toast or, better still, two baskets of those Swedish crispbreads.

AND DELEGATE
Whether it's a roast or a casserole, you can serve from a sideboard onto warmed plates if your table simply isn't big enough to accommodate everything. Put the vegetables on

the table and delegate the serving duties to one of your guests, who will enjoy the responsibility. This avoids the endless passing round of serving dishes which anyway ought to be too hot to handle and avoids some guests taking too much (not often) and some who are too shy to take enough (even less often).

WASHING UP
At dinner party time keep a large pan in one sink and pop all the used cutlery into it, course by course. Scrape left-overs straight into the bin, or the waste disposal, and stack all the plates in a neat pile. Saucepans and dishes are stacked in another pile and the whole debris looks so organized that the washing up after a dinner for ten looks like the scene after tea for two.

If you have a dishwasher (and no cop-out cook should really be without one) you *can* load the plates and bowls etc. into your machine course by course – quietly!

Cheat

As often as possible, and particularly with soups. Add a can of shrimps to any tin of good fish soup whether it's crab, lobster or prawn. Experiment with flavourings – brandy, a little cream, soy sauce, curry powder, tabasco or paprika. And always serve extremely hot. Warm soup is awful. Do not feel compelled to serve toast – it's a last minute chore and a bore. Serve chunks of granary or wholemeal bread. Or Swedish crispbreads.

Be a specialist

Whether it's fish, meat, salads or pasta, concentrate on be-coming familiar with about half-a-dozen simple recipes and their variations.

Sometimes you may not need to serve a starter and can plunge straight into the main course, followed by a green salad with the cheese and then the fruit salad. Ample and also nicely balanced.

Keep the balance

For some reason some hostesses are tempted to serve more than one pudding as though in a restaurant. This is totally unnecessary, but becoming increasingly popular due, perhaps, to our preoccupation with health and slimming, and if one pudding is fattening and sinful we salve our consciences with the other and let the guest make the deadly decision. Although it's by no means essential, it may be a good idea to have an alternative to cholesterol-crammed cherry cheesecake or calorie-rich rum baba. Suggested alternatives include fruit fools or mousses served with sweet biscuits like ratafias or *langues de chat*.

A better alternative is never to serve the megabaddies at all, and concentrate instead on the most elegant and serendipitous fruit salads that delight the eye as well as the palate. All should be served with fresh lemon juice mixed with a sugar-and-water syrup and a dash of liqueur. You may like to try the following:

- Chunks of pineapple, red water melon and slices of kiwi fruit.
- Raspberries and blueberries on a bed of sliced bananas – which must be soaked in lemon juice to stop them discolouring.
- Blueberries, raspberries and kumquats soaked in Cointreau. (When you see these tiny orange-type fruits in the shops buy a couple of pounds, slice them and soak them in Cointreau before freezing in small portions.
- In winter, honeydew melons with chopped ginger, sultanas soaked in liqueur with a handful of flaked almonds.

Arrange contrasting fruits in circles so that their colours sing out from the dish. Nuts also can be used – they improve most fruit salads and mousses and give a nice surprise in that extra crunch.

However, there will be times when there is no acceptable alternative to scrumptious profiteroles so to hell with it and just try to make the preceding courses a shade less sinful. (Three fattening courses are not only unnecessary but also indigestible.)

There is a current vogue for serving a sweet dessert wine with the pudding course. A favourite is Beaumes de Venise at around £5 to £7 a bottle.

What about cheese?

The British way is to serve it *after* the pudding; the French prefer it the other way round which harks back to the time when it wasn't considered a good idea to take your turn round the dance floor with the partner of your choice while smelling of Camembert. Solution: simply produce both cheese and pudding simultaneously and let the guests decide the order.

Avoid a cheese board covered in itty bitty portions of too many different kinds. Three is maximum, two even better. A nice generous piece of each, one blue and soft, one traditional and hard. Brie and Cheddar, Cambozola and Gruère or Emmental, Stilton and Double Gloucester. One British, one not. Surround them with shiny, wet radishes, their green stalks still intact, plus chunks of celery and/or fennel and lots of watercress. If any of these 'crudités' have been served as a starter, replace them with fresh dates, whole almonds, dried apricots or figs and a small bunch of black grapes. Served on a wicker platter it looks – and tastes – delectable. Serve a pot of cottage cheese, bound with a little Greek yoghurt, a pressed garlic clove or two, a load of chopped chives, salt and ground pepper, and perhaps some fresh thyme. (Cottage cheese is also good mixed with a few drops of Worcester sauce.) Guests like to spoon the mixture out and either eat it with a fork as an end-of-meal savoury or pile it on to crispbread or biscuits.

It's nice to offer a choice – crispbread, wholemeal crackers and highbaked water biscuits make a good and contrasting combination, and let's not forget Bath Olivers. For those who care about being 'in', it's very 'in' to serve both margarine and a low-fat spread as well as butter and to leave them in their garish plastic containers so that your guests can be calorie and/or cholesterol conscious or not, just as they fancy.

And coffee?

Buy the very best – it's worth it to finish off the meal well. Offer caffeine-free coffee, too, and/or one of the herb teas which are becoming increasingly popular.

To go with the liqueurs – no more than a choice of three or you run the risk of being flash – serve some crispy mint chocolates or sticks of chocolate covered ginger. Or those sinful fresh cream chocolates that are too wonderful to think about and if you have any left, give them away the next day so that gluttony will not go unconfined.

The Three Card Trick

Most enthusiastic cop-out cooks read recipes voraciously but when it comes to choosing a menu for guests – starter, middle and pudding – inevitably fall back on old favourites. There are a number of tried and trusted ones that you will know (a) will never let you down, (b) your guests will enjoy even immoderately and (c) are as simple to make as any cop-out cook could possibly wish.

Despite the incalculable number of different foods now available, the categories into which each course will invariably fall are really quite few. They go like this:

Starters	Main Course	Pudding
Soup	Poultry or game	Eggs
Fish	Meat	Fruit, cooked or raw
Fruit	Fish	Cereals (rice, flour)
Vegetable or salad	Pasta	including pastries, flans,
Meat	Vegetarian	pies, puddings etc.
Eggs	Pulses	Mousse
Pasta		Fools
Pulses		Icecreams, jellies, sorbets

Texture and colour

The final balance is what matters and the textures and the colours are every bit as important as the content. You can't start with an egg mayonnaise and finish with crème caramel, and if you have baked grapefruit to start with it's not the best idea in the world to end with a citrus-based fruit salad. If you have been to a dinner party where every individual dish was delicious – and beige – fish pâté followed by blanquette de veau with rice and boiled potatoes followed by zabaglione – you'll long for a green bean or even a tomato. Clashes can most easily be avoided if you choose your middle dish first and then work forwards and backwards.

Deciding your menu

The best of the first courses are those which can be (a) bought ready to serve, (b) made the day before, (c) taken from the freezer and thawed (make twice as much as you need if it's that kind of recipe eg., fish pâtés), (d) decanted from a can. If you decide to start with fish buy granary or wholemeal bread the previous day so that it's not too fresh and crumbly if you want to make toast. And don't forget to cut the slices in half when they're done so that the steam escapes and you get nice crispy slices instead of rubber mats. Alternatively, just serve the bread fresh or choose those Swedish wholegrain rolls. Not only do they form the perfect basis for both sweet and savoury spreads, they also last for months.

Working out menus, I believe, is as personal as working out your wardrobe or your make-up. Cast iron rules about what-goes-with-what are inhibiting and unnecessarily constricting but we all like suggestions that we can consider, change according to our whims and fancies and come up with memorable meals that are particularly *us*. So here for your consideration and, optimistically, your delectation are some tried, tested and trusty favourite combinations. For easy reference, they are separated into summer and winter; spring and autumn creep in whenever the weather seems suitable for a change of menu and the new season's foods make their first appearance in my local shops.

Summer Recipes

Starters	Main course	Pudding
(1) Watercress soup	Cold fresh salmon boiled new potatoes, tzatziki	Blackcurrant fool with langues de chat biscuits
(2) Mozzarella/tomato and avocado salad	Baby chickens roasted with bacon, mangetout	Rhubarb fool with blueberries
(3) Egg mayonaise	Vitello tonnato boiled new potatoes, green beans	Summer pudding Greek yoghurt

(4) Smoked salmon pâté	Roast leg of lamb with mint sauce *and* redcurrant jelly, baked potato halves, courgettes	Red, white and green fruit salad
(5) Gazpacho	Fish pie broccoli	Nectarine or peach salad – or a mix of both – with raspberries

Menu 1

Watercress soup

3 bunches of watercress
1 large onion
2 medium sized potatoes

¾ pint of milk
1½ pints stock made from a vegetable cube
Salt and freshly ground pepper

Wash and clean the cress discarding the 'hairy' coarse stalks. Keep a few sprigs for garnish and chop the rest. Peel, chop and gently 'sweat' the onion in the butter. Do *not* brown. Add the chopped cress, the potato chunks, the stock and the milk. Cook gently for about 15 to 20 minutes or until the potato is quite soft. Season to taste, allow to cool and pass the lot through your blender. Serve hot or cold (more seasoning needed if cold) with sprigs of cress on the top. A swirl of single cream looks nice too.

Boiled salmon

You need about 2 lbs for six people, depending on your generosity and their appetite.

This is a magic recipe. It never fails no matter how big the salmon piece. Wrap it carefully in foil. Several layers if necessary to make sure it's sealed. No seasoning is required. Put it in a fish kettle, saucepan or large iron casserole, cover with water and bring to the boil. Let it bubble away for about 5 minutes and then remove from the heat. Allow it to cool all on its own, overnight or all day. Then remove it first from the water and then its metal overcoat and you will have the most perfect, the moist fresh salmon you ever did taste. Put it gently on a dish, peel off the skin, decorate with a few thin slices of lemon and cucumber and serve with your best silver fish slice so that you can remove elegantly separate sections. Salmon is a precious fish so be gentle.

This is best with baby new potatoes scrubbed, served in their skins and sprinkled with either finely chopped chives or parsley. New potatoes should be put into cold, salted water, brought to the boil and cooked for about 15–20 minutes. Test with the tip of a fine knife and if done pour off the water, cover with crunched-up kitchen paper or a clean cloth, put the lid back on and go and join your guests until they and you are ready. The cloth will absorb the steam as well as keeping the potatoes nice and hot. Add a knob of butter if you must.

Instead of a cucumber salad or mayonnaise serve tzatziki, a classic Greek dish that can also make a lovely fresh summer starter. Peel and chop up a cucumber. (Some people salt the cucumber and allow it to drain with a weight on the top to make it more digestible. Wipe it dry before using.) To a large tub of Greek yoghurt add 3 crushed cloves of *fresh* garlic (or more or less according to your degree of abandon about the breathy aftermath). Whip in ½ cup of good olive oil, a good handful of chopped fresh mint and salt and pepper to taste. You can use spring onions instead of the cucumber.

Blackcurrant fool

Blackcurrants are the most fragrant wonderful summer fruit and full of vitamin C. All you need to do is to pull 2 lbs of them off their stalks, wash and put them in a heavy pan with just an eggcup of water. Cover tightly and simmer gently for about 10 minutes. Don't add the sugar until they're done, thereby saving you the risk of a burnt-out pan. When they're soft push through a coarse sieve – or blend if you don't mind the pips and I don't – and mix with ½ lb sugar – or more according to taste, and a large pot of Greek yoghurt. (You *can* use cream if you'd rather.) I add a slurp of sloe gin or Kirsch to give it an extra fillip. Serve in individual wine glasses. Keep a few berries to scatter on the top. A mint leaf or two on the top looks extremely appealing.

Menu 2

Mozzarella, avocado and tomato salad

Try to find the little 'blind' avocadoes from Israel which can be peeled and used whole. Slice them and douse them in a vinaigrette sauce (more gentle than lemon juice) so that they don't discolour. Make up individual plates of slices of mozzarella cheese, avocados and tomatoes with oil drizzled over and sprinkled with fresh basil (wonderful!) fresh thyme (delicious!) or parsley (not bad!). Very colourful, very tasty.

Baby chickens

With luck you can find these poussins small enough to serve one per person which cuts down on the work and the pre-dinner anguish since cutting them in half requires time, a sharp pair of poultry scissors and asbestos fingers.

Today's chickens need a lot of loving care to give them flavour. Stuff an onion and rosemary or tarragon inside along with salt and pepper and a knob of butter. Rub their skins with either a lemon or a cut garlic clove, smother them in butter and then place pieces of streaky bacon over their breasts.

Set them in a pan along with more tarragon and rosemary, salt and pepper and a drizzle of oil. Put them into a hot oven for about 20 minutes, then demote the bacon to the bottom of the pan so that it can crisp up and the breasts can brown. Baste and leave to cook for about another 10–15 minutes.

Remove, place the birds round a dish, ovenproof if possible, and put back in a cool oven along with the bacon and brown crispy onion pieces to await your pleasure. Add a small glass of sherry or red wine to the roasting pan and the sliced raw chicken livers and make the kind of gravy that never could come out of a packet. Do this by letting the liver cook for a minute and then attacking it with a fork to smash it to a paste in the bottom of the pan.

Serve with bread sauce that could perfectly well come out of a packet, sprigs of watercress and the crispy bacon bits and fresh or frozen mangetout. The frozen variety need a minimum of cooking and often put to shame the bruised and stringy 'fresh' kind. Fresh green beans are a good alternative. Both go well with chopped parsley or flaked almonds scattered over them.

Rhubarb fool

The leaves of rhubarb are poisonous, the pink stalks are nectar. Stew them gently with one or two slivers of lemon and orange peel. Add a mixture of sugar and honey to sweeten to taste and blend, again with a carton of Greek yoghurt, to make a smooth purée. A small glass of Cointreau is a magic extra. Chill and serve in individual glasses with a few toasted almonds or rose leaves scattered on the tops. Buy these in little glass tubes at your local Italian delicatessen.

Menu 3

Egg mayonnaise

Allow 1½ eggs per person. Boil them gently for about 8–10 minutes – *not* straight from the fridge or they will crack. Run them under cold water and shell. Cut them in half lengthwise and place them, sunny sides down, on a large crispy lettuce leaf. Now make them look inviting with a good dollop of mayonnaise – home-made or Hellmans mixed with cream to 'gentle' it slightly – and criss-cross them with anchovies. Sprinkle with parsley, add a sprig or two of watercress and a couple of slices of cucumber.

Vitello tonnato

For this you need a piece of veal – leg or shoulder – which should be gently cooked in salted water with an onion spiked with cloves, a stick of celery, a carrot and a sprig of parsley. If the meat is 'untidy' tie it into shape before cooking. Simmer for about 2 hours and leave to cool overnight to 'settle'.

Slice on to a serving dish and cover with the tonnato sauce. This is made by blending a tin of tuna fish in oil with an equal amount of both mayonnaise and olive oil until it forms a smooth cream. Sharpen the flavour with lemon juice and pour over the sliced veal. Scatter with capers. Serve with warm new potatoes. Fine green beans are also delicious and add colour as well as an extra taste.

Summer pudding

This is a favourite summer dish and when the necessary berries are in season prepare enough to form the fillings for half-a-dozen future puddings. The fillings can vary but black-currants and redcurrants are vital. These must be lightly cooked with sugar while other fruits, including raspberries, strawberries and loganberries can be included raw. (Black-berries are also good but as these are often very tart they should be tasted and cooked if necesary.)

Once you have your gorgeous dark red filling – check for sweetness and flavour and if too sweet, squeeze a few drops of fresh lemon juice – take a glass or china pudding basin and line it with sliced white bread from which you have removed all the cursts. Pretend it's a jigsaw puzzle and all the pieces must fit exactly, pushing and persuading to make a perfect lining up to the rim of the bowl. Pour in your fruit mix, right to the top and cover with a crustless bread jigsaw 'lid'. Put a heavy plate on the top and leave in the refrigerator overnight. If you have any spare juice left, keep it to serve separately.

When ready to serve take off the weight, put a deep plate on the top and speedily invert. If it doesn't budge give it a gentle shake. Still stuck? Turn it back again, run a fine knife round the sides and repeat the upside down process. Serve cut in wedges with a bowl of Greek yoghurt or double cream.

If for any reason the bread is white in patches where it hasn't become totally soaked, just pour over the spare juice. And if you haven't any spare juice use crème de cassis. And if you haven't any crème de cassis, Ribena with a squeeze of lemon will do nicely.

Menu 4

Smoked salmon pâté

Take two ½ lb (230g) packets of salmon pieces, trim away any skin or bone and blend with ½ cup olive oil, 1 tablespoon *fresh* lemon juice, 1 clove garlic and lots of freshly ground black pepper. Some cooks also add double cream, but Greek yoghurt is better – about ½ a cup. When it's smooth put into one large pot or individual ramekins, sprinkle with cayenne pepper and serve with crispbread or hot brown toast.

Roast lamb

When English lamb is in season there is little to beat it. Insert slivers of garlic and fresh sprigs of rosemary here and there under the skin and around the bone. Pepper it liberally and stand on a grid in a pan full of roughly chopped onion scattered with rosemary and thyme, salt and pepper and drizzled with oil. Put it into a *hot* oven for 20 minutes and then reduce the heat slightly until done. A mere 20 minutes a pound is all you need unless you like your lamb grey and well done.

Remove the lamb to a carving dish along with the delicious crispy onion bits and pop back into the rapidly cooling oven while you make the gravy by pouring off the excess fat, adding some stock or a little of the water from the green beans.

Scrape the pan, add a small glass of wine if you feel inclined but do *not* thicken with flour. Serve in a separate jug and let your guests pour their own generous helpings, which they will.

Serve with green beans which can be fresh or frozen – you can't tell the difference if you don't overcook, and sprinkle with a generous sprinkling of parsley. Toss them in butter before serving if you're not too cholesterol conscious. Flaked almonds look good on *al dente* vegetables but they're merely an optional extra. Parsley, chives or nothing will do just as well.

Note: if you leave hot cooked vegetables drained in a hot saucepan they will go on cooking so douse them under the cold tap and heat them through when they're needed.

Red, white and green fruit salad

Arrange slices of immaculately trimmed fresh pineapple with the core removed. Cut into crescents and placed round the edge of a shallow glass bowl. Fill the centre with whole or cut-up strawberries. Pile some thin slices of peeled kiwis on the top, and pour over a syrup made with sugar, lemon juice and Cointreau and leave to steep for at least 2 hours. No cream please – it just blunts the wonderful clean taste. Do not make this dish with (a) woody, tart pineapples or (b) tasteless too-early strawberries.

Menu 5

Gazpacho

There are umpteen recipes for this cool summer soup. The following is an easy one:

2 lbs ripe tomatoes	
2 onions	*2 or 3 slices stale bread*
2 cloves garlic	*½ cup olive oil*
1 green pepper	*1 tablespoon white wine vinegar*
1 red pepper	*Salt*
1 peeled cucumber	*Lemon juice*

Peel tomatoes, onions and garlic. Deseed peppers. Cut every-thing into pieces and feed into blender with all other ingredients. It should still be 'bitty'. Leave to chill for at least 2 hours. Serve poured over 2 or 3 ice cubes and sprinkled with peeled chopped cucumber. If the texture is too thick it can be diluted with stock or water – or the ice cubes will do the job if left to stand for a while. But stir before serving or the top layer will be watery.

Fish pie

Simmer the fish of your choice in milk with salt, peppercorns, a bay leaf, until it's barely cooked – just a few minutes. (Cod, haddock, plaice, sole, monkfish – they're all good and the pie will be even more delicious if you add some scallops, prawns or scampi.) Drain gently and put into a large pie dish.

Make a cheese sauce with the remaining milk and a glass of white wine. A packet sauce will do nicely but do add an extra cup of mild grated fresh Cheddar or Gruyère. Add a packet of defrosted sweet corn – or a drained tin. Pour over the sauce and top the lot with a purée of mashed potatoes into which you have added a large knob of butter, and a raw egg. Sprinkle a little grated cheese on the top, add a few knobs of butter and heat in a gentle oven for at least an hour, turning up to high at the last moment to brown the top.

A green vegetable goes well with this – steamed broccoli or green beans. Or just a crispy green salad made with iceberg lettuce, watercress and lots of parsley served with a sharp French dressing.

Nectarine or peach salad with raspberries

Every summer it suddenly happens – a glut of wonderful peaches or nectarines. Pour boiling water over them – quickly remove them or they'll boil and brown – peel and arrange them in a circle round a large glass bowl. Sprinkle them with sugar and Cointreau and fill the centre with a huge pile of raspberries or blueberries. Top with a sprig of mint and serve with a big bowl of yoghurt.

Winter Recipes

Starters	Main course	Pudding
(1) Spiced grapefruit	Chicken in red wine purée potatoes, green salad	Chocolate mousse
(2) Baked eggs with shrimps	Veal Marengo rice and salad	Pears in red wine
(3) Cold cuts and pâté	Spaghetti alle vongole mixed green salad	winter fruit salad
(4) Fish soup	Boiled brisket of beef with vegetables	Apricot mousse
(5) Mushrooms à la grecque	Chicken and ham pie broccoli	Grapes galore

Menu 1

Spiced grapefruit

This is an unexpected way to start a meal, both refreshing and not too filling. Allow one whole grapefruit per person. Cut off a 'lid' and then cut round the sections to remove the whole centre 'wheel'. A curved sharp grapefruit knife will shorten the time this takes. Whirl round the edges, then each side of the sections and pull. It should come out in one go. Make sure no pips are left. Stand the fruit in a baking tin, sprinkle generously with brown sugar or drizzle in some runny honey. Add a knob of butter to each, pour in as much sherry or marsala as each will hold and bake for about 15 minutes in a hot oven. Serve fairly quickly because they're *not* nice cold. Pink grapefruit are sweeter and easier to section.

Chicken in red wine

1 roasting chicken cut into sections
½ bottle red wine
4 oz butter
½ lb unsmoked bacon cut into cubes

12 small onions, peeled
½ lb button mushrooms
2 cloves garlic, chopped
Seasoned flour, cornflour
1 bouquet garni
Parsley

In a large deep ovenproof pan brown the bacon then add the onions and mushrooms. Remove from the pan with a draining spoon. Flour the chicken – easy to do by putting the flour, salt and pepper in a plastic bag and shaking it – and brown them in the same pan. Put the onions, mushrooms and bacon back, add the garlic, seasoning and bouquet. Bring to the boil, cover and place in a moderate oven for about 45 minutes.

Remove the chicken pieces and warm while you thicken the sauce by boiling fast for about 10 minutes. If it is still not thick enough, strain off a little of the liquid, say, half a cupful. Allow it to cool and mix with a tablespoon of cornflour to make a paste. Add this to the liquid and boil furiously once more. Now it should be beautifully thick so return the chicken pieces to the pot and place it back into a low oven until you're ready to eat – at least half an hour to allow the flavours to blend.

Serve sprinkled with a great deal of chopped parsley, accompanied by puréed potatoes, followed by a green salad – just crisp lettuce and watercress.

Chocolate Mousse

¼ *lb best dark chocolate* (Menier or Bournville)
4 eggs
Brandy, Cointreau or Rum

Break the chocolate into pieces and melt in a double boiler – or over a pan of boiling water. Remove from heat and gradually stir in the egg yolks. Stir in a measure of liqueur. Beat the egg white until stiff and fold into the mixture. Serve in individual ramekins with some especially delicious little biscuits. *Crèpes Dentelle* are a favourite, closely followed by ratafias or Palmiers.

Menu 2

Baked eggs with shrimps

Butter individual ramekins and scatter some fresh or frozen shrimps (or potted ones) on the bottom. Break an egg very gently into each one and stand in a roasting pan filled with about an inch of water. Bake in a moderate oven for about 8–10 minutes. The yolks should still be soft and the whites set but not rubbery. This is good served hot or cold. You can pour cream on the top if you must, plus a sprinkling of cayenne.

Veal Marengo

This was supposedly served for the first time to Napoleon in battle. You need:

2 lbs lean veal cut into smallish pieces	Olive or corn oil for frying
2 onions, sliced	Garlic
4 tomatoes, roughly chopped	Salt and pepper
½ pint good stock (veal, vegetable or chicken)	Bouquet of herbs

Slice the onions and fry gently in the hot oil. Remove and gently fry the meat until browned. Replace the onions, add the wine, stock, garlic, herb bouquet and the roughly chopped tomatoes. Taste, season. Cover the pan and cook for about 1½ to 2 hours on the top of the stove. This is even better cooked for only 1 hour and then reheated the next day in the oven so that it gets that lovely 'baked' taste. Not truly traditional but quite delicious.

Serve scattered with lots of finely chopped parsley and plain boiled rice. A salad of endive and watercress makes a nice accompanying 'refresher'.

Pears in red wine

There are several variations on this. The classic way is best and don't make it with anything other than top quality fruit as misshapen hard pears are a waste of time – and do use good red wine. Choose big perfect pears (Comice, not *too* ripe are best) and allow one per person.

Peel them carefully leaving the stalk intact. Arrange them in an ovenproof dish just large enough to hold them standing, stalks up. Pour in at least ½ pint of wine (a half and half mix of wine and water will also do nicely.) The pears should be covered almost up to their necks. Cook for about 1½ hours in a slow oven, basting every now and then so that their colour is uniform.

Remove them gently from the liquid, stand on a pretty dish and chill. Boil the liquid quite fiercely until it reduces to a lovely goo-ey syrup. Allow to cool, pour over the pears and serve either warm or ice cold with *tuiles d'amandes* biscuits.

Menu 3

Cold cuts

This is an unattractive name for one of the most popular ways to start a meal. From a good delicatessen buy at least four kinds of smoked meats, and/or sausages. A good choice is prosciutto, mortadella, two kinds of salami and a good garlicky pâté. Serve on a dish with green and black olives and shiny red radishes still with their green stalks. Forget the toast and serve crunchy French bread instead. Delicious.

Spaghetti alle vongole (*cockles*)

Cook your spaghetti, either fresh or dried, according to the instructions. Allow 1 lb for four people.

If you use tinned vongole, which are excellent, drain off the water before you use them. If you use fresh ones, you'll need about ½ pint. Wash them thoroughly under the tap to remove grit and excess salt.

Make your sauce with a chopped onion and 2 cloves or garlic, gently cooked in olive oil until they are 'sweated' but not brown – about 10 minutes. Add a tin of chopped Italian peeled tomatoes, season to taste and cook for about another half an hour or until the sauce is nice and thick. Add the vongole and heat through – just a minute or two. Do not overcook. Pour over the spaghetti and serve.

To cut down on any last minute panic you can cook the sauce well in advance and reheat it while the pasta is cooking. Add the vongole only at the last minute. Sprinkle with *lots* of chopped parsley – the Continental kind is best as it's less fierce in flavour.

Always serve a really good salad after pasta – lots of greenery, iceberg lettuce, watercress and endive. A red and green salad with watercress and radicchio is colourful. Serve two cheeses, one should be hard and English and one soft and Italian or French.

Winter fruit salad

There are many variations. This is a favourite. Cut a melon into chunks and mix with pieces of stoned dates, sultanas soaked in a liqueur and tiny pieces of ginger in syrup. Add a slurp or two of the special syrup which you can keep permanently on hand in a tightly stoppered bottle. It's just sugar and water to which you can add fresh lemon juice before using. Scatter the salad with flaked almonds and serve with Greek yoghurt.

Menu 4

Fish soup

This one is a real cheat. Buy some good quality lobster, shrimp or crab bisque and add some fresh prawns or small scampi, a modest quantity of sherry or brandy and a pot of single cream and some extra milk to dilute. It becomes quite spectacular. Do serve *very* hot – with chunks of granary bread if your guests are gluttonous.

Boiled beef and vegetables

For this you need a piece of salt beef weighing about 5 lbs for six to eight people. Brisket is better but silverside will do. Put the meat into tepid water, bring to the boil, take off all the scum, add a dessert spoon of brown sugar and cook *very* slowly for about 3 hours.

Cut your vegetables – carrots, baby turnips, and celery, into smallish chunks and about half an hour before the meat is ready, pour off some liquid into another pan and gently boil the vegetables. Boiled potato or potato purée is also

117

delicious, and so are brussel sprouts which should be cooked separately. Serve with lots of mustard, French or English.

There are those who like dumplings but these are totally unnecessary as well as being both filling and fattening – what a deadly combination.

The meat is wonderful cold with pickled dill cucumbers and a beetroot and horseradish sauce known in Kosher delicatessens as Chrane.

Apricot mousse

This is best made not with the fresh (doubtful) almost tasteless (certainly) kind from the greengrocers but with the soft, flavourful dried kind from health food shops.

Stew the apricots with a twirl of lemon rind. You can mix apple juice and water for extra flavour. Taste for sweetness, add a carton of Greek yoghurt and put through the blender. You may prefer to use whipped white of egg in place of the yoghurt but this merely adds bulk. Pile into a large glass dish or individual small ones and sprinkle liberally with toasted almonds.

Menu 5

Mushrooms à la grecque

Best when the mushrooms are no bigger than your thumb nail. For six people you need:

1 lb mushrooms
3 large ripe tomatoes (or a tin of peeled Italian ones)
1 cup of olive oil
¼ pint dry white wine

1 teaspoon crushed coriander seeds (they're elusive little chaps so cover them with a cloth and tackle with a rolling pin)
2 cloves fresh garlic
1 bay leaf
Salt, pepper and parsley

Clean the mushrooms and trim the stalks. If you are using fresh tomatoes put in a basin, pour boiling water over them and peel at once. Remove the seeds and chop roughly. Place all the ingredients except the mushrooms and tomatoes into a pan and cook gently for about 5 minutes. Add the mushrooms and tomatoes, cover and cook gently for another 4 or 5 minutes. Remove the mushrooms and boil the sauce to thicken and reduce it slightly. Sprinkle with lots of fresh parsley and serve with crusty French bread.

This dish is best made the night before so that the flavours develop. It will keep for several days, getting better all the time.

Chicken and ham pie

Of all the variations this is a favourite. Boil a good quality roasting chicken with an onion, a stick of celery, a bay leaf, salt and peppercorns. About 1 hour is enough. Allow it to cool and remove all the flesh. (Keep the skin and bones for stock.) Break or cut the chicken into chunks and layer into a pie dish alternated with strips of cooked ham. Make a white sauce using the liquid from the chicken plus a glass of white wine and pour over. For the pie crust use frozen puff pastry which comes in sensible 1 lb packs.

Dark green broccoli looks lovely with this – or small brussels if they're in their prime and if not, baby frozen ones are excellent. Good alternatives: frozen baby-sized mangetout which are twice as delicious as the fresh ones and infinitely more reliable. They need the barest minimum of cooking to preserve their *al dente* texture. Add boiled potatoes only if you must.

Fresh green or black grapes

Preferably a mountain of them, these are really all you need after such a meal – lots of the sweet seedless kind are best. A tricolour pile is also a good idea, green, black and those lovely red ones that taste so wine-ey. You may also serve just a sliver or two of cheese if you must. And pile some shelled almonds onto the same dish. Finally, perhaps, some chocolate-covered ginger to go with the coffee and liqueurs.

God, I've been so busy
I've approached my boss about Maternity leave
And my ad for the nanny goes in next month
And I've started decorating the spare room like a nursery
But you're not even pregnant yet
I know. I haven't had the time.

Working Mother

Returning to Work

If you are a working mother you can rest assured you are not alone – nor even in a minority. Statistics show that 50 per cent of mothers with dependent children are now working either full or part-time. And women who do return to work are doing so after shorter and shorter 'baby-breaks'. This could be for economic reasons as fundamental as meeting mortgage repayments; it could be for fear of missing out on promotion, or even back-sliding; it could be because you miss the stimulus and the rewards of paid work and, as one woman put it – the satisfaction of doing 'something for me'; it could simply be that having had your children you realized that you are not cut-out for full-time mothering. As a journalist, Jill Tweedie put it: 'One of the great lies told to women is that motherhood is the best thing you can do. This assumes everybody is good at it, which isn't true. Motherhood is a vocation not everyone has.'

Whatever your reasons, the decision to return to work will probably not have been an easy one. And once taken, the realities of being a full-time working mother will not be easy either. To succeed in the role there are three essentials: a good back-up team, persistent juggling skills (both of these are covered later in this chapter) and perhaps most important, the determination not to waste time in guilt-stricken worrying.

Don't feel guilty

In avoiding this there are various things to remember. First, there is no significant research to show that the children of working women are more affected than their peers with full-time mothers. Second, children accept and feel comfortable with what they are used to – and that will include your absence from the home. They are not going to feel disadvantaged unless you keep telling them that they are. And finally, the years for which your children are yours – in terms of full-time care – represent only a tiny proportion of your life span. If, during those years, you put all your emotional and intellectual 'eggs' into your offspring you endow them with a terrible burden of guilt when the time comes – as it surely will – that they don't need you any more.

What about the children?

It is a difficult thing for a new mother to give over the care of her young baby to another. She will regret, she will feel guilt, and she will think that it really can't be done as well as she would do it. Well, perhaps it can't be done quite as well – were she the perfect caring all-understanding mother, leading solely by example, and never ever shrieking 'because I say so'. But those of us who are not perfect may well find that with the right person helping you, although the caring may be done differently, it will probably add another dimension to the loving world of your child. Whoever heard of a child, big or small, getting too much love. Not a common complaint.

In their earliest years your children will obviously need a continual and constant caring figure but, for the bulk of each day, this need not necessarily be you. It is increasingly believed that it is not the quantity of time spent with your child that it is important – rather the quality of that time. A couple of hours devoted completely to him will provide as much emotional feedback as hours spent dividing your attention between him and the housework.

Nor should you worry that the child will become more deeply attached to your nanny or childminder than he is to you. Research has shown that the most significant steps in the bonding process are taken in the hours immediately after birth, and subsequently children will recognize their parents not by voice or even smell, but through the awareness of a deep instinctive caring that only a parent is able to give.

Another major source of worry is the idea that you are

missing out on vital stages of the child's development. Here again it is important to remember that the first word your child says is not the only one he will ever utter, nor his first steps the only ones he will take.

It is probably true to say that the emotional loss – if any – is yours rather than the child's. The mother of a thirteen-year-old girl, who had worked during her pre-school years, opted to remain at home following the birth of her second child. Was the decision based on the assumption that her first child had missed her while she worked? 'I don't remember that I did,' said her daughter, 'I think it was more that she missed me.' This is likely to happen, but you can minimize the feelings of loss by acknowledging the rewards that paid working gives you – and consequentially your child. These are not only financial, but more important, emotional. Endless hours spent nurturing your child, together with feelings of frustration, resentment – and quite frequently boredom – are not going to do either of you any good.

You should also reorganize your priorities so that you can devote as much time as possible exclusively to your child. Relax a little when it comes to standards of house-keeping and the preparation of gourmet meals – the time would be much better spent enjoying yourself with your family. Conversely, remember that having elected to 'have it all', you have got to give it all you've got. Therefore, no matter how tired and ratty you might feel when you get back from the office, you can't just collapse into an armchair with a stiff drink. You owe it to your children to make the time you do spend with them as interesting as possible.

Fathers can help

Of course, every aspect of the working mother's life is going to be easier if she has a sympathetic and supportive partner, and luckily it's increasingly likely that she will. The most devastating ploy for domesticating men has been the invitation to fathers to share in childbirth. The invitation has rapidly become a command, the rite of passage of proper responsible fatherhood.

However, the price you have to pay for paternal involvement is quite high. You are likely to find yourself suddenly up-staged in what has traditionally been regarded as a women-only theatre – you are going to have to share the reins in what was perhaps the only area of your life in which you felt completely confident and in control. You are also going to have to allow your partner to do things his way (no matter how different his standards are from yours) and you're going to have to find the confidence to let him iron out his own mistakes. For instance, if after he's bathed the children the bathroom looks as though it's been hit by a typhoon, don't automatically feel *you* have got to mop it up. The chances are he'll tire of paddling over to his toothbrush as quickly as you do, and if he doesn't, you'll have to accept – without sulking – that because you mind most you will eventually clear it up.

In recent years there has been talk of marriage 'contracts'. This is the sort of arrangement whereby you come back from your honeymoon, sit down and draw up a set of rules along the lines of 'I'll mow the lawn if you change the sheets'. These tend to lead to demarcation disputes and go-slows (or do-it-badlys, as they're known on the domestic front) in the best-ordered two person families. With the advent of children they are well-nigh impossible to maintain. It's better to let the frontiers draw themselves of their own accord, based on the ideal that everybody does what he or she is best at, according to how they can fit it into their schedule. It's also a good idea to get your children into the habit of contributing their bit towards the running of the household – even if it's just making their own beds or helping with the washing up.

If you do manage to run a 'co-operative' household in this way, you are bound to beset by a niggling guilt that you are not fulfilling your natural role, and that if you can't manage to run your house and career you ought to stop working. Don't give in to your doubts – remember that you are refusing to bring up your children in near-isolation from their father (which must be a good thing), and that you are sensibly fitting your children to be – or live with – working mothers. It *is* possible to have it all and enjoy it.

The debate continues, and doubtless will continue long after our children are grown, about whether or not women who work are damaging their children. Most mothers think at some time or another, 'I should have been around. I should be around.' Many mothers then think exactly how they would be if they were around all the time. And the answer is all too often none too pleasant. It would be a hard mother indeed not to feel positive spasms of guilt if, when she leaves for work she leaves a wan child plucking at the sheets, and whispering, 'Bring me back a paper doll, please'. But that is not an argument for never working. It is perhaps an argument for not working all of the time, but jobs are few and far between that allow most mothers the luxury of chosen time and place. There are born mothers, and they possibly shouldn't work. There are not so born mothers who nevertheless love their children dearly, and are thrilled to be with them most of the time. Would the children of the latter mother benefit by having a bored crabby woman marching round the place and kicking at the fitted carpet? A lot of people ignore the basic enjoyment of life when debating this point. If you are happy, your child is more likely to be happy. If you think of life, and work in particular, as one long grind, a series of ever more exhausting scenes, then it is likely that children and everyone else will be damaged by your attitude. But if as much pleasure as possible is gleaned from every aspect of life – home, work, and free time, then that must reflect on those you are trying to show the world to. An optimistic view perhaps, but one that is necessary to contented working mothers.

Your Baby-Break – Your Rights Considered

The decisions involved in taking the 'baby-break' – if, when and how long for – are without doubt the hardest that most working women are going to have to face in the course of their careers. Children are now almost universally acknowledged to represent the biggest stumbling block between a woman and the boardroom and yet, it remains a woman's right to have her children whatever her occupation.

It is very important that you give yourself time to weigh up that crucial 'if' decision. Try, if possible, to get some exposure to babies and small children beforehand so you have an idea at least of what it will all involve. Then, assuming you have been through the 'if' decision, and come out with an affirmative answer, you will need to know exactly what your rights are as far as maternity leave is concerned.

Your rights – in theory

Maternity leave – time off from work to have a child – is every woman's right by law. Provided she has worked for her employer for two years full-time (i.e. at least 16 hours a week) or five years part-time (8–16 hours a week), she can leave work 11 weeks before the birth of her child, and return 29 weeks after the birth to the same or a similar job.

By law, those women who qualify get six week's maternity pay at 90 per cent of earnings less tax and national insurance, and the flat rate maternity allowance. This is paid to you by your employer, who then claims it back from the government, and you are eligible for it whether you actually take the leave or not. You may also qualify for maternity allowance at a standard rate of £29.15 per week, paid from the 11th week before the expected week of the birth (unless you carry on working, which disqualifies you from the allowance) until seven weeks after your baby is born. An additional maternity grant of £25 is supposed to cover additional costs like clothes for the baby – although these days it won't get you far. (Form NI 17A from the DHSS gives a more detailed explanation.)

You are also entitled to time-off with pay whilst you are still working to attend anti-natal clinics.

In practice

Whilst some women do find it works smoothly, others believe that career considerations such as continuity, reliability, and credibility in a male dominated world can be shaken or even shattered by taking the baby-break. In spite of their legal rights, some women will go to extreme lengths to play down their pregnancy and the birth of a child, mostly for career reasons. One top executive worked until a week before the birth of her child, returned very quickly, and (unknown to her staff) regularly expressed her milk in the ladies' loo and sent it to her home by motorbike messenger to be fed to her child.

A break in your career is likely to be seen as more of a problem if you work for a small firm. A break of six months for any reason can be dangerous as in that length of time you can easily get out of touch. In a personal business dealing with clients, large companies may have the resources to make arrangements when someone leaves for a long period, but most small firms have to work for a living, to pay their overheads, for example, and cannot easily adapt to the loss of a member of their team, even temporarily.

In fact, firms with less than six employees are exempt from the obligation to reinstate a woman after maternity leave, if they can show there is no available job which is equivalent to the one she left. Large concerns, however, should have the human and financial resources to cope well with maternity leave. (See 'Useful addresses' for details of firms which now offer good maternity schemes.)

You must also bear in mind that, in spite of the 'Superwoman' efforts made by working mothers not to allow their children to disrupt their careers, there is still an assumption that a woman is unreliable *because* of her children. Men taking time off for their wives' illness is acceptable – women taking time off for children is not. A woman is resented if she is absent through pregnancy. Perhaps it's something to do with the fact she chooses to be pregnant.

It is worth mentioning here that if you *are* forced to go home to deal with a domestic crisis, *never* refer to the reason why you have to leave the office early and don't expect to be back – 'I have an appointment' will suffice.

Some aspects of the legislation covering maternity leave can confuse both employers and employees. For example what happens to the employment contract while a woman is away? What about the pension scheme, holiday entitlement and the employer's obligation to create a suitable job if necessary upon her return? It is your responsibility to work all these factors out with your employer.

There is one main reason why employers sometimes take a jaundiced view of maternity leave. This is the statistic, established by the Department of Employment and illustrated by the experience of companies such as IBM, that only a small proportion of women who take maternity leave fulfil their declared intention of returning to work. The government's figure for those who return is 17 per cent compared with IBM's 'healthy' 39 per cent. But a 1981 report by the Policy Studies Institute suggests that this figure is likely to be small compared with overall staff turnover where 'an employer of 200 people may, on average, expect one notification of return per year', compared with 'overall rates of staff turnover of over 20 per cent'. The report points out that 'covering the jobs of people who are absent due to sickness, holidays . . . and so on is part of the normal business of staff management'.

To avoid any objection to your claiming your legal rights discuss your maternity leave with your boss. If you would like to change your working hours after the birth of your baby – to work part-time perhaps – be sure you do this in good time. As a general rule three weeks before you stop work (and some doctors consider it inadvisable to work after the 32nd week) tell your employer, in writing, when you intend to stop work, the week the baby is due, and whether you wish to return to work after maternity leave. (You are entitled to maternity pay even if you do not intend to return to work, because this is ultimately paid by the government not by your employer.) After the birth (usually about seven weeks after) you may receive a letter from your employer asking if you are going back to work. You should reply in writing within two weeks. Remember that 29 weeks after the beginning of the week of the birth is the latest time by which you still have the right to go back to your job – write to let your employer know you will be returning three weeks before you do so.

Many women who fully intended to return to work find, when the time comes, that they cannot bear to leave their baby – and vice versa. The decision whether to return to work or not should be shared with your partner, but ultimately it rests with you. However, in fairness to your employer (and to other female employees following in your footsteps) you should inform him/her of your intentions as soon as possible.

If you are self-employed you will have to subsidize your own pregnancy and recovery period. You are still entitled to basic state financial aid, and if you are a single parent you might also be able to claim supplementary benefit.

There are also efforts being made to persuade the government to introduce 'parental leave'. (This should not be confused with paternity leave for which there is little official provision at the moment.) Paternal leave is currently available to working parents in Belgium, Germany, France, Luxembourg, Denmark, Greece and Portugal. Early in 1985 the EEC produced a directive suggesting that it should also be made available in Britain, and should allow both the mother and the father three months' leave per child, not to be taken by both parents simultaneously, and to be taken before the child is two years old. (Variations occurred where the child was handicapped, adopted, or the leave taken part time.) Nothing, as yet, has been done to advance this proposal.

How Soon Should You Return to Work?

There are an increasing number of women who, rather than taking advantage of maternity leave, decide to take all their annual leave after the birth of their baby and return to work within, say, six weeks. If you are contemplating doing this you might be interested in current medical opinions about such swift returns to work.

Professor Chamberlain, consultant obstetrician at St Georges Hospital, London, says it depends on the mother, the baby and the job. 'If a woman has a job which is physically demanding, she may need the full 40 weeks' leave in which to prepare for the birth and recover after it. But I have known women whose work was more intellectually demanding who have wanted to be back in a couple of days. I don't think you can make any hard and fast rules about it.' (When maternity leave was introduced into the Employment Protection Act in 1975 it seems that the figure of 40 weeks was more or less an arbitrary one. It was not based on any research about what was best for the mother and baby because at that time there was none available.)

Mr John Malvern, consultant obstetrician at Queen Charlotte's Hospital, London, feels that medical attitudes to maternity leave must be flexible. 'I would just watch the mother carefully at her antenatal visits and see how she was coping. And I would advise her to warn her employer that she intended to work on up to the birth unless she began to get too tired.' He feels that it is the baby who needs the mother rather than vice versa in the first few months. 'We're very keen on maternal contact, reassurance and the baby being as near the mother as possible,' he says. 'While you can't be dictatorial about it, I would say two months is the minimum the mother and child should spend together.'

Bonding

This is the forming of a close relationship between the baby and the significant people in its lives and is always a subject of controversy when it comes to mothers leaving their babies, particularly in the first few weeks. One pediatrician believes that as long as babies are not passed around constantly, but can relate to a small number of people during the early months, it's unlikely to do them any harm.

But a child psychotherapist from a leading London clinic is less emphatic. In her experience, linking later psychological problems in children to being left at 20 weeks rather than 29 weeks would be far too simplistic; nevertheless she feels that from the baby's point of view, the longer it spends with the mother the better. 'There is also evidence that the less women see their babies, the less they want to. I would always advise women to take full advantage of maternity leave. If a woman is going to fret at home, however, then returning to work may be best for mother and child.' She also advises mothers, wherever possible, to leave their options open about when they might return to work. Some women get 'hit' by mother-hood and, contrary to their pre-birth ideas, do not want to return to work. If their income is vital to mortgage repayments, though, there may be no alternative.

The doctors, it seems, are happy for women to start working whenever they feel able after the birth. Apparently there's no medical reason why women can't do three jobs at once and straight away if they wish. But that's not to say that being a mother, holding down a job and keeping both a home and a relationship going is easy.

Organizing Child-Care

A working mother, outside her work, is a thing apart: regarded with suspicion by non-working mothers, as a strange animal of odd habits. At work, she is careful to hide all references to nannies, nappies and night feeds. The only people who understand her distracted looks and silent mutterings are other working mothers.

Enjoying work without carrying the heavy burden of guilt about leaving the children at home, has of course everything to do with who is taking your place at home. For, if you find the right person to look after your child in your stead, the chances are that you will be able to cope with all the other parts of your life – both at work and at home – with a degree of calmness, not to say contentment, that you would never otherwise achieve.

There is no point in replacing guilt (about working) by worry (about young children). Given properly organized care, they are not going to grow up into delinquents or depressives. Hellish teenagers maybe – just like the offspring of doting round-the-clock mothers whose children can't wait to be free. There's something to be said for scarcity value (yours) and sociability (theirs) cultivated early.

What then are the alternatives?

Daytime care away from home

PLUSES
Officially recognized creches and nursery schools have professional staff plus some untrained helpers. Young babies should be in good hands and three- to five-year-olds might

even learn something useful. They'll also have company and may learn that aggression doesn't – and sometimes does – pay.

Registered child minders look after under-fives in their (the minders') own homes, which means that hours are more flexible. An efficient well-staffed local authority won't register anyone until every conceivable check has been made.

MINUSES

Creche and nursery school hours are usually restricted – mornings only, or full days that stop at 5 p.m. You have to deliver and collect, and late collection, except by very special arrangement, would earn disapproval.

Nursery schools often observe school holidays, including half-terms, which means you need to make alternative arrangements.

With a minder you still have to collect and deliver and you may be expected to take food – or may prefer to. Some minders also like to have nappies supplied daily – no chore to take clean ones along in the morning, but take dirty ones home at night can't appeal to many people.

The minder's own children can be a minus if they're rough, inclined to tease the baby, or grow jealous if he/she gets all the attention from their mother.

And, as in all walks of life, the quality of minder can vary – some are marvellous but there are some you may be less than happy with.

CONDITIONS

All creches and nursery schools should be regularly inspected – check this via the Social Services but also do your own checking. Find time to go along at collection time and chat to the mothers. Request a daytime visit to see whether the children seem happy and busy. Note the treatment handed out to the naughty ones, and if there aren't any, try to work out why. Too happily occupied, or too scared of authority perhaps?

Try to see a minder when her own children, if any, are likely to be around, and notice how she handles them, as well as any she may be minding.

Make sure that she has a telephone. Ask how she copes with the odd times when she has to be out – emergency shopping, trips to the doctor or dentist. Can she be sure of a suitable 'sitter'? Is there a garden where a young baby can sleep, or a toddler can play, in full view, and behind a securely locked gate? How much experience has the minder had, and is she happy to put you in touch with at least one local mother who has employed her? Has she a washing machine that will actually boil, or near boil nappies? How much does it matter if you're kept late at work? Does she find the time to play with your child? Much of the above can be handled most tactfully as a cosy chat.

Daily nanny

PLUSES
You get her training and experience without losing evening and weekend privacy, and she may be able to give you an occasional evening's babysitting. She might possibly work part-time if you do or she might even be shared with another part-time worker.

MINUSES
You have less chance to spend time with her, get to know her and discuss problems. Evening babysitting may still have to be laid on separately, involving more money and still more organization.

Any nanny can wake up with a streaming cold or a sky-high temperature, but at least if she lives in she's there, and you know about it in time to call up reinforcements. Don't take on a daily nanny who doesn't have a telephone or at least guaranteed access to one.

A daily nanny is likely to be an expensive alternative, as she will have her own flat, utilities and expenses to pay for.

HOW TO FIND:
Ask your nearest reliable nanny/domestic agency. If they can't help, try advertising in your local paper, and *The Lady* which is known internationally as *the* paper for nanny jobs. It also carries advertisements for nanny agencies. (See 'Useful addresses'.)

Don't forget newsagents' noticeboards, but do make your requirements very clear. You will avoid a lot of unnecesary phone calls if you state you are looking for NNEB (Nursery

Nursing Education Board) or equivalent qualifications. An experienced nanny, whatever her qualifications, will know what that means. Hopeful amateurs probably won't.

FINANCE
Expect to pay a daily nanny between £55 and £80 per week, perhaps more if you live in central London. (For more about finance see under 'Living-in nanny'.)

CONDITIONS
Qualifications, experience, personality and references that can be followed up by telephone are particularly important, especially if you'll be working when your new nanny takes up the job. (And don't forget your needs may not be the same as her previous employer's.) Once she's started work try to plan things so you don't simply dash past each other twice a day. One working – and commuting – mother gets herself and her four-month-old baby all set to go out as soon as the daily nanny arrives at 8.30 a.m. All three walk – well, the baby rides – to the station, and this provides them with a useful time to chat and exchange any plans for the day. Remember to warn your nanny about any happenings – 'Gas man soon after 1 o'clock to mend the boiler if we're lucky' is the sort of thing that should already be written on the kitchen pad – that way she won't be taken unawares.

Living-in nanny

PLUSES
She's there. No need to panic if you have to work late, unless it's her evening off. (See 'Conditions' below.) She's trained and/or experienced; you can relax and enjoy the baby and, at the same time, pick up the kind of professional know-how that doesn't arrive as a package deal with motherhood. With luck and foresight (yours), she'll be pleasant company and a rich source of anecdotes about the local goings-on that you've missed while out at work.

MINUSES
Some loss of privacy is the first and obvious disadvantage. There will also be vastly increased household bills: no one

who isn't paying ever remembers to switch lights off, economize on hot water or minimize their phone-calls. The wrong nanny is also, to put it bluntly, a very trying business.

Nanny-sharing

An increasingly popular solution for women who don't want their entire salary to go straight into their nanny's pay-packet! It is usually arranged by the individuals themselves: one person finds a nanny that suits her requirements, and then looks for another family who would like to employ her for two or three days a week. (At least one London agency will do this ground work for you; see 'Useful addresses'.)

The specific arrangements will vary: does one of you want a live-in nanny, or will daily help suit you both? Do you only need help three days a week, or would you prefer that the nanny looked after both sets of children every day in either one of your houses? What are the nanny's evening obligations? All this should be clearly worked out in advance.

PLUSES
One obvious one: it halves the cost. (It will also halve agency fees.) It could also give your children a chance to play regularly with other children, if the nanny is going to look after all the offspring concerned in one house.

MINUSES
No matter what arrangements you make there are bound to be occasions when one or other family feels they need the nanny at a time when she is not officially 'theirs'. The more often this happens, the more resentment it is likely to cause, and the system becomes increasingly likely to break down. To avoid this make clear schedules and try to stick to them.

How to find a suitable nanny

Start looking, if it's at all possible, at least three months before you need your nanny. If you use agencies, they may take their time. Some less good ones might even try to give you their less promising candidates, on the principle that, as you're a working mother, you won't be around to spot the mistakes.

Agencies often charge the earth – or a month's nanny salary, which comes to the same thing – for a successful introduction, so be prepared to wait for total satisfaction. You could send a stamped addressed envelope to the Federation of Personnel Services (see 'Useful addresses') for their country-wide list of recommended agencies. They're also the people to whom you should report any really awful behaviour by an agency, like claiming to interview nannies when they don't, and leaving it to you to take up references, both of which you'll need to do anyway. Some also have the nasty habit of placing a good nanny and then 'keeping in touch' with her. An acquaintance was sent a very good (and luckily very straight and loyal) nanny. The introduction fee was £150, not returnable after three satisfactory months. Very soon after the three months had expired they approached the girl with 'A marvellous job: ultra-rich family, swimming pool, all the trimmings . . .' This is actually illegal under the 1973 Employment Agencies Act (section 5, regulation 2) and should be reported if it can be proved that the agency made the first move.

Another alternative is to advertise. Your best bet is *The Lady* magazine (published weekly), or try the *Daily Telegraph* and *The Times*. If you go for all three, don't place all your advertisements at once. You could get heavily involved in correspondence and interviews.

OBTAINING REFERENCES

Once you think you've found the right candidate, take up references by telephone – even if the previous employer is in the Outer Hebrides. Most people will say far more than they would ever write in a formal testimonial. Enlist the sympathy of the previous employer: tell her how disastrous a less-than-ideal nanny would be in your circumstances, raise carefully – and impersonally – any doubts you may have and nudge her into talking.

Working mothers need nannies with previous experience. There are plenty of non-career or part-time working employers to give a newly qualified NNEB her first job. However well she has coped with the 'practics' and can cope with health or feeding problems, she still has to find out how she can fit in with a family and accept the wishes – or most of them – of an employer who probably knows less about current child-care theory than she does.

136

Even if the first applicant seems good, do interview more than one. Apart from the fact that she might not take the job, this kind of interview is different – far more personal – than the ones that you may have conducted in your office. You get better with practice. For example, you must ask about her health. Is she ever laid low by migraine or period pains? You are going to feel guilty going off to work leaving a sick girl with no one, except possibly a cleaning lady, to offer warm drinks and sympathy. And is she, incidentally, going to be tactful with such a cleaning lady should you have one? You need to know her holiday plans, and also what her own family arrangements are.

PAYING YOUR NANNY

A nanny who has her NNEB certificate or good hospital experience will expect about £50–£69 per week in her first job, rather less if you live outside London. After three year's experience this should rise to £70–£80.

Just in case you think that Norland or other privately trained nannies are expensive and toffee-nosed, Norland recommends £50 per week for a first job, and doesn't award its trainees with a certificate until their first employers have vouched that they've provided a trouble-free nine months' work. Most of the girls will like to wear their uniform while the baby is small and probably messy as it is easily washed. Later, a lot of them prefer to wear their own clothes.

Don't slide carelessly past the deceptively innocent-looking word 'clear' after a salary figure. It means that you pay whatever tax is due (one third of anything over £34 per week) plus the whole, not just the employer's part, of the National Insurance Stamp – a weekly sum of fractionally over 20 per cent of her salary. There is no need to queue at the Post Office for stamps, you can arrange with your local tax office, which also handles National Insurance, to pay by cheque. And talking of cheques, many employers and nannies find it convenient to pay part of her earnings directly into her bank or Building Society, the rest in cash. This helps the nanny save as she earns and saves her a lot of time queuing for ready cash.

CONDITIONS

A nanny must have her own room. Make it as much like a bed-sitter as possible – for instance a sofa-bed will save on both cost and space, and a bright, felt-covered notice board for photographs, postcards and magazine tear-outs will go down well. 'Own bathroom if feasible' is specified by agencies, and it certainly eases the early-morning rush. Failing this and given enough space, it's worth asking a plumber to quote for a hand-basin in the bedroom. Enclose it in a cupboard if at all possible. Colour television is also specified. This may seem an unnecessary luxury that you'd rather not afford, but it means extra privacy for you. To these items you could add an electric kettle, three or four pretty cups and saucers and a table for writing at.

Be totally frank with your nanny from the start. She'll like you and the job better if you are. Tell her exactly what you expect her to do and not to do. Cooking for young children? Tell her. Ironing other than for her charges? Tell her. Bed-making? Tell her. Eating arrangements: with you, or if she prefers, in her own room. The answer is probably a mixture, and will probably depend on what's on television. If you prefer her to eat separately when you're entertaining tell her in advance: don't wait until the situation arises, or she may think you've decided that she's a social disaster. In any case, do ask her to 'drop in for a few minutes and have a quick drink' to be introduced to friends and, more especially, your relations.

Is she allowed to entertain friends in her room? In your quarters when you're out? The occasional friend for lunch? The one thing you must say, carefully but firmly, is that you'd rather she didn't bring in absolutely new male acquaintances who might be bad news for her and you.

Should you impose a curfew? That rather depends how old she is. For a young nanny who has to be up early in the morning, and perhaps during the night with a young baby 11–11.30 p.m. seems sensible. You could extend this on her official evening off, and of course at weekends. Does she smoke? Never ever in the nursery or in bed. Is she a sound sleeper? If you are doing a long day's work you shouldn't have to get up in the night if the baby cries. But if a young child is ill and fretful, you should be prepared to take over for one night in three – to give your nanny a break.

Au pairs

PLUSES
They cost less than nannies. They can, if you're lucky, be good company, and might even help you to improve your French/ Italian/Spanish or your children's faltering beginnings in foreign languages at school. They are sometimes interesting cooks. And you will also find that you learn a lot about your own language.

MINUSES
They are definitely a gamble, unless they're available for interview. It's neither sensible nor fair to expect a young, inexperienced girl to be responsible for a young baby, so unless your children are at least four years old au pairs are not for you. The times of their English classes tend to coincide exactly with the times that you need them most. And on top of that they do get homesick, and like it or not, you will feel responsible for cheering them up. One way to alleviate this problem is to suggest that your au pair recommends a friend of hers from home who is willing to work for a friend of yours with children of similar ages.

HOW TO FIND AN AU PAIR

Through an agency preferably recommended by friends, or by advertising in European newspapers – or through *The Lady*. (See 'Useful addresses'.) If you're lucky you might find a girl who's already in this country, and has genuinely good reasons for wanting to change jobs. Don't consider one who hasn't given an employer or locality a fair trial – at least two to three months.

FINANCE

Au pairs acquired through agencies come in grades. 'Demi-pairs' should do two or three hours' work daily for a five day week and two or three evenings babysitting in exchange for free board and lodging but no 'pocket money'. 'Au pairs' should do five hours daily for a six day week at £20 a week, and 'au pairs plus' get £25 per week for an additional two or three afternoons. (These are obviously guide-lines.)

Agency fees will cost you from under £20 for a short-term demi-pair to over £50 for a year-long au pair plus. The agency should also handle 'import' arrangements for you.

CONDITIONS

An au pair needs her own room – as for a nanny – which should be absolutely private and barred to children except by invitation. She'll expect to live 'as family', *but* again, her own television might cut down on the sort of conversation that begins 'In your country do you have . . .'. You should include her in at least some of your family outings – you may well find yourself seeing the sights for the first time!

As well as your office number, if you have a secretary give her name and the name of at least one other office friend, and if possible, one non-working local friend who could be appealed to in a crisis. It's also useful to write down a few stock phrases.

Making it all work

Whatever type of child care you use, the occasional let-down is almost inevitable. Even a living-in nanny could walk out in a huff or be called away by a family emergency, so a tight network of reinforcements is essential. Mentally listing friends and neighbours who would probably help in a sudden crisis is not good enough. Talk to some of them – especially those who have help with their children – and arrange a cut-and-dried mutual pact *before* things go wrong.

You may not be able to contribute your help in person, but you can explain what you've arranged to your nanny, your minder and even your nursery school teacher. It's also useful to ring round the agencies as some of them specialize in providing emergency nannies at crisis time.

Only widowed mothers – as opposed to married, unmarried or separated ones – can claim a 'Housekeeper's' tax allowance, as can widowers, but it is small. It's far better for a single mother to go for the Additional Personal Allowance (APA) – which brings her tax reliefs up to those of married couples. Apply too for child benefit, which isn't taxable, and is available to everyone. These items won't pay the nanny's salary, but they'll certainly help to offset it.

Don't ask your nanny to do a lot of household shopping as it's hard to manoeuvre a pushchair or toddler in crowded supermarkets, and 'picking-up germs' isn't mere nanny lore. But she'll feel part of the team if you sometimes let her buy clothes for a toddler, whether or not you agree with her taste. Name your shops and your price range and let her get on with it.

Useful addresses

Several organizations and companies have special schemes which enable women (and men) to take extra time off to be with their children. Here are some examples:

National Westminster Bank: has two schemes. Re-entry is for those of high management potential, whom the bank will guarantee retaining and re-employing at the original grade within five years of resignation. Also within that time anyone on the Reservist scheme (available to those of lesser potential) can apply for suitable vacancies and is guaranteed consideration. All re-entrants and reservists must do at least two weeks' paid work each year.

IBM: has a competitive scheme allowing 20 women each year to work part-time three years after birth.

BBC: offers employees the chance to apply for internal jobs before they are publicly advertised, up to five years after resigning. The scheme is not only available to maternity leavers but to all employees who want to leave for strong domestic reasons.

Times Newspapers: looks favourably upon applications for job-sharing and part-time work following a birth.

Nottinghamshire County Council: offers its teachers three years' maternity leave with a job guaranteed at the end.

The Maternity Alliance, Ruth Evans, 59–61 Camden High Street, London, NW1 7JL
Tel: 01 388 6337
This body campaigns for improvements in the health care social and financial support offered to parents-to-be, mothers, fathers and babies, and for improvements in the legal rights of parents during and after pregnancy. It conducts research and organizes seminars on key maternity issues. It provides an information resource for organizations, groups and individuals with an interest in maternity services and maternity rights. They produce a useful publication called *The Maternity Rights Handbook* by Ruth Evans and Lyn Durward (Penguin £4.95).

Child-care

This list is *not* meant to be exhaustive but a guide to known and tested agencies which may be able to help you in your search for the right person to care for your child.

The Lady Magazine, 39–40 Bedford Street, London WC2E 9ER
Tel: 01 836 8705

AU PAIR AGENCIES
An au pair does not need a work permit provided she falls within the Home Office's definition of an au pair, i.e. an unmarried girl (aged 17–27 inclusive) who is a national of a western European country, including Malta, Cyprus or Turkey, with no dependants who is entering the country as a guest of a family to learn the English language and live as a member of an English family. For further information there is a pamphlet called *A Guide for the Hostess* available from HMSO bookshops. The agencies below all specialize in finding au pairs. They will require you to fill in a questionnaire and will all charge a one-off fee. Always check when fees are payable and what the conditions are should you find the au pair you have chosen unsuitable.

Bliss Service, 1 Sussex House, Raymond Road, London SW19 4AH
Tel: 01 946 8705
Open 9–9 p.m. (telephone calls taken until 9.30p.m.). Bliss au pairs are over 18, English-speaking and usually from Sweden, Austria or Switzerland. They arrive in September, January or April (English language school term time); holiday-only au pairs can also be found. Bliss charge a £50 introduction fee. Two-week free trial period.

Edgware Au Pair Agency, 74 Lake View, Edgware, Middlesex
Tel: 01 958 8188
Open 9.30–5 Mon–Fri. Can supply three types of au pair for one month or more (introduction fee £15–£80) and two types of demi-pair and mothers' helps for six months or more (£35 per week plus £100 introduction fee). Once you have completed their questionnaire, Edgware will send details of a suitable au pair for your consideration.

Ianda Employment Agency, 501a Walmer House, 296 Regent Street, London W1
Tel: 01 580 1949
Ianda will send you questionnaires that would-be au-pairs have filled in for you to choose from (mostly from France, Spain, Italy and Scandinavia). They come either during the holidays or for a six-month or longer period. They also offer an au pair plus who will do housework as well. Ianda charge a £50 plus VAT introduction fee.

Mary Poppins Nanny Agency, Abbots Hills Chambers, Gower Street, Derby DE1 1SD
Tel: 0332 369177
Open 9–5 Mon–Fri. Charges sheet available. Mary Poppins provides a personal service with interviews instead of mailing lists. Their au pairs are mainly French and will travel all over England.

NANNY AGENCIES
Barncrofts of Belgravia, London House, 26–40 Kensington High Street, W8 4PF
Tel: 01 589 3990
Open 10–6 Mon–Fri. All domestic personnel including fully qualified nannies. They also offer a 'learner' nanny service in which parents are asked to monitor their trainee's progress for six months. This works out cheaper but is unsuitable for families with small babies.

The Childcare Agency, Uppleby Road, Poole, Dorset BH2 3DE
Tel: 0202 737171
Open 8.30–2, 6–7. Family fills in details. Introduction fee is 5% nanny's annual salary. Refund period of 6 weeks. Replacement not guaranteed, but they will try to organize one if required.

Harrow Nanny Agency, 42a Roxborough Park, Harrow-on-the-Hill HA1 3AY
Tel: 01 422 3999
Open 9.30–6.00. Family and girls fill in details and the two are matched and introduced. Once placed there is a flat fee of £120 but there is a reduction if this is paid within 7 days. Replacements and refunds available during the first 10 weeks.

Minder, The Old Rectory, Marsh Baldon, Oxon OX9 9LS
Tel: 086 738 277/0491 651 687
Open 9.30–5 Mon–Fri. They charge £5 registration fee; the family fills in a questionnaire and an interview is arranged. Once the nanny is placed, the family pays an introduction fee of £95 for a qualified girl and £80 for an unqualified girl. You have a three-month trial period during which you can get a refund on pro rata basis (minimum fee £20) or they will organize a replacement.

Nannies (Kensington) 177 Kensington High Street, London W8
Tel: 01 937 3299
Open Mon–Fri 10–5. They arrange interviews with the nanny and the clients. There is a hefty engagement fee when the nanny is placed. Families are sent three or four different people to choose from. They will try to find a replacement or return money should it not work out.

The Nanny Services, Oldbury Place, London W1M 3AH
Tel: 01 935 6976
Open 9.30–6. There is a lengthy introduction over the phone. The placement fee is 4 weeks' salary (average salary £45–£80 per week). Nine-week guarantee enables the family to get a replacement or a refund of half the fee.

Sloane Bureau of Chelsea, King's House, 25 Kings Road, London SW3 4BR
Tel: 01 730 8122
Open Mon–Fri 10–5. Families and girls fill in forms stating requirements and are matched and introduced. There is a scaled fee – 6½% of nanny's income (average £50–£60 per week). One year's guarantee of replacement free of charge.

Tinies Agency, The Stable House, Lammas Lane, Esher, Surrey KT10 8PN
Tel: Esher 67447
Open Mon–Fri, 24-hour answering service. Clients' details are taken and given to the girls who then phone up the family and arrange to meet them. There is £155 introduction fee to pay for successful placement which is refundable on a sliding scale up to 6 weeks or they can organize a replacement.

Details of further agencies can be found in *The Lady* magazine, which is also the best way of advertising for a Nanny directly yourself – see p. 00

I love travelling. It's so interesting meeting completely different types of people
Eating exotic food in picturesque surroundings
Breaking down the language barrier
And really getting to know their culture
Where are you?
Middlesborough

Travelling – for Business and Pleasure

Business Travel

Travelling on business is traditionally regarded as a perk in any job. And so it should be. At best it involves new challenges and adventures; at least it broadens your horizons and breaks the routine of sitting at your desk. But that is not to say it's all a dizzy whirl of exotic destinations, smart hotels and champagne on expenses. The bulk of business travel involves getting up at sparrow's fart to catch the train or shuttle to places no more exciting than Birmingham or Reading; working through a day of meetings and then dashing to catch the last train home to a waiting family . . . If you are going to cope successfully the most important thing is to be organized well in advance.

Getting ready

AT HOME
Start with your life outside the office. If you've got children your first priority is to ensure that there is somebody reliable who can deliver and collect them from school at the appropriate times, and then look after them until you or your partner gets back.

If you are not lucky enough to have a full-time nanny, try and arrange a network system with other local mothers. Even if they are not themselves working, they will probably be glad of a few hours' peace and quiet at weekends when you are at home.

If you can't get a network going you could try enlisting the services of a student, or there are lots of agencies – Universal Aunts for example – who can arrange a few hours' child care as and when you need it. (A list of these agencies can be found in 'Useful addresses'.)

One of the easiest ways to help keep your family happy while you are away on business is to keep their routine running as smoothly as possible. If, for instance, you are worried about the children missing you at bedtime when you normally read to them, why not tape the next chapter of the book you are reading together. The novelty of working the recorder will probably more than make up for your absence.

If you live alone getting away will probably be a lot simpler to arrange. But if you are often away overnight or longer do leave a set of keys and a telephone number either with a neighbour or the police in case they need to contact you quickly. When you're going to be away for more than a couple of nights you might want someone to keep an eye on your home, water your cat, feed your plants, forward your telephone messages . . . Minders will do all that – for about £25 for the first week, and £15 per week thereafter.

AT WORK
Having sorted out your home-life you can prepare for business. And prepare you must. If you are to impress your clients you have got to be 110 per cent on top of your subject – and confident enough to prove it. You're not likely to be relaxed and refreshed enough to do that if you've been frantically scrabbling through your papers in the cramped quarters of a train or plane. Anyway, unless you've got extraordinary powers of concentration, constructive work while travelling is not a realistic option. A couple of hours' overtime in the office the night before you leave will save you a lot of worrying while in transit.

Time saving

Do make sure that you make the most efficient use of your time and money. Unless your job involves frequent travelling to a variety of places in the same region it is probably wisest not to take your own car or hire one. Navigating your way round strange towns and finding parking places will contribute to the wear and tear on your nerves, as well as cutting into valuable thinking time between appointments.

On the other hand, if your trip involves visiting several cities in a couple of days, having your own transport will save you hanging around at stations and being tied down to train or plane timetables.

If you are travelling through London to Heathrow or Gatwick taking a taxi will do nothing but enhance your status. Even taking your own car is not a very satisfactory option as the long-term car-parks are always some distance from the actual terminals. Unless you are travelling at very unsocial hours train or tube are the quickest and the cheapest methods of getting there.

Check in at the last possible moment. One of the main arguments in favour of splashing out on business class tickets is that they do give you speedier check-in and priority disembarkation at the other end. Many airlines also allow their business class passengers to use a separate lounge, which helps enormously if you do have to make some last minute notes or telephone calls to the office. (In some cases this only applies to people who have joined the appropriate business class club.)

The most important time-saving trick of all is to take only hand-luggage. Soft-sided sail-bags or hanging suitcases are lighter and easier to carry than solid suitcases – and airlines often take a lax line on passing their dimensions as suitable for hand-luggage. Their other great advantages are that you can put them in the washing machine when they get dirty, and they don't look important enough to slash or steal. And if you're travelling by plane and can't manage with just one piece of hand-luggage don't whatever you do, rely on the luggage you have put in the hold arriving with you. Carry all vitals on to the plane so that if you travel in casual clothes, make sure you have one executive suit with you if you have a meeting as soon as you arrive.

Practical packing

Even the most efficient packers will find their clothes get creased in suitcases, but this does happen less if you avoid packing immediately after ironing. However, an increasing number of hotels now have irons available from the reception, so if you are due to have a quick change on arrival ask for an iron to be waiting in your room when you make your reservation. (Some up-market hotels also have curling tongs and heated rollers – it's always worth asking.)

Make a list of what you are going to need – try to do it by event and occasion. You can cut your luggage literally in half if you remember that, be it a business meeting or a dinner with clients, the top half of you is going to be most visible. Dramatic jewellery and a selection of shirts and sweaters will dress the same skirt up or down.

Take small, unbreakable bottles of skin- and hair-care products – you may like to keep a set specially for travelling. The Body Shop has a good range with products suited to most sorts of skin, and if you prefer to stick with your regular brand you can always use their products once, and then refill the bottles yourself. You can save more space in your case – and money spent on hotel laundry bills – by packing a tube of Dylon's Travelwash. It's unbreakable, inexpensive and available at most chemists and department stores. Take a supply of sanitary products with you whenever you are travelling. In under-developed countries they are non-existent or unbelievably expensive, and even in the western world ignorance of brand names can lead to embarrassment. Remember also to take a small medical kit (vitals are aspirin, Alka-seltzer and Rennies), a needle and thread and a small pair of scissors.

Deciding where to stay

When booking your accommodation choose a hotel that is as close as possible to where the bulk of your business will be. If that involves staying in the centre of town it is obviously going to cost more, but if you calculate the time and money wasted on taxis you'll probably find it's a few extra pounds well spent.

Most of the big hotel chains now have executive floors. Like the airlines with their business class tickets, they tend to promote these on the basis of the luxuries they provide which will probably include larger, better-equipped rooms and a lounge reserved for guests on that floor only. However, the biggest advantage to the business traveller working to a tight schedule is the fact that they offer express check-in and -out.

150

It's done on the executive floor or in your room, so you don't have to wait in reception with tourists who, while they are paying their bills are anxious to practise their German or discover the best route to the local *piscine*. Executive floors will frequently be able to provide secretarial services too, but even if you are staying in standard rooms and you are going to need to type up reports or contact the office before your return, do make sure that the hotel you have chosen has a business centre. In some of the larger hotel chains these facilities are available on a 24-hour basis, and some even provide typewriters for use in your room.

Making the best use of money

If you are travelling overseas, carrying a combination of cash, travellers' cheques and credit cards is the best way to ensure that you'll never be caught without a valid form of currency. Remember that US dollars are welcome almost everywhere – it's a good idea to carry some in case of emergencies. If you are taking travellers' cheques make a note of all the cheque numbers in the back of a notebook or diary, and try to change them at banks. Hotels and airports often operate an unfavourable rate of exchange and money-changers are a positive rip-off. Remember to keep the receipts you are given when changing money: in most countries you will need them to substantiate insurance claims for lost or stolen money. (You will also need to obtain written confirmation that you have reported the loss to the local police.)

If you are travelling within the western world much the simplest and – comparatively – the safest way of paying for everything is with credit cards. You can of course use your own cards to do this. VISA and Access cost nothing to obtain, and you could always have one for business and one for personal purposes. However, that will involve you in settling the account each month and then claiming the money back on expenses. More important, as these cards have a pre-set credit limit (usually between £200 and £1,000) they are not always sufficient to cover air-tickets or the total cost of a series of trips within one month. It is much easier therefore to have charge cards (American Express and Diners Club) at hand as well. These have joining and annual subscription charges and if you

151

are using them solely for business purposes you will need to persuade your company to obtain a corporate card for you. Only about one third of UK companies issue their travelling employees with credit cards, although about a quarter of them pay the annual fees for charge cards of employees using personal cards for business purposes. These low figures are absurd for several reasons. First, because it is estimated that at any one time £780 million of company money is in employees' hands in the form of cash advances. At a notional interest rate of 12 per cent this costs British business about £94 million a year. Corporate cards not only reduce this cash flow problem; they also allow for easier expense administration by providing a precise monthly account of both individual and total expenditure. It's a good argument to use with a reluctant company secretary or boss. Also if your boss claims that providing corporate cards is an unviable expense you should point out the fact that the companies which do charge for their cards operate a sliding scale for annual subscriptions. (Thus American Express charges £20p.a. for 10–24 cards, sliding to £8p.a. for 750–999.) Another point often raised by bosses who don't want to issue corporate cards is the fear that employees will use them for personal purposes. This is also unjustified: most companies issuing charge cards offer a waiver clause exonerating companies from responsibility for non-business expenses.

Do consider the following points before choosing which company's card you will carry. Among the most important is how widely it will be accepted both at home and abroad. The answer is that while VISA and Access claim to have the largest number of co-operating establishments, American Express and Diners have broken into marginally more countries. For the purpose of most infrequent travellers VISA and Access should be sufficient – anybody else should carry a selection.

It is worth bearing in mind that certain organizations – particularly bucket shops – will only accept Access or VISA because the other companies' levying of a commission charge (on total revenue rather than profit) may render their cards uneconomic to handle.

When you buy airline tickets on credit or charge cards you generally receive some automatic insurance. Check the policy carefully. Although it will be good (if probably unnecessary) value, some of them will cover you only while in transit.

You will need a separate policy to cover you while staying abroad.

If you use your cards to buy goods abroad remember that fluctuating exchange rates can alter the cost of your purchase. Charges are made according to the exchange rate at the time receipts reach the billing centre, not on the date of purchase – a fact by which you stand either to gain or lose. With VISA and other cards in certain countries there is a double gamble, as the currency is converted first into dollars and then into sterling. But, in spite of this, the rate of exchange operated by credit card companies tends to be better than average.

Two final warning notes. Be sure you have the emergency numbers for the issuing numbers of your credit cards. (See 'Useful addresses' for details.) Wherever you are, if your card is lost or stolen you should report it immediately, and most companies operate a 24-hour telephone line for this purpose. When you are paying with plastic it's a good idea to ask for the carbon copy of your receipt. If you don't, it will be dumped at the end of the day and anybody scouring the dustbins will have instant access to your card number and signature.

Insurance

If you are travelling only within the EEC the standard cover of about £25,000 should be adequate as there are reciprocal health arrangements with these countries. You can get details and the relevant forms from the DHSS. If you're travelling further afield the amount of health cover you want to buy should depend on your general state of health. If you have a chronic condition which might flare up abroad – asthma or diabetes for instance – you should take out more comprehensive cover than people with a clean bill of health. Be sure to check that pregnancy does not invalidate your cover, and if you are taking time off to relax by windsurfing or riding, for example, make sure that your policy covers you for these 'dangerous' sports. A less specific form of insurance involves keeping your passport universally inoffensive. If you are visiting politically sensitive countries ask the passport control to stamp a blank piece of paper rather than your passport as you enter and leave the country. Most will be happy to do this.

Keeping fit

If you travel to countries where you need inoculations, it's a good idea to keep them up to date rather than having a last minute panic. Full vaccination packages are available (see 'Useful addresses'), but if you are caught out you can have them done just before you fly in Heathrow's Terminal Three Departures building.

Check that the water in the country you are visiting is safe to drink. (According to the British Medical Association it will be in reasonable sized towns in the United States and Canada, Scandinavia, Belgium, Luxembourg, the Netherlands, Switzerland, northern France, Italy, mainland Greece, Australia and New Zealand.) If you are unsure, stick to boiled and bottled water, or use water sterilization pills (available at chemists). Remember in these cases to avoid ice in your drinks too.

Unless you are very unlucky the only major health hazard you are going to have to face is jet lag. A great deal has been written on how to cope with this problem – and it is a very real one. Solutions range from the complex – stuffing and starving yourself on alternate days before the flight – to the simple – avoiding all alchohol and most food while you are actually in flight. However, as a working executive your schedule probably won't allow you to indulge in eccentric eating patterns before you go away, and once you are locked in the aircraft there is very little to relieve the tedium apart from eating and drinking!

Put your watch to local time in the country you are flying to as soon as you take off, so your brain if not your body has time to adjust to the change. Get up and move round the plane as often as possible – it helps to reduce the swelling in your feet and ankles. You'll find it easier to sleep if you are wearing something comfortable – take a tracksuit to change into. And unless you're the sort who can sleep anywhere, eye shades and earplugs both help. Healthcrafts produce some sleeping pills called Night Time – they are made up from vitamins and herbs and are neither harmful nor addictive: these are useful both in flight and when you arrive. Once you've reached your destination you will adjust best if you fit in with the local time scale immediately. For instance, if you normally go to bed at 11 p.m. try not to crash out at 7 p.m. just because your body is telling you that it's 4 a.m! And when you do go to bed, if you find you can't get a proper night's sleep don't worry. Being tired is not a dangerous illness. The best thing you can do is get up and use the time constructively – read a book, prepare the day's work, or explore the city before your first meeting! Nevertheless, after flights of more than about 8 hours you should try and leave at least 24 hours before making any vital decisions. If possible, build an extra day into your itinerary to allow for this.

If you are used to taking regular exercise there's no reason why a business trip should mean a break in your routine. Always take a swimsuit with you – more and more hotels have swimming pools, and it is a marvellous way to wake up in the morning or to unwind at the end of the day. And if you pack your jogging kit the receptionist should be able to advise you of the nearest pleasant route. Exercise is the best way to combat the excesses that often accompany business trips!

The most important thing to remember is enjoy your trip. An important lesson for all business travellers to learn is that for a day or two – even a week – you are dispensable. Once you've realized that your office and your family will go on functioning without you, you can relax and get on with the business you've been sent out to do.

Travelling alone

Coping with foreign languages, different customs, finding your way round strange places and relying only on yourself can be daunting if you're not used to it. Whether travelling alone on business, or on holiday, remember you're on your own out of choice. The fact that you're alone is a privilege not a penance, and has many advantages. There is no need to feel self-conscious. People are not looking at you because you're travelling alone, they're not interested.

You may find it a novelty having time to spend as you choose. Working women's evenings are usually a whirl of after-hours meetings, children, husbands, lovers, shopping, housework, dinners . . . an endless list of obligations which prevent you ever having to think what you would actually *like* to do. It's useful to spend some time preparing yourself for solitude. While it's not always practical to take your hobby with you (most hotel bedrooms aren't very conducive to painting, and cellos are expensive to transport!), everybody must have at least three books they have been longing to read. And how many times have you promised yourself you would keep a diary, but have never found the time to fit it into your schedule? Making notes on the places you visit, the people you meet, even recording the cost of meals can all come in useful if you suddenly decide that you want to make a little money on the side through freelance writing.

Perhaps at the end of a day of meetings all you want to do is collapse and watch television – most major hotels have video channels too now. When was the last time you could do that at home, without the niggling knowledge that you really ought to be doing something more important? In a hotel bedroom you don't even have to rush about fixing yourself something to eat during the commercial breaks. Roomservice is at the other end of the telephone.

Eating alone

If you creep into a restaurant behaving as though your presence there is an embarrassment you will no doubt be seen as one. If, on the other hand, you walk in as if you own the place you will be accorded exactly the same respect as the next man. And bear in mind that most men don't enjoy eating alone any more than women.

Frequent complaints from single women diners are that they are always seated behind a pillar/against a wall/beside the kitchen door. Many women prefer to read a book or do a crossword (it's often useful to have something to hand to discourage unwelcome 'companions') and both these pursuits are better achieved outside the crowded centre of the restaurant. If you really do dislike your table, don't sit there fuming – ask to be moved. Simply point out the table you prefer and ask if there is any reason why you should not sit there. If you are quite firm they are unlikely to object.

Once seated the solo diner might encounter one of two difficulties. The first is being rushed through the meal. Couples tend to consume more than singles and therefore spend more – it's worth encouraging them to linger. But remember, you've paid for the right to sit as long as you like (within reason), so be firm. If you want a pause before coffee, say so! The other problem you might meet with is quite the opposite – being totally ignored. Again it's up to you to take the initiative. Don't ever click your fingers – it's rude, irritating and likely to be counter-productive. Try and rely on eye contact and/or raising a hand. If things get really bad get up and start walking out – you won't make it to the door, and it should jolt the waiters into action. There is a lovely story about a woman called Frances Michaelis, a buyer for a major group of stores. She was breakfasting alone in an hotel, when she became so frustrated by the waiters who ignored her that she pulled a pair of knickers out of her briefcase and put them on her head. Within seconds she was getting the instant attention she had wanted some 25 minutes before. (History doesn't relate why she had a pair of knickers in her briefcase; one can only assume that she is a staunch advocate of the 'hand-luggage-only' theory!)

If you are eating alone and suddenly find yourself with an unwanted companion you have a variety of options. You can smile sweetly and pretend you don't speak English – it's useful to learn a phrase in something obscure like Norwegian to illustrate this point. You can explain that you are travelling on business and don't have time to chat as you must read through a document. A business suit and trappings like a briefcase are extremely helpful in these situations. Or you can remind yourself that this person is unlikely to be either a closet rapist or a white-slaver in disguise: he's probably just another lonely business traveller, and it's an even chance whether he will enhance your evening or ruin it. Even if you do take this last option, you don't have to feel that you've embarked on a course from which there is no return, and in a strange place you have the advantage that, because this man is not somebody's friend or brother, you can always resort to rudeness.

The same advice applies to women in bars. Most women business travellers say that although they have no objection to eating alone, they still feel uncomfortable going into bars on their own. It may be due in part to the guilty notion that it's not quite right to drink alone, and therefore if you're in a bar you must have an ulterior motive which is, of course, rubbish. Although a drink may not be the best way to unwind at the end of a hectic day, it is certainly one of the easiest and most accessible. It is encouraging to know that, at least in hotels, barmen are now almost always trained to realize that single women don't want to pick up more than a drink. They are also taught not to follow a strange man's instructions to pour a woman a drink without first checking that she actually wants to accept it.

Staying away

With the sudden growth in the number of female business travellers, hoteliers have been tying themselves in knots wondering how to treat them. Some of their efforts have been rather too extreme – the introduction of all female floors in hotels for example. But, beside the somewhat excessive measures there have been some very constructive changes in the last year or so.

Some of these are practical measures: hotels should now provide skirt-hangers, full-length mirrors and hair-dryers. And more and more have realized you need proper lighting for face make-up. An iron is a possibility. There is also a growing tendency to put salad bars in dining-rooms. However, the best move hotels have made is towards re-educating their staff. Receptionists are now trained not to assume that the woman holding a briefcase is simply holding it for the man she's standing next to – who must be her husband. They are also taught not to bellow your room number out across the foyer, thus informing all those interested of your whereabouts. The importance of unisex service is instilled into waiters almost before they have mastered their silver-spoons and, as we've already discussed, barmen are now made to realize that thirsty women aren't all call-girls. Knowing that the hotels are on your side should allay most of your fears.

GENERAL SAFETY
If you are nervous about staying alone in a hotel ask to be put in a room near the lift – your worst jitters strike when you are wandering through gloomy passages trying to find your room number, so the less you have to do that the better. More and more hotels now provide dead-locks and peep-holes – use them. If you have to take valuables with you it is unwise to leave them in your room, no matter how inconvenient it is not to, so use the hotel safe.

Once you have left your hotel the possible sources of danger increase, but remember you are used to getting about cities on your own. The statistics for crime in England's largest cities are nothing to be proud of, so looking after yourself should by now be second nature. It is an established fact that meek and nervous looking people are much more likely to be mugged than those who appear purposeful and confident, and you are less likely to be scared if you've learnt the rudiments of self-defence. The police force runs a series of self-defence courses which will teach you how to protect yourself, and if you do get into trouble you shouldn't hesitate to use the techniques you've been taught. (See 'Useful addresses'.)

But the best way out of trouble is to avoid it by taking sensible precautions. Wherever you are don't flaunt your affluence: wear your jewellery inside your clothes, or better still leave it at home. (That includes things like fake pearls. You bought them because they look real, didn't you?) Buy handbags that can be firmly closed, and keep them tucked under your arm rather than dangling from shoulder straps. Whenever possible avoid quiet, unlit streets at night and, wherever you are walking, stick to the outside edge of the curb.

Do conform to the dress-codes of the country you are in – particularly if you are travelling in the Middle East. Although you might be keen to get as tanned as possible you should note that Western women wearing T-shirts and shorts in Muslim countries have been stoned by crowds of indignant locals – including women.

In under-developed countries you are more likely to be pestered than attacked. Don't react. Anger, fear or embarrassment are what these men are after, and if you appear oblivious they will soon get bored. If you are pestered or followed for a prolonged period go into a shop or café. Don't accept the protection of the first respectable looking man who offers it – you may just substitute the unwanted attentions of one person for those of another.

But don't be too wary and start thinking that every local you come across is a would-be mugger. Some people are genuinely friendly, and if you are too suspicious, you won't enjoy yourself.

Without doubt the most difficult situation to deal with is that in which the unwelcome attention comes from a colleague or client. If this is not too serious or consistent, it's best to treat it as light-heartedly as possible. Laughter is a very effective passion-quencher – it's extremely disconcerting for the would-be-Lothario, and yet it cannot be considered offensive. If the situation has gone beyond that, your best recourse is to Head Office. You may hate the idea and feel you are whingeing, but remember that your boss respects you enough to send you out on business, and should therefore respect any complaints you might make.

ENTERTAINING AND BEING ENTERTAINED

When you are travelling on business a great deal of the work that has to be done will take place outside office hours – probably over large meals and copious drinks. Whether you relish this prospect or loathe it you have to accept it.

In most countries business people rely on a few hours' socializing to establish whether or not they trust, and have respect for the person with whom they are dealing; and in the East getting drunk together is considered to be an essential part of doing business. The Japanese, in particular, regard it as a time in which you can air your views and try out theories without being held responsible for them later. Therefore, no matter how much you are longing to go back to your hotel, wash your hair and put your feet up, you have got to stay the course.

Again, it shouldn't be regarded as a penance. Evening entertainment will usually give you a much greater insight and understanding of the country than hours in an office would do. It can also lead to some interesting situations: Janice Hughes, an economic consultant, then working in Africa was sent on a trip to Timbuktu. The business concluded, she and twelve men retired to have lunch on a balcony facing out over the desert. Above them the ceiling fans swished, below a whole sheep was being barbecued on a spit. When the time came to eat the twelve men, as custom dictated, got up and carved a portion of lamb for 'their' woman and then sat back to watch her eat it before they could eat themselves. Twelve portions of lamb later Janice staggered off with indigestion – and the men went home with their national pride intact!

Whenever you travel on business you are acting as an envoy of your company, and once you leave the UK you're responsible for the reputation of the British as a whole. But when you are travelling outside the Western world – in countries where women still have a lowly status – you will be seen as such a strange phenomenon that you'll probably be accorded the status of a third and separate sex. It's up to you to live up to it.

All well and good, but what happens when you are the host? Agreed, it's a much greater responsibility, but does entertaining in a restaurant really present a greater challenge than leaving the office at six, collecting the shopping on the way home, and having a three-course dinner for eight prepared by 8.30, having bathed and changed in the meantime? If you can manage that you can manage most things, and the important thing to remember is to keep calm.

When you make the booking at your chosen restaurant or hotel dining-room (and if you don't know where to go you can always seek the advice of the receptionist) make it clear that you are the host and, if possible, state your table preference. As previously discussed, most waiters are trained to realize that women might well be the host. They should, therefore, put the bill in the middle of the table allowing whoever wants to to pick it up. If this doesn't happen and the bill is given to your guest, just point out that you'd agreed that you would pay the bill, and take it from him.

The same goes for the wine list. But, in that instance, unless you pride yourself on being what Americans would describe as a 'wine-buff', it may be just as well to allow your guest to choose the wine anyway. It's generally one of the prerogatives that men loathe losing, and if it will keep your guest happy and allow the meal to run smoothly you have gained an advantage.

TIPPING

It's impossible to lay down a set of ground rules about tipping because in each country the procedure is different – in Japan if you tip anybody you cause them grave embarrassment, in Egypt if you don't tip everybody you incite great wrath. However, tipping is something that women are notoriously bad at, so if it's something you worry about, rest assured you are not alone. There are some general guidelines by which you can operate. For a start tipping should be a gesture reflecting appreciation – not an obligation. But nowadays, when the service charge is so often added to the bill automatically, it is definitely expected. Therefore, if you are genuinely dissatisfied with the service you should complain to the manager or head-waiter. If you just skip the tip you will simply be regarded as mean.

It's a good idea to tip generously in places you intend to go back to regularly, and if you are staying in a hotel tipping early will ensure better service. Whenever you are paying by cheque or credit card, if you leave the tip rather than simply adding it to the total figure it is much more likely it will reach the person for whom it is intended. (It also simplifies the company's tax administration.) And finally, while you are in transit carry loose change in your pockets – it saves the embarrassment of grappling in your handbag while the porter hovers discreetly.

Making the most of it

Having sorted out all the essentials of your trip it's time to concentrate on the things you can do to change the days from a business obligation into an adventure. Read up about the places you are going to before you set off – you may well have a spare hour in which to visit a museum or art gallery. The relevant tourist board in this country should be able to tell you about any particular events or exhibitions that are going on. If your trip ends on a Friday see if you can change your return ticket and stay an extra day. Your family and friends will still be there when you get back, but you might not get a chance to visit that particular city again. (And if cost is a deterrent factor bear in mind that most business hotels offer very favourable weekend rates.)

If you get the time spend some money. You may feel obliged to bring back presents for family friends and perhaps even colleagues, but don't forget yourself. You haven't financed your trip, so you can afford to spend a little money on yourself. And although the eye quickly becomes jaded and local artefacts soon appear to be simply piles of tourist tat, if you look carefully you will find things that do retain their attraction. Unusual foreign products can also make inexpensive and original presents – collecting a small stock will save you a great many last minute panics.

A final word

It's true to say that travel is frequently synonymous with trouble – and the more often you travel the more this becomes likely. Whenever you run into a problematic patch there is one golden rule to remember: nothing is ever as bad as it seems, and few things are fatal so KEEP CALM. Of all the advice given in this section that alone is imperative! And as your luggage gets lost, and the taxi breaks down so you miss your plane and your visa has run out so you've got to leave the country . . . take heart from the fact that while smooth running trips don't make good stories, you can dine out on disaster for years!

Holidays – a Complete Break or a Family Holiday?

The more responsible you get the more you need holidays and – conversely – the less likely you are to get them. Of course, you still get the time off and the chance to go away. But once you've got a family it's no longer a matter of flinging a bikini and a few T-shirts into a clutch bag and catching the first flight south. Simply leaving the house becomes an event to rival the retreat from Moscow. And once you've reached your destination you are going to need the combined skills of watch dog, Redcoat, nurse and banker while, quite possibly, still carrying on in your normal role as chief cook and bottle washer! After two weeks of a family holiday you are unlikely to come home relaxed refreshed. Therefore even the most devoted parents mother are likely to want – just occasionally – to take a complete break.

Weekend breaks

The easiest, and increasingly the most popular, way of doing this is by taking several two- or three-night breaks. If it's just for a couple of nights you can probably rely on friends or grandparents to help out with the children. Short breaks also avoid the pre-holiday panic at the office.

Luckily the British travel industry has responded to the demand for this type of holiday with alacrity. Most of the big hotel chains – anxious to fill the rooms left by business travellers on Fridays – now offer attractive weekend packages. Large tour operators see them as a lucrative source of income outside peak holiday seasons, and firms specializing in short breaks are mushrooming.

Among the most obvious routes to retreat are health farms. Increasingly, these are frequented not so much by over-indulged wives of the rich and famous, but by harrassed executives who need a re-vitalizing rest. Many of them will not necessarily want to lose weight – which is fortunate because most health farms do provide gourmet meals for non-fatties. And most of these establishments are to be found in beautiful surroundings, with grounds that are completely conducive to rest and recreation or just plain recuperation. The cost varies according to the treatments you take on top of your basic meals and accommodation, but health farms are not cheap.

If you are looking for something further afield and more adventurous, dozens of firms offering weekend breaks in Europe. (See 'Useful addresses' for suggestions on these and other weekend breaks listed below.) Paris and Amsterdam are obvious choices but while you are doing your research it's worth considering more unusual destinations – Budapest, Geneva, even Athens – if you've got three nights to spare. If you're counting the pennies bear in mind that prices shown in brochures are usually only for bed and breakfast, so look into exchange rates and comparative costs of living. And if you are really being thrifty and you're a reasonably intrepid traveller remember that lots of European destinations can be reached by coach or train. (Sealink is one of the companies that caters for this market.)

If all you want is peace, quiet and a lot of good food the obvious answer is to drive across to France. You can either organize this independently or you can buy a complete package (see 'Useful addresses').

If you plan to stay in the UK the best value breaks are in London, in fact they are the only way to get a cheap bed in the capital. You can buy packages which include return rail tickets to London, bed and breakfast, tickets to a West End show and a travel pass that allows you to move about the place free (see 'Useful addresses').

If on the other hand you are trying to avoid the Metropolis, there are a wide variety of packages available all over the country.

However, the real growth in the industry is in 'special interest' breaks. These range from a plethora of sports, arts and crafts weekends to exceptionally silly gimmicks: snowman building near Oxford, psychic healing in Kidderminster and hang-over breaks in Cumbria, to name but a few. You will find details of these, and many less bizarre weekends in the *Let's Go* Booklet and Best Western's Getaway Breaks brochure. It would probably be true to say that whatever your interest you can find a holiday company that will allow you to indulge in it. Lots of these will be small companies that are not necessarily well-publicized, so your best bet is to decide what you want to do – cooking, photography, trekking, cycling – and then scour your local newsagent for specialist magazines on the subject. These should carry advertisements from the relevant companies, and if they don't, ring the editor and seek his/her advice. Alternatively ring the travel editors of general magazines and national newspapers – they should have up to date information on what's available.

If you are genuinely interested in spending a weekend constructively, The Earnley Concourse offers weekend courses in subjects ranging from 'the work of the Meteorological Office' to computer programming and calligraphy. General facilities at the centre include a bar, indoor swimming pool, squash and tennis courts. West Dean College operates a similar set-up, although their courses are much more craft-oriented, and will include more unusual skills such as mosaic work, lettering on stone and batik printing. The college is set in an impressive stately home in a very attractive part of Sussex.

For those people who really want to spoil themselves the best bet is to splash out and stay in one of Britain's country house hotels. These will give you gourmet food and gracious living in some of the country's finest houses.

Of course you might want to go away for longer, and if this is the case the first thing you must do is make arrangements for the children. You're not going to enjoy sunning yourself on a beach unless you are sure that they're having a good time.

Taking care of the children

RESIDENTIAL AND DAY CAMPS
An excellent option for many people will be 'Parents Get Lost' holidays – so nicknamed after the founders in the field, PGL holiday camps for unaccompanied children. These have been going since 1957 and there are now dozens of residential and day camps to be found all over the country. Some are run by small organizations and some by family firms. They are not simply child-minding services. The aim is to educate and instruct as well as to amuse. To this end the various camps now cover a wealth of activities ranging from canoeing and abseiling to painting and drama – all taught by qualified instructors. The vast majority of them offer multi-activity holidays which allow children to try their hand at six or seven options in the course of a week and several of them also specialize in, for instance, pony-trekking, soccer, swimming or computing.

Day camps are the only option for the under sevens and often the best bet for children who haven't been away from home alone before. Several hold open days so that children can try out all the activities and decide what they want to do during the week. This also gives the parents a chance to view the facilities and meet the instructors. Most day camps last from about 9.30 a.m. to 4.30 p.m. and provide transport from various pick-up points in the vicinity. The travelling itself can add up to an hour onto the stated time, but those who need to have their children off their hands for longer periods should take advantage of the extra activities and specialist courses which some camps provide in the early mornings and late afternoons.

Children choosing to do a specialist course such as computing will still spend about half of each day doing a variety of other activities. Although at the end of one week they are unlikely to have become experts in their chosen subject, they will certainly have a sound working knowledge of it. Almost all camp directors work to a flexible schedule, however, and so if a child starts a course and then decides he hates it, he will be allowed to change if at all possible.

At the residential camps accommodation is usually dormitory style, and food of the school variety – plain and plentiful. There are usually tuck-shops on the premises, and so some pocket money will be required. The most important things to look for when choosing a camp for your child are locations and options available – prices do not differ enormously.

Last-minute getaways

It's quite likely that your decision to get away from it all will be made at the last minute – the result of a slack period at work, the children being invited to stay with friends, a blast of summer sun or, quite simply, a sudden desire to get away from the endless English winter.

You may want to spend a week acquiring a new skill, perfecting an old one, or simply setting out in search of adventure. The choice of activities now is endless: photography in Wales, cookery courses in Avon, cycling in France, wine-tasting in Germany, trekking in the Himalayas. And that doesn't even scratch the surface. To even attempt recommendations would be to do the market an injustice, but you can get ideas and information from your travel agent or tourist bureaus.

The same applies to those who are simply sun-seeking. If this is the case there are a variety of options. As far as flights are concerned your best bet is the back of *The Times*, London's *Standard* or *Time Out*. Be prepared to do a lot of ringing round – competitive prices and availability don't always go hand in hand. And cautious types should also be warned that agents advertising in these publications will not necessarily be ABTA bonded – which means that if they take your money and then go bust before you've travelled you have no recourse. However, if you've paid for your ticket by credit card (VISA or Access) they will be obliged to pay up in these circumstances, provided the cost of travel was more than £100. Charge card companies (American Express and Diners) are not similarly bound, but sometimes agree to do so 'as a gesture of good will'.

Many of the holiday operators offer knock-down prices for late and last minute bookings – and if you don't have set ideas on where you want to go you will probably have a wide selection. Equally, if yours is an organized life-style and you can book early, you are likely to be offered favourable rates.

Travelling alone

If you ever travel alone you will know that hotels tend to penalize 'single' guests. If you want a break from your loved ones but you don't want to pay a hefty single room supplement ask your travel agent for the major tour operators' brochures – these will show you who places the heaviest charge on solo travellers.

The ultimate getaway?

Finally, if you want a complete break, but you haven't more than a day to spare, why not do something really indulgent? Hire a chauffeur-driven-Rolls Royce for the day to go on a shopping spree, take a picnic into the country or have lunch at your favourite out-of-town restaurant. There is a firm called The Lynton Group which will arrange it all. Take a day out on the Orient Express. You could visit a local stately home and

which ever you choose the cost will include lots of good food
to be washed down with champagne.

Family holidays

As a general rule small children loath sight-seeing, long
journeys and foreign food. As an absolute rule exposing them
to any of these things is expensive. Therefore, unless you and
your partner are insatiable travellers you might be best ad-
vised to spend your small-fry's formative years exploring quite
close to home.

Camping and caravanning

These are both inexpensive, and nowadays most sites have all
the amenities to keep you and your clothes clean. If the idea of
purpose-built campsites appals you there's still lots of
common ground on which you can pitch your tent, and even
the odd farmer who is not averse to the occasional visitor,
provided permission is sought first.

If you are planning to rough it, it's a good idea to camp
within striking distance of a pub equipped with a sympathetic
landlord. When your fire-lighting skills aren't quite up to
scratch, pub food suddenly becomes very appealing and –
even for the most intrepid – a proper loo is sometimes a very
welcome sight.

Consider going with another family with children of a
similar age to yours. This will instantly halve the parental
responsibilities and (hopefully) the children will entertain
each other.

Self-catering accommodation

The same applies to self-catering, which needn't mean staying
in egg-box blocks of modern flats. There are all sorts of
agencies offering self-catering holidays in country cottages,
gate-houses – even wings of stately homes. The Sunday
papers are also a good source, but probably the best is *The
Lady* magazine which is published weekly. (Accommodation

arranged thus may well be cheaper because you avoid agency fees.)

Before you book be sure to check on things like clothes-washing facilities, whether bills are to be paid on top of rent, accessibility to shops and, if your children are teenage or there is only one driver in the family, nearby bus stops.

House-swapping

An extremely sensible but scantily publicized option is house-swapping. You can do this within the UK and almost any-where abroad, it removes all accommodation costs and it ensures that your house will be protected from burglars and vandals while you are away. All it takes is the faith to believe that, although you are giving strangers the run of your house, they are also giving you the run of theirs and therefore re-specting each other's property is a mutual interest. (See 'Useful addresses' for a list of the companies involved in organizing house-swaps.)

As a general rule, once you've found a suitable family to swop with, the details are all a matter of individual taste. You ought to compile a small dossier on your area; perhaps alert a neighbour who would be prepared to lend a hand if necessary. You might or might not want to include cars, pets and toys in the arrangement and you will have to decide whether or not you are going to clear out cupboards, and how you'll sort out the bills.

You don't necessarily have to exchange identical sorts of property – large country house owners might well be happy with small, but central, town houses. You'll definitely feel closer to the local community than you would do staying in standard holiday accommodation – and you may well make some new friends.

Holiday centres

Another alternative is a holiday at centres like Club Mediter-ranée and Butlins. You might blanch at the thought but your children certainly won't. Having been brought up in a family where holidays meant climbing steep hills and looking at old churches, I well remember the back-seat chorus everytime we passed a Butlins of 'Can't we go in there just for one day?' The main advantage of these centres is that prices in the brochures are almost all inclusive, so you know in advance exactly how much you are going to have to pay. Another point to consider is that if you get tired of the computer camp, the knobbly-knees competition and all the myriad other options, you can always abandon base for the day. What do you suppose all those jolly GOs (at Club Méditerranée, Gentils Organis-ateurs) and Redcoats are there for if not to entertain your children for the day? Sometimes the only problem can be that parents feel abandoned by their children. There is so much going on that they feel lucky if they catch a glimpse of them at meals!

Single parent holidays

There are more than one million single parent families in this country (and probably as many more parents with access), so it seems strange that tour operators do little to cater for their needs. Very few offer the relevant discounts, and even if single parents are not counting the cost, they are unlikely to enjoy themselves in a resort where they are ignored by the singles because they have children, and spurned by the families because they are single. Children are just as likely to be upset by well-meaning but thoughtless questioning as to the whereabouts of Mummy or Daddy.

However, if the 'go-it-alone' approach doesn't appeal, there are a few tour operators and organizations dealing specifically with single parent families (see 'Useful addresses'). Prices are set bearing in mind the financial strains on single-parent families. And because you'll be surrounded by people in similar circumstances a lot of the burdens of baby-sitting can be shared.

Finally, wherever you are travelling with children do take an emergency kit. Not just sticking plaster and TCP, but things that will make them feel at home in unfamiliar surroundings: a favourite book or toy and, perhaps most important, a couple of packets of something that, when all else fails, you know they will eat.

Useful addresses

TRAVELLING ON BUSINESS
Answering Ltd. Telephone Answering Service, 11 Rosemont Road, London NW3 6NG
Tel: 01 435 0066
Branches around the country. Will answer your telephone, other services include providing postal and telex address.

Baby-Sitters Unlimited, 271–273 King Street, London W6 9LZ
Tel: 01 741 5566/7

The Body Shop, outlets all over the country. See telephone directory for your local branch.

Childminders, 67a Marylebone High Street, London W1
Tel: 01 935 2049/9763

The City Bag Store, 3 South Molton Street, London W1 and branches

Department of Health and Social Security, Alexander Fleming House, Elephant and Castle, London SE1 6BY
Tel: 01 407 5522

Minders, 33 St George Street, London W1R 9FA
Tel: 01 499 8929/4717

Solve Your Problem Ltd., 1a Droyson Mews, London W8 4LY
Tel: 01 937 0906/7 and 937 2526/7

Universal Aunts, 250 Kings Road, London SW3
Tel: 01 352 5413

Emergency numbers for credit cards:
Access: 0702 352255 (24 hours a day throughout the year)
American Express: 01 222 9633 (24 hours a day throughout the year)
Diners Club: 0252 516261 (recorded message outside office hours)
VISA: 0604 21100 (24 hours except Christmas Day)

IMMUNIZATIONS:
British Airways Travel and Immunization Centre, 75 Regent Street, London W1
Tel: 01 439 9584

PPP Medical Centre, 99 New Cavendish Street, London W1
Tel: 01 637 8941

Thomas Cook Ltd., 45 Berkeley Street, London W1
Tel: 01 499 4000

All inoculations can also be done by your GP which will be cheaper, but probably not as quick.

TRAVELLING ALONE
Self-defence courses are run by: A6 Branch, Metropolitan Police Force, New Scotland Yard, London SW1H 0BG
Tel: 01 230 2432
For those outside London they should be able to supply details of courses in your area.

Holiday breaks

WEEKEND BREAKS – CITY
Stardust Mini Holidays, Kiln House, 210 New Kings Road, London SW6
Tel: 01 736 5500

Time-Off, 2a Chester Close, Chester Street, London SW1
Tel: 01 235 8070

Travelscene, Travelscene House, 94 Baker Street, London W1M 2HD
Tel: 01 486 6411

WEEKEND BREAKS – GENERAL
Getaway Breaks, Best Western Hotels, 26 Kew Road, Richmond TW9 2NA
Tel: 01 541 0033

Superbreak Mini Holidays, 305 Gray's Inn Road, London WC1
Tel: 01 278 9646

Winter Inn, Park Street, Hovingham, York, YO6 4JZ
Tel: 065 382 425
They offer a particularly attractive programme in Flanders, Picardy and Normandy and specialize in charming tucked-away hotels.

SPECIAL INTEREST BREAKS
Celebrated Country Hotels, Oakley Court, Windsor Road, nr Windsor, Berkshire SL4 5UR
Tel: 0698 37230

The Earnley Concourse, Earnley, nr Chichester, Sussex PO20 7JL
Tel: 0243 670 392

Let's Go, free from Tourist Information Centres, or post free from: Let's Go, English Tourist Board, ADMAIL 14, London SW1W 0YE

Pride of Britain, c/o Jenny Paton Philip, Maison Talbooth, Stratford Road, Dedham, Colchester, Essex, CO7 6HN

West Dean College, West Dean, Chichester, Sussex PO18 0QZ
Tel: 0243 63 301

LATE TRAVEL
Hogg Robinson, 176 Tottenham Court Road, London W1P 0DE
Tel: 01 636 8244

Pickfords, 576 Mile End Road, London E3 4PH
Tel: 01 981 1141

UNACCOMPANIED CHILDREN'S HOLIDAYS
Camp Beaumont, 9 West Street, Godmanchester, Cambs. PE18 8HG
Tel: 0480 56123

Dolphin Adventure Holidays, Grosvenor Hall, Bolnore Road, Haywards Heath, West Sussex RH16 4BX
Tel: 0444 458177

Millfield Village of Education, Street, Somerset BA1 60YD
Tel: 0458 45823

PGL, Station Street, Ross-on-Wye, Herefordshire HR9 7AH
Tel: 0989 65556

THE ULTIMATE BREAK
The Lynton Group, 73 Elizabeth Street, London SW1 9PJ
Tel: 01 730 8545

Orient Express Pullman Tours Department, Sea Containers House, 20 Upper Ground, London SE1
Tel: 01 928 5837

FURTHER READING
Activity and Hobby Holidays, produced by the English Tourist Board, £1.25 from Tourist offices.

Adventure Holidays, published by Vacation Work, Oxford. £2.95 from W.H. Smith.

The Weekend Away Book, published by Weekend Away, £1.95, is a good source of ideas plus some useful addresses, in both Britain and Europe. If you want to go further afield and don't know what possibilities there are in the country of your choice ring the relevant tourist board, who will have brochures on all sorts of options.

Family holidays

SELF-CATERING
The Helpful Holiday Agency, Coombe Farmhouse, Chagford, Devon TQ13 8DF
Tel: 06473 3593/2478

Home Interchange, 8 Hillside, Farningham, Kent
Tel: 0322 864527

Interchange Holidays, 29 Highfield Road, Derby DE3 1GX
Tel: 0332 42664

Intervac, 6 Siddals Lane, Allestree, Derby DE3 2DY.
Tel: 0332 558931

SINGLE PARENT HOLIDAYS
Gingerbread Holidays, Empire House, Clarence Street, Swindon, Wilts. FN1 2JF
Tel: 0793 613220
A registered charity offering holidays in Europe (hotel and chalet accommodation), holiday camps in the West Country, caravans in Wales, and activity holidays for children only.

HELP (Holiday Endeavour for Lone Parents) 25 Stephyns Chambers, Bank Court, Hemel Hempstead, Herts HP1 1DA
Tel: 0442 47151, ext. 226 (Mrs Bray)
Another registered charity, it organizes UK holidays at very reasonable rates, on set dates and at a limited number of destinations which change each year.

N.B. This list does not attempt to be comprehensive. To cover the entire market in any area would require a great deal more space than is available here. Your local travel agent should be able to give you details of similar companies in any one field.

What to Do with Your Well-Earned Money

Few people have either the time or the inclination to constantly tend their hard-earned cash. Even reading about it gets a high yawn ratio. But you owe it to yourself to make the most of it, so a shortish amount of time spent streamlining your money management is worthwhile – to take care of the pennies so the pounds can grow with only occasional nurturing, and to free you for better things. The first steps are to assess your money profile, define your goals, and plan a budget.

Your Financial Profile

Start by drawing up a financial profile of yourself – the personal equivalent of a company's annual report and accounts, complete with balance sheet (see below). In one column, write down your assets – if you own your home, its approximate market value; plus any savings and investments, insurance and pension policies you may have. In another column put your debts – mortgage, credit card accounts and so on. Also write down your gross annual income.

Next, write down your financial goals. Be as frivolous as you like at first – this exercise can tell you a lot about yourself, your current financial position and your spending patterns. The more serious purpose is then, bearing in mind the sort of financial animal you are (thrifty, entrepreneurial, downright reckless or so unadventurous you think Premium Bonds are for compulsive gamblers only), to determine the right goals for you. This means tackling them in order of priority and achievability so you can work out how to get there.

Personal Financial Profile

As at (insert date)

Assets	£	Debts	£
House, market value approx	42,000	Mortgage outstanding	27,470
Building society:		Credit cards	850
Ordinary shares	130	Overdraft	220
Short notice account	600	Revolving credit	
Three month notice account	1,500	account	2,350
Premium Bonds	25		

Insurance
Home: Buildings cover to £75,000, premium £126
   Contents covered to £12,000, camera separately insured,
   total premiums £90
Personal: Endowment mortgage, but no other cover

Income
£11,000 gross

Goals
1. Must pay off debts – seem to borrow faster than I save.
2. Would love (ideally) to give up present job and go travelling for six months, but still have a base to come back to.

One essential is saving, a fundamental but often neglected element of money management. But to build up sufficient capital to meet your targets, you must first accumulate cash to work with. This doesn't mean that if your ultimate ambition is to lie in a hammock, reading and sipping champagne while someone else manages your millions, that you have to save those millions pound by pound in the building society – clearly impossible unless you're on an astronomical salary already. But you can save enough to *invest*, or perhaps (aided by a bank loan, having impressed the manager with your astuteness) start up the small manufacturing company that could make your fortune . . . It's what's known as a gearing effect: using your money to make more money. The more ambitious you are, the more adventurous you'll eventually have to be: but make sure you build on firm foundations.

Planning a Budget

List your outgoings

Using the checklist below to jog your memory, list all your possible outgoings for the year. Base costs on last year's bills plus inflation (around 7 per cent at time of writing, but if you're extra cautious round it up to 10 per cent). Where applicable, add the dates of when the payments are due.

If you want a truly accurate picture of where your money goes to day by day, you could also keep an account for, say, a month, of everything you spend, and on what. Then you can see where to cut costs – though don't overdo it and leave yourself nothing for deserved luxuries; just try to restrict them to the ones that give you most pleasure.

Checklist of expenses

Home
Mortgage or rent
Rates
Electricity
Gas
Coal
Telephone
Water rates
House insurance –
    building and contents
TV licence
Repairs and maintenance
New household items
Service charges
Ground rent

Personal
Life insurance, e.g.
    endowment policy, term

insurance, permanent
    health insurance, etc
Pension plan
Subscriptions to clubs,
    trade organization,
    journals
Season ticket
Clothes
Holidays and travel
Birthday and other
    presents

Car
Road fund licence
Insurance
MOT
Subscription to AA/RAC
Petrol
Maintenance

Good managers delegate

Increase your efficiency by using your bank and/or building society to run your day-to-day finances as much as possible (the same principle applies with investment, which we discuss later). So pick out and list separately all the bills that can be paid by standing order or direct debit, to save you the trouble of doing it yourself – so long as you don't pay out too much before you need to.

For example, it's in your interest to pay your rates monthly (in 10 instalments). If you settle in full as soon as you get your annual or half-yearly demand, you're paying in advance and effectively giving the recipient an interest-free loan of your money (which could be better used to earn interest for you).

The reverse applies with gas, electricity and telephone bills, where you're paying for what you've already used. So resist any monthly budgeting schemes offered by the organizations concerned to help you save *towards* the bills for these services, as there's no point in paying in advance or even as you go, when you can pay in arrears.

And don't, whatever you do, buy savings stamps towards your bills, TV licence or whatever. Again, it's payment in advance – but what is worse, you could end up paying twice if the savings stamps are lost or stolen.

Planning for bills

As you do need to save towards bills, tot up the costs on your own checklist of expenses and divide by 12. You've now got the minimum amount you should set aside each month in a separate account to cover costs not paid by standing order. Add that sum to your monthly standing order and direct debit outgoings, then – assuming your salary is paid in fixed monthly amounts – deduct the total from your net monthly earnings and treat the remainder as your *true* net income. If you're self-employed, earn a merit badge (and, more important, peace of mind) by setting aside something for your tax and National Insurance.

Liquid accounts

There's plenty of choice as to where to keep your liquid funds, from bank current accounts to the newer breed of 'high interest bank accounts' offered by over a dozen financial institutions. They usually require a high minimum deposit (£2,000 or more) but offer interest linked to money market rates, plus a cheque book. Most of them, however, insist on a minimum cheque withdrawal of £250 or so, making them suitable only for large purchases, and they're not really designed to handle day to day current account transactions (with such exceptions as Midland Bank's High Interest Cheque Account, which throws in a separate current account as part of the deal; and Save & Prosper's High Interest Bank Account with bankers Robert Fleming, which provides for standing orders and direct debit payments).

For these (assuming you want to earn interest on your liquid funds) you could try a building society. A number of them now offer accounts with standing order facilities, statements, chequebooks and cash dispensers (or, to give them their correct title, as they generally do more than merely dispense cash, Automated Teller Machines – ATMs). If you want a full banking service, including cheque guarantee card, direct debit, credit or loan facilities, you're better off with a building society/bank linked account.

A good example is the excellent BankSave Plus account offered by the Alliance & Leicester Building Society and Bank of Scotland. It consists of a building society share account paying an above-average rate of interest, and a full bank current account which is free of all charges so long as it's a mere £1 in credit. As for covering your outgoings – provided there's enough in the Alliance & Leicester account it will automatically top up the current account (to £350) if the balance falls below £100. Yearly savings can be considerable.

Keep it flowing

Bills have an irritating habit of arriving in droves – usually when your reservoir of liquid funds is virtually dry. A separate account which allows you to meet the demand(s) can be worth its weight in final reminders, and there are two types designed for such moments:

BUDGET ACCOUNTS
With a budget account you estimate the total bills you would want to pay from it, divide by 12, and pay in that amount each

month. If, during the year, you find you need to pay out more than you've accumulated, you can – but your account should square up at the end of the year (and as both you and your bank manager keep copies of your estimated bills there should be no surprises).

The finer points vary from bank to bank: you may have to pay interest, or a service charge, or both; you may be able to arrange insurance cover for outstanding debts if you die; *but*, you won't earn interest on your credit balances.

REVOLVING CREDIT ACCOUNTS
These, on the other hand, allow you to pay in and borrow on a continuous basis, with a higher credit limit – commonly £3,000 – and without the obligation to balance your books once a year (which could be a pitfall, without that discipline . . .). They're flexible and, while you're in the red, generally cheaper than major credit cards or in-store credit cards, so you can have the occasional splurge. Moreover, if you manage to save through the account, you can usually earn interest on the credit balance (again, the details will vary slightly from bank to bank).

Borrowing

How do you know which is the cheapest form of borrowing, should you need to? The simple answer is to check the APR – the Annual Percentage Rate. This is a truer reflection of the interest rate at which you repay than, say, the monthly percentage rate – 'only 2 per cent a month' amounts to an APR of 26.8 per cent.

Keeping tabs

Budgets are not for planning and forgetting. You can keep an eye on outgoings by filling in cheque stubs and noting credit card purchases (easiest if you tape a small card in your wallet, in front of the plastic card itself, and jot down all the details on the spot).

If your diary has pages for financial accounts, use them (even if you just record your business expenses). If you're self-employed, you should keep proper accounts or, at the very least, a monthly record of your income (setting aside a proportion for the taxman as you do so), plus a large file into which you put all invoices, receipts and other relevant documents, so as to minimize scrabbling and head-scratching when you prepare your annual returns.

As for the budget itself (see below), write it somewhere instantly accessible like the flyleaf of your pocket diary so that you can remind yourself of its details (updating when necessary) at a moment's notice – it's amazingly useful and goes down well with bank managers.

And, while on the subject of bank managers: it's worth cultivating a good relationship, which means keeping him or her informed of any problems and not overdrawing except by prior arrangement. When you want anything from a loan to investment advice, go prepared with the relevant information and questions. The occasional lunch doesn't go amiss, either (use your credit cards to pay the bill), and nor does a little modest trumpet-blowing – if you're doing well, say so. It's especially important if the bank is backing you in a business venture (and if it has just helped you through a rough patch, it's simple courtesy to say thank you). But it's not a bad practice for personal customers to adopt – and the more you use and rely on your bank, the more important a good relationship becomes.

A well planned budget

Monthly outgoings as from (insert date)

	£ p	
1st	100.00	Revolving credit account
15th	22.44	Endowment premium
25th	80.75	Rates
26th	220.00	Mortgage
26th	50.00	Unit trust regular savings
Total	473.19	

Annual payments

	£ p	
Jan 1:	80.00	Professional subscription
Feb 3:	25.00	Subscription to trade journal
Mar 31:	41.22	Term insurance
Apr 1:	58.00	TV licence
May 27:	200.00	Personal accident policy
July 31:	100.00	Road fund licence
July 31:	127.00	Car insurance (approx)
Oct 26:	136.00	Buildings insurance
Dec 19:	90.00	Contents insurance (approx)
Total:	857.22	

Saving

You should, of course, be saving – possibly in several different ways, for different aims. If you want to buy your own home, you should have a regular savings account with a building society to stand you in good stead for a mortgage – if you can, putting in the amount you might expect your monthly repayments to be, so both you and the society will know you can afford them. Building societies are also a good home for short-term savings. For the longer term – perhaps ten years ahead – you might consider an endowment insurance, with its element of life cover; or, for pure investment, a unit trust regular savings plan.

If you're self-employed or in a non-pensionable job, you should also have 'pension premium' somewhere among your outgoings. If you're self-employed you should be setting aside part of your income to provide for tax: do so in a separate account so that you know how much you've got for the taxman and how much for you.

Taking stock

Like any business, you should take stock and review your financial plan every now and then – preferably on a regular basis. Consider whether you are making the most of your income. Are you paying out more in interest on an array of credit purchases than if you got a bank loan, which might work out cheaper, to pay off the lot? Have you a lump sum lying idle in a current account which could be earning you interest elsewhere?

If you haven't already got one, try to build up an emergency fund – the amount depending on what you can afford and how much you need to give you peace of mind. Some people feel uneasy if they've less than £20,000 they can get on demand, others are happy with £500. Remember that the longer you can commit your money, the more you can make from it – without even taking any risks. So you can put it in a range of building society accounts to get the most advantageous spread of terms and interest rates, or into nice safe National Savings, for example.

To give yourself the chance of higher returns, though, you have to take risks – and the classic advice, which needs repeating, is never to put money into a risk investment if you're likely to need it in a hurry. You could be lucky – who knows? On the other hand, if you're forced to cash in when markets are low, you could lose at least some of your hard-earned money.

To help you assess your position, consider the steps below before turning to the next section.

Strategic planning

Step 1: regular saving

Risk-free, and with interest to help build cash into capital.

CHOOSE:
Building society (regular savings account or, if you can get more interest that way, a higher rate account), or National Savings (the Yearly Plan gives a tax-free guaranteed return, currently 8.19 per cent over 5 years, but isn't as flexible as a building society account).

Step 2: emergency fund

Take care of short-term needs with a lump sum that's safe, accessible – and earning interest, of course.

CHOOSE:
Building society ordinary share account (or, if funds allow, a higher-rate account allowing instant access without any loss of interest, such as the Cheltenham & Gloucester's Gold account).

Step 3: the meanwhile fund

You're building a lump sum towards the new car/dream holiday/cottage/own business, which isn't a big enough lump (yet) and which you don't want to risk. So, meanwhile . . .

CHOOSE:
Building society high-rate account; National Savings; or local authority bonds which can also offer a fixed return. You can get a list of those on offer by contacting the Loans Bureau (see 'Useful addresses').

Step 4: hedge your bets

You might not have an accident/fall ill and lose your income as a result of disability – but there again, you might. You might not live to see retirement – but hopefully, you might. Insurance and pension planning will cover the 'ifs' and 'buts': if disaster strikes, you've got some cover; and if it doesn't, you'll have money to come from your own pension scheme. See pp. 195–202 and 202–9 for further discussion and advice on these aspects of financial planning.

Step 5: risk and reward

You've got money you can set aside – either on a regular basis, or as a lump sum – and you don't mind an element of risk for the chance of a better return. Now read on.

How to Invest Your Spare Cash

You've budgeted for the basics, and you've got an emergency fund or two. You've also got a bit you can afford to play with –

a small amount set aside each month can be enough, if you haven't got a lump sum – which can go into your investment pool. Whether it sinks or swims depends largely on you.

Of course, there are many factors which could affect your investment, including national and international economic and trading conditions, currency fluctuations, market forces, and even natural disasters which you cannot assess. But you *can* look at the risk/reward ratio for each investment medium, getting expert guidance where necessary, before you put your money into it.

Start at the shallow end – unit trusts

Before you consider jumping in at the deep end of buying shares or speculating on the gold price, take a look at the possibility of unit trusts.

For those who don't know, unit trusts are pooled funds which are invested in a large number of securities, usually 50 to 100 different stocks or shares. Instead of buying individual shares yourself, you buy units in the fund, thereby getting the benefit of professional investment management, and also spreading your risk.

Most unit trust companies offer a variety of trust funds in which you can invest, ranging from general UK or international funds to specialized markets such as the Far East, smaller companies or technology. As a rule of thumb the more specialized the sector, the more volatile the fund's performance is likely to be: this year's high-flier could be next year's crash victim, and vice versa.

Trusts are also designed for particular money-making aims: capital growth, income or a balance between the two. Income can often be either rolled up to accumulate in the fund, or paid out, according to the investor's wish. It is paid net of basic rate tax, but if you don't fall within the taxman's grasp you can claim it back.

BUYING AND SELLING
The price at which you buy units is known as the offer price; the price at which you sell is the bid price; and you buy and sell through the trust company. The difference between the two prices on any one day, known as the bid-offer spread, is

generally about 7 per cent – so if you bought some units and resold them immediately you'd be 7 per cent worse off.

If you want to switch between a company's funds, you still have to pay to do so, but you'll be given a discount on the offer price of your new fund.

The unit trust company includes an initial charge in the offer price – 5 per cent is the standard rate. It also makes an annual management charge, generally from ¾ to 1½ per cent plus VAT (management charges are always quoted in fractions). Both these charges are deducted directly from your trust income.

There are two drawbacks to unit trusts. One is that unit prices, like the share prices they reflect, can go down as well as up, so that timing is very important. The other is that the minimum investment for most trusts is £500, and not everyone has that amount to put into a risk investment. If you have, however, and you can afford to leave it for some time, then as bets go, unit trusts are less risky than most. Which doesn't, of course, mean that every one's a winner, or that the current winner tops the performance tables every year. A trust that doubles your money in a year — rare, but it has been done – might collapse during the longer stretch of, say, five years, when quite a number of companies could be reasonably expected to have doubled your original stake.

CHOOSING A FUND
There are well over 700 funds to choose from. Leaving pins and guesswork aside, you can make a shortlist by deciding on your investment aims, the amount of volatility you can stand, and examining the track records of the funds over a number of years. Read the financial press, especially specialist investment magazines, which regularly publish performance tables. You can also get information and guidance from the Unit Trust Association (see 'Useful addresses'). And don't hesitate to contact companies for their promotional literature either.

LONG-DISTANCE PADDLERS
If you haven't got the minimum for an individual trust, or you're worried about timing your jump, you can enter the water a toe at a time with the aid of a unit trust regular investment plan (RIP).

These have several virtues. The minimum investment can

be as little as £10 a month, giving you a piggy-bank entry into the Stock Market with the added advantage of the unit trust's spread of risk. Furthermore, price fluctuations are evened out by an impressive-sounding process known as pound cost averaging – your money buys more units when the unit price is low, fewer when it is high, so by feeding regular amounts into the chosen unit, timing is less important.

RIPs offer good returns, particularly over the longer term, when building society and bank deposits are left far behind. The Unit Trust Association regularly produces statistics for a theoretical £50 a month invested in median general funds, where the 5-year gain (on past performance) is in the 60 per cent bracket and the 10-year gain more like 160 per cent. The building society regular savings account, by comparison, takes a 10-year trudge to do as well as the unit trust did in just 5 years.

Theoretical examples and past performance figures are no guarantee for the future, of course, but they're a reassuring indication – so look for consistency.

A bigger splash – stocks and shares

Undoubtedly, there are rewards to be gained from sharing via the Stock Market in a company's fortunes (and it can happen as speedily as with British Telecom), but you may find yourself sharing in its misfortunes too. In 99.9 per cent of cases you'll have to accept a greater element of risk – so think out your attitude and aims before you leap in.

At first, the aim appears simple: more money. But are you prepared to lose everything if the short-term fortune you want doesn't materialize and you have to sell your shares in a hurry? Do you want steady if unspectacular growth from an already well-established company? How long are you prepared to wait for a profit before you need the money – or simply get bored? Discuss your own favoured approach with a broker who will make recommendations and give you an opinion on any shares you might fancy.

WHAT WILL IT COST?
The normal stockbroker's commission is 1.65 per cent, but as a big deal involves no more effort than a small one, many firms have a minimum charge – partly to recompense their efforts and partly to discourage the more miniscule business. The London average is £15, but provincial brokers generally charge less and are probably more willing to deal in small amounts – of, say, under £500.

The recent changes in Stock Exchange rules won't have such a sudden or explosive impact on the sharebuying public as might be supposed from references to the 'Big Bang'. Its effects are unlikely to filter through to the punters before October 1986 at the earliest, for administrative reasons. And even then, the replacement of fixed commissions by negotiated commissions doesn't imply that you'll have to go to a succession of brokers and haggle over their commission charge as though bartering in a Moroccan souk. It's more like the ending of retail price maintenance – instead of knowing the price in advance, you have to go into the shop and ask, as the same item can vary in price from shop to shop. And to some extent you'll also get what you pay for – a simple dealing service will cost less than one where you also get advice. If you know precisely what you want to buy and sell, you can go for the cheapest dealing service you can find; but for most people, it'll mean shopping around for the best combination of price and advice.

The smaller your purchase, the higher your relative costs and the bigger the jump you will need to see in the price of your shares before you can make a profit. Should you want to buy overseas shares, the charges can be even higher. So it's generally cheaper (and safer) to start investing with home-grown companies.

If you buy your shares through the bank, it may be slightly dearer than going to a broker direct as several banks charge the broker's commission, plus £5 (or thereabouts) for acting as your intermediary.

Not that your dealing costs end with commission. VAT is slapped onto the commission charge, and there's a 1 per cent stamp duty to pay on the cost of the shares; and finally, the contract stamp – the official seal for your share purchase – a snip at 10p minimum, 60p maximum.

Our example below shows the costs on a purchase of 1,000 shares at £1 each. Buying costs usually average around 3 per cent of the purchase price of the shares. When you come to sell you'll be liable for all the same costs except the stamp duty, bringing the bill down to around 2 per cent. It may not sound much, but remember that your investment has to put on 5 per cent before you can make a penny – so never leave your costs out of the equation before selling.

HOW TO BUY SHARES

You can use a stockbroker, or your bank, which will deal through a broker on your behalf. The advantage of this is that the manager knows your financial state and won't need to take up references; but if you intend to be an active Stock Market trader you may prefer to establish a relationship with a broker right away. If your friends can't recommend anyone, write to the Stock Exchange, London EC2N 1HP, and explain that you are 'a small investor'. They will send you at least three names.

Having found your broker, discussed your aims and made your choice, you're ready to place an order. The broker then deals with a stock-jobber – they are respectively the retailers and wholesalers of the Stock Market, but just as discount warehouses have blurred the demarcation lines of the shopping scene, so the new concept of 'dual capacity' will gradually result in brokers and jobbers being all things to all Stock Exchange investors.

The broker is under an obligation to get his client the best price possible, so when you ask for, say, Marks & Spencer shares, he may approach several jobbers. He won't say whether he is buying or selling, but merely ask the jobber how he's pricing M & S. The answer might be 144p/146p. The first is what he would pay if you were selling the shares, the second what he would charge if you were buying. (The price quoted in newspapers is the 'middle price'.)

Total cost of buying 1,000 shares at £1 each

	£ p
Basic cost	1,000.00
Broker's commission at 1.65%	16.50
VAT on broker's commission	2.47
Stamp duty, 1% of shares	10.00
Contract stamp	30
Total cost	£1,029.27

(Buying cost 2.93% of share purchase price)

Depending on your instructions, the broker might come back to you to check before going ahead and dealing on your behalf. Then you will get a contract note showing that you have bought the shares, followed by your broker's statement of account. One of the delights of shares is that you buy first and pay later. The Stock Market has its own calendar, divided into fortnightly 'Accounts'. No matter at what stage of the month you buy, you are not expected to settle until the end of the account. And eventually you will be able to clasp an official share certificate proving that you are the proud owner of a tiny bit of Marks & Spencer.

All this can be accomplished on little more than a telephone call. Once you are established as the stockbroker's client, the ancient idea of the 'gentlemen's agreement' comes into play. Your word will be your bond, so don't get carried away with Stock Market euphoria and tell him to buy you a 25 per cent stake in ICI.

LOOKING FOR GOODIES

You can, if you like, simply ask for your broker's recommendations. But sharewatching can be fun as well as lucrative, so look for tips in the press and in newsletters and study any research material sent to you by your broker. Allow yourself the odd hunch, too, particularly – and preferably – if it's something you know about. If you're interested in a particular company, you can send off for its report and accounts as well as watching its progress in the financial press.

Some companies with an eye to shareholder loyalty offer 'perks' (which also help to increase their business, as they're usually in the form of discounts on the company's goods or services). These range from cheap ferry fares (Townsend Thoresen), discounts on clothes (Burton Group, whose shops include Peter Robinson, Top Shop and Principles), discounts on certain hotel accommodation, whisky, jewellery, textile goods, Audi and Volkswagen cars, plus more (Lonrho) and even Centre Court seats at Wimbledon (All England Lawn Tennis Club).

Whatever your passion or however strong your hunch, do take the precaution of asking your broker for his opinion of any shares you fancy – he's in a better position than you to assess the company's situation in the Market, and it's only worth buying shares if you stand to make money on them, however tempting the perk(s) might appear.

Bullion and baubles

There's something intrinsically pleasing about having your wealth in tangible form. Share certificates and the like are all very well, but their value seems a bit remote – and, like cash, they aren't aesthetically appealing.

So it's understandable if you have a hankering for something more enduring – like a bar of gold bullion to use as a paperweight, or a diamond chunk dangling from each ear (plus a permanent security guard to keep an eye on them!). Gold, moreover, is the traditional safeguard against ruin for nations and private investors alike.

However, that is not to say that its market price always goes upwards, never down – it peaked at £371 an ounce in 1980, fell back to a low of £172 during 1982, recovered to steady at an average of £270 during 1984, and by mid-1985 had fallen back to around £228.

COINING IT
If you're able to take a longterm view and want to include gold in your portfolio, the most marketable form of it is the Krugerrand – a pure gold coin available in one ounce, half-ounce, quarter- and even one-tenth of an ounce sizes.

If you also want to look at your Krugerrand, it'll cost you more than the gold price, as UK residents who buy and take delivery of bullion – even one-tenth of an ounce of it – have to pay VAT. You can get round this by having your pile stored overseas, though the bullion dealers who arrange it are likely to look askance if you've fewer than 10 one-ounce coins. And, to trade at the nearest to the spot metal price and make the cost of your numbered vault worthwhile, that's probably the minimum you should start off with. Otherwise, to compensate for the effect of VAT and – on the smaller coins – quite a high premium above the metal value, the underlying price will have to rise by about 20 per cent before you begin making any sort of profit.

The one-ounce Krugerrand, which carries only a 3 per cent premium and is thus the best value, was being offered in mid-1985 at £237 including VAT, while the tiny one-tenth coin cost £30. If you were selling a one-ouncer, though, you'd have got only £229. You can check the latest price by telephoning Teledata (01-200 0200); and if you want to buy, you can do so through coin and bullion dealers and even the banks. A list of dealers is included in The Krugerrand Directory (see 'Useful addresses').

WEAR IT WELL
The mark-up on gold jewellery makes the one-tenth Krugerrand look like the bargain of the year. On top of the gold content, you pay for workmanship, the retailer's cut, fashion and (hopefully) enough beauty to console you in place of investment value.

The same applies with precious stones, but more so, as they are much less marketable than gold. Buying is hard enough even if you've got several thousand pounds to spend, as individual investors have to buy retail – and if a retailer tells you that a stone is perfect, are you qualified to argue? If you want to sell you'll be lucky if you get more than the current wholesale price of the stone; which, if you buy and sell the same day, will probably cost you around half your money.

Wearable wealth is fine, so long as you don't count on more than its scrap value. If you love it for its beauty regardless, the pleasure it can give you is the return on your investment – so go for it, but insure it.

Insurance for Women

The insurance industry was begun by men and is still largely dominated by men – which is why the traditional view of men as sole protectors and providers tends to persist, and why female policyholders don't always get a fair deal.

That said, we all need some form of insurance cover for the people and things we hold dear – whether our families, our homes and possessions, or ourselves. If we are to be protectors and providers, it's also up to us to *be responsible*. And if that means gritting your teeth when an insurance brochure refers to the person you've married as 'your wife', or you're told that women are ill more often than men so you'll have to pay half as much again for your health insurance, complain, campaign – but take out a policy meanwhile.

Life insurance

You need some sort of life insurance if:
- You have got financial dependants, whether children or elderly parents
- You are financially interdependent with your husband/partner – relying on both salaries to maintain your home, support children etc.
- You have got a mortgage
- You are a non-earning wife and mother – it could cost a lot to pay someone to do your work

If you're in a company pension scheme, it may automatically include life cover, so check before taking out a life policy yourself. If you're self-employed or in a non-pensionable job, you might find it cheaper to get life assurance as part of a personal pension plan package – where you can still get tax relief on your premium.

There are various types of life insurance available. These plans are:

TERM ASSURANCE
The simplest and cheapest life cover. You pay regular premiums to the life company for a set number of years (10, typically), whilst it pays out a lump sum if you die during that time period.

There are several variations on the term assurance theme. With **decreasing term assurance** the sum assured decreases over the years – which is why this type is used only for mortgage protection policies, matching the decreasing debt.

Convertible term assurance is a little more expensive, because it gives you the right to 'convert' the policy at some time in the future, as a born-again endowment policy, for example. It's a good option to have, because it also means that if your health worsens later on – when you most need assurance and the companies are least willing to give it – the life company will be obliged to take you on, and at the normal rate for your age.

Renewable, increasable and convertible assurance policies give the rights their name suggests, often with the increasable bit automatically built in to counter the effects of inflation.

Family income benefit (FIB) is another form of term assurance. Instead of a lump sum, it pays an income to your dependants who won't have to pay income tax on it, as payments under an FIB policy count as return of capital and are thus tax-free.

The above are all 'pure protection' policies. Next come the hybrids providing a protection/investment mix.

WHOLE LIFE
Another type of policy to look after your beneficiaries, whole life policies are designed to last the whole of your life and pay out *when* you die, not *if*. As the company knows it will have to pay out eventually, it therefore charges you considerably more in the meantime and invests part of the premiums on your behalf to provide for the sum assured.

Unlike term policies, whole life policies acquire a surrender value after a number of years, though if you surrender after only a few years you'll get very little back.

ENDOWMENT POLICIES
Much-loved for mortgage purposes, endowment policies are almost entirely investment oriented. They are designed to last for a set number of years, and a conservatively small capital sum is assured at the outset. If you die before the end of the endowment period the sum assured will be paid to your dependants: if you survive till the policy matures, the money is yours to spend as you will.

Endowment policies taken out in conjunction with a mortgage are mostly of the conventional kind, where the life company builds up reserves to withstand the vicissitudes of investment performance over the years and pay up as promised. If you take out a 'with-profits' policy, which is marginally more expensive, they'll also give you a small share of their own profits – both annually, when they declare a cautiously small 'reversionary bonus' which is then permanently added to your sum assured, and when the policy matures, when you also benefit from the 'terminal bonus'. The latter reflects the company's investment performance to a greater extent, which despite its dreary name is often cheeringly large.

For the more adventurous, however, unit-linked policies are the insurance industry's whizz-kids – from which you may assume that despite turning in impressive results, they're not universally admired. The reasons for both stem from their much-vaunted flexibility. For a start, they give you more control over where your premiums are invested, usually offering at least five funds to choose from, with options to switch if desired. This is fine if you're confident of your ability to predict the markets, because if you get it right you can do very well indeed. If you're not so sure, a safer option is to plump for the company's own Managed Fund.

The second and possibly more significant factor is that not only do you get what you buy, but also what you get back depends on what you have to sell, and when. So, if your policy matures when markets are high you will get proportionally high returns on your investment. Conversely, if it's maturing in a year when investment values are depressed, you also may feel depressed at getting less than you'd hoped for.

To give them their due, unit-linked policies have significantly outperformed conventional with-profits endowments in recent years. However, they don't have a long track record (unit-linked plans have only been around since the late 1960s – a short time, in insurance industry terms) and as ever, the future cannot be predicted.

What you *can* do – apart from trying to be your own actuary and assessing whether your lifestyle will allow you to last as long as your policy – is to weigh up the comparative risks in endowment versus unit-linked, look at what track records there are (you can do this by watching the specialist financial press, or asking a broker) and comparing them – and in the case of unit-linked, look at the performance of the Managed Fund, which should best reflect the company's overall invest-ment expertise. If you do feel bold enough to count on a unit-linked policy to pay off your mortgage, read the small print carefully to see how much of a risk you may be taking. Some companies, to their credit, are now attempting to in-corporate the element of guaranteed mortgage repayment offered by conventional endowments, and some adopt a re-assuringly cautious approach to the assumptions they use for illustration ('assuming 7 per cent growth throughout the life of the policy, you should get returns of . . .' etc). Beware of over-confident assumptions. You should also look for a policy that offers flexibility in the choice of maturity date – so you can have a bit of leeway on when you cash in, and can thus (hopefully) manage to do so when the markets are favourable for you.

Health insurance

Most sensible people give due consideration to their eventual – and possibly untimely – end. Few give as much consideration to the possibility of accident or illness happening in between, and the loss of income that would result from being unable to continue working.

Yet you are more likely to be incapable of working for a long period than of dying before retirement age. Government statistics for 1982, for example, revealed that 400,000 people had been off work for 6 months or more as a result of injury or illness – some of them for as long as 15 years. The financial effects of being unable to work for even 6 months can be pretty dire. Longterm, they can be devastating. It doesn't, therefore, take much imagination to realize the importance of providing insurance cover.

You will, of course, get some state benefit but it's unlikely to be generous. More significant is what you might get from your employer, so it's worth checking out what you might be entitled to – and if you can persuade your employer to take out a group scheme if there isn't one already, as you would get cheaper cover than if you arranged it as an individual. For those not covered by group schemes, and for the self-employed in particular, health insurance is a must.

ACCIDENT INSURANCE

The main purpose of an accident insurance policy is to pay out a lump sum in the event of a disabling accident or, possibly, illness (depending on where it's contracted – exotic parts of the world are usually excluded). You may also be able to arrange for some income to be paid, but only for a limited period of time.

PERMANENT HEALTH INSURANCE

This should be the grand cover-all. It isn't, but it goes a long way nonetheless. Permanent health insurance (PHI) guarantees to provide an income should accident or illness keep you off work for more than a certain period (four weeks is the usual minimum 'deferred period', but the longer you can afford to manage, the lower your premium will be). And unlike accident insurance, it guarantees to keep paying until normal retirement age.

Now for the snags. Women have to pay higher premiums than men – 50 per cent more is not uncommon – and there are umpteen restrictions and exclusions. You shouldn't, for example, get involved in a war or insurrection, catch something nasty on your tropical travels, engage in hazardous sports, become ill as a result of something self-inflicted (drink, drugs etc), or become pregnant. And you shouldn't get ill as a result of pregnancy either, as most companies won't pay up even for that – and those that do, impose a deferred period (usually 3 months on from the end of the pregnancy).

When making a claim, you may be required to provide proof of income – and if you're self-employed and you've had a bad year that could be tough. When you eventually get your money, the most you can get is 75 per cent of your income, and the company will probably lop off a sum equivalent to any state or company benefits due to you before it pays up. The final insult is that if you receive the benefits (for which you've paid premiums) for longer than a full tax year, the Inland Revenue treats it as unearned income and may start demanding tax on it. (This doesn't apply with group schemes, where the payments are regarded as earned income and subject to PAYE from the start.)

Yet aside from its considerable drawbacks, PHI is good value for money – a woman aged 35 could buy cover of £500 a month (subject to a 13-week deferred period) up to age 60, for as little as £120 a year. You do need to examine the contents of the package with great care, and to shop around to find the best deal for you – which may not be the cheapest. Check too what happens if you're able to work again but have to take a pay cut, as some companies will merely reduce the benefit accordingly and others cut it completely. Ask questions about claims procedure – you don't want to have to cut through kilometres of red tape before you can receive any payment, so the simpler the better.

As with life assurance, a good broker will help you to select the best cover for you – possibly by taking out both a cheap accident insurance or accident/illness insurance to see you through the short term, and a PHI policy with a long deferred period (26 or 52 weeks) to cover the longer term.

Insuring your home

If you're a homeowner you should insure your property. If you have a mortgage, the building society/bank will insist on it – and they'll stipulate how much cover you must have. It sounds perversely flattering if you are told that your dilapidated Victorian edifice is being insured for a sum nearly three times as much as you paid for it – though sadly, this isn't an assessment of its true market value. Buildings insurance is to cover the cost of rebuilding your home to its previous standard should it collapse, burn down, be blown up by a gas explosion, or suchlike. Lesser damage, naturally, would be dealt with proportionally.

If you feel your home has outstanding features of which the

200

insurance company might not be aware and which might be expensive to replace, do point this out rather than find out too late that you were under-insured. The same applies if you add value by installing central heating or making other improvements to the house.

The Association of British Insurers (ABI) has two free leaflets on the subject: *Buildings Insurance for Home Owners* and *How to Make a Claim*. If you want to double-check that your cover is sufficient, you could also employ a surveyor: contact the Royal Institution of Chartered Surveyors for a member in your area.

Contents insurance

A quarter of all householders in the UK have no insurance cover for their house contents, and it's estimated that an equivalent number are under-insured. In either case it is false economy for the owner, not to say plain daft, as the loss of just one item can cost you more than the premium for insuring all your moveable possessions.

Contents policies cover a variety of risks, notably fire, flood and of course burglary: but you should read the small print in case you need to pay extra for covering accidental damage.

Check whether personal money is covered, and up to what amount; and whether you're covered for items lost or stolen outside your home. You can play it safe with an 'All risks' policy, which means what it says – but not even that includes the risk of under-insurance, so make sure costly items such as camera equipment or valuable jewellery are fully covered under the terms of the policy. If they form more than a stated proportion, such as 5 per cent of the total sum insured, you should mention them specifically and if necessary pay an extra premium.

There are two types of contents insurance to choose from:

INDEMNITY
This is cheaper because it allows for wear and tear on your cherished chattels and thus pays out less.

REPLACEMENT AS NEW
This means exactly that . . . except in the case of clothing and linen, which are usually excluded from replacement cover and

insured on an indemnity basis, irrespective of which type of policy you're paying for.

Tot up the cost

To get an accurate assessment of how much you should insure for, you can't beat doing a room-by-room inventory – which you should keep, updating as necessary and including the serial numbers of TV sets etc., as this can be an invaluable reference if you have to make a claim, or give the police a list of stolen goods. Do get an expert valuation where appropriate, as with art and antiques.

Most companies rate by postal districts, but what one considers a 'high risk' area may be rated lower by another with a smaller incidence of claims from there. So again, shop around or ask a broker to do so on your behalf. And, as with buildings insurance, the ABI has leaflets on contents insurance and how to make a claim.

Complaints

If you have a complaint against your insurance company, take it up with the company (write to the chief executive if necessary); then, if you're still not satisfied, you can appeal to the Insurance Ombudsman Bureau. This is an independent body funded by the industry, but not all companies belong to the Ombudsman scheme, so you should check beforehand.

Pensions

It's easy to put off planning for the future. If you're under 35 especially, retirement seems a long way off and anything could happen before then. But the future has an unsettling way of sneaking up on you; and when it is suddenly too late to make advantageous arrangements and you may pay dearly for your neglect.

Much has happened in the last decade – and is happening now – to affect our financial anticipation of retirement. Between 1978, when the State Earnings Related Pension Scheme (Serps) came into being with the promise to spread jam on the basic state pension's bread, and now, when the present government is partially dismantling it, it has become clear that by the turn of the century Serps would be placing an intolerable burden of pension support on a diminished work-force. Its partial disappearance once again places a question mark against our future security, but better now than too late.

The recent discussion over phasing out of Serps has at least focussed attention on the adequacy or otherwise of state pension provision – and made it clear that we cannot afford to be complacent about laying in our own stock of preserves. From 1987, women under the age of 45 (and men under the age of 50) will have to make their own pension arrangements. Employees will by law have to contribute a minimum of 4 per cent of salary to a pension scheme (company or 'personal portable'), with the employer meeting at least half the cost. But if you're self-employed or in a non-pensionable job, you can set up your own pension arrangements now.

Don't kid yourself you could do as well by investing the money yourself. Pension plans attract tax relief at your highest rate, and you'd have to be an investment genius to outdo the benefits accrued through that advantage, coupled with the plans' professional management. If you've already got a pension plan, don't feel smug about it – remember to top up your contributions in line with salary increases, or else the plan you proudly tucked away at 25 won't be nearly as im-pressive by the time you reach 60. And as a woman aged 60 has, on average, another 20 years ahead of her, that's not the time to realize that you should have done more to take care of yourself.

The rules

You can put up to 17.5 per cent of your earnings into a Personal Pension Plan. Below are two illustrations of typical pension plans.

PERSONAL PENSION PLANS – COST AND PROJECTED BENEFITS
The quotations below, from two of the most well-established and consistently well-performing companies in the pensions field, are based on an example of a self-employed woman aged

35 next birthday, paying basic rate tax, and who can afford a premium of around £50 a month, with waiver of premium option and 226a life insurance, and retirement at age 60.

Legal & General (unit-linked)

LIFE INSURANCE
under 226a, Income and
Corporation Taxes Act 1970

Guaranteed sum £25,000.00
payable on death before
retirement

Cost
Gross monthly premium 5.00
Net monthly premium 3.50

PERSONAL PENSION PLAN
including waiver of premium
after six months' incapacity

Fund at retirement £72,791.00
assuming growth at 12%

(if we assumed growth
   at 15% 119,971.00)

which would buy a pension
   for life of 8,978.00

or a tax-free sum of 20,542.00
plus a pension of 6,442.00

Cost
Gross monthly premium 50.00
Net monthly premium 35.00

**Total net
   contribution** 10,710.00

National Mutual Life (with profits)

LIFE INSURANCE
under 226a, Income and
Corporation Taxes Act 1970

Guaranteed sum £25,000.00

Cost
Gross monthly premium 5.00
Net monthly premium 3.50

WAIVER OF PREMIUM
waived after six months'
incapacity

Monthly benefit £50.00

Cost
Gross monthly premium 2.00
Net monthly premium 1.40

PERSONAL PENSION PLAN
**Guaranteed cash
   fund** £18,091.00

Regular bonus
assuming growth of
   6.2% 68,346.00

Final bonus 41,008.00

**Projected total cash
   fund** 127,445.00
which would buy a pension for
life of 15,331.00
or a tax-free sum of 35,439.00
plus a pension of 11,068.00

Cost
Gross monthly premium 50.00
Net monthly premium 35.00

Total net contribution 10,920.00

You can also make up for lost time by paying in a lump sum to cover premiums to the permitted maximum for the last 6 tax years. And, in both cases, you'll get tax relief on your contributions at your highest rate – so the higher your tax bracket, the lower your actual payout, and the better your value for money.

When you reach retirement age you can, if you wish, commute part of your pension – that is, take a chunk of it as a tax-free lump sum in return for a reduced pension. (The pension itself counts as income and so the taxman does eventually get a chance to claw back some of your carefully accumulated cash.)

How to buy

Don't just plump for the first plan you see, however impressive the projected pension appears. All of them look like Continental telephone numbers from 20 years or so away, and however appealing the advertisement, your pension is too important to be bought 'off the page'.

Consult an insurance broker or other professional adviser – including your accountant, if you're in any doubt about your tax position and what you can declare as earnings for tax purposes. Remember that being clever and lowering your tax bill can backfire in the long run if it gives you a low pension base – a quandary for many a self-employed person. And do get as many quotations from different companies as you want, before making your choice of scheme . . . so long as that doesn't become an excuse for procrastinating.

What to look for

Your Personal Pension Plan can and should be tailor-made to suit your own requirements – and, as your circumstances may change, you should choose one that offers maximum flexibility as well as a good return. (Fortunately, most personal pension plans are now designed to be as portable as possible.)

There are two types of pension plan investment – with-profits and unit-linked, which operate on the same basis as their equivalents in life assurance policies.

WITH-PROFITS

A with-profits plan is like the familiar endowment policy: at the outset you are guaranteed a minimum sum at maturity (both your own and the policy's, in the case of planning for retirement) and meanwhile, during the life of the policy, the company adds annual reversionary bonuses. Because the actuaries have to take future payouts into account they err on the side of caution but, once granted, these bonuses cannot be taken away and accumulate on top of the guaranteed minimum. When the policy matures you should also get a final or 'terminal' bonus reflecting the investment performance of the fund over the years you've been paying contributions.

OR UNIT-LINKED

Unit-linked plans offer a potentially greater return, but at greater risk – because more of the investment onus is placed on you, the policyholder. Instead of your contributions pouring into an unspecified investment pool, you are offered a range of investment funds from which to choose, and the relative success of your chosen fund (or funds – you can switch) will partly determine the size of your pension at the time you retire. The last phrase is significant: as with unit trusts, the value of your investment fund can go up or down, with no reversionary bonuses to cushion you in case it falls. However, a unit-linked plan aims to be equally 'with profits' and could well rise far above its more cautious fellow. It's unlikely to be 'with losses', either, as insurance companies offering unit-linked pension plans have a cash fund or guaranteed fund where the value is guaranteed not to fall below your entry point. A few offer the option to convert to a with-profits basis, say, 5 years before retirement – reassuring if you're worried you might retire during a falling market.

With both unit-linked and with-profits schemes, your contributions build up a fund which is used to purchase a pension at retirement. The amount of pension you are able to buy will depend not only on the size of the fund, but on annuity rates at the time you retire; and the type of pension you buy. You can also, if you wish, commute part of your pension as a tax-free lump sum up to a maximum of three times the residual level pension – equivalent to about a quarter of the fund.

A word of warning: don't be too seduced by the future projections quoted. They can be misleading – firstly because

206

they all look so impressive that one might be tempted, wrongly, to pay a lower premium or not increase the contribution as time goes by. Secondly, with-profits quotations will appear better as these companies are allowed to 'roll up' their anticipated bonuses when making projections, making them look like sure-fire winners, whereas in reality unit-linked policies have recently tended to outstrip these more conservative runners, and in the longer term might prove more startling performers.

If you can afford it, it might be worth splitting contributions between with-profits and unit-linked companies, though it means that you'll be covering two sets of administrative charges. But if you can put more than £100 a month with each company (which in real terms might cost you only £40 for each, if you're a 60 per cent taxpayer) you'll be getting a good deal, especially as unit-linked plans give an extra allocation of units for larger investments.

Standard options

There are various options built in or which can be tacked on to either type of plan.

WAIVER OF PREMIUM
This is a must for anyone who's self-employed. You pay a little extra for the waiver of premium option but it means that your premiums will be credited by the insurance company if you are unable to work for any reason, apart from an exclusion period, generally the first 3 or 6 months.

LIFE INSURANCE OPTION
You can take out life insurance under section 226a of the Income and Corporation Taxes Act 1970 – the only area where it is still eligible for life assurance premium relief; and, as it's linked to a pension plan, you get tax relief at your highest rate of tax.

SINGLE OR REGULAR?
You can pay into a personal pension plan either with regular monthly or annual premiums or with a series of lump sum 'single premiums'. The first has several advantages. For a

start, it's a good habit to get into – whereas if you reckon you'll just pay in single premium chunks according to what you can afford year by year, you'll probably always find many other causes making demands on your available cash, and not put away as much as you should. More importantly, single premium policies are ineligible for waiver of premium benefit or section 226a life insurance, both useful options.

Single premiums do have their uses, though. They can take up unclaimed contribution allowances for the previous 6 tax years, or be used to maximize input as your retirement date gets close. Should you ever be unemployed and therefore excluded from the regular premium policies, you are also allowed to make a single premium provision for your old age.

It's a good idea to start with regular monthly or annual contributions at a level you know you can afford, and if your circumstances change you can increase or reduce your contributions, have a 'premium holiday' or make the policy paid-up. A good financial adviser should review your plan annually and suggest constructive changes according to your circumstances.

If you change jobs and enter a company pension scheme you may have to make your own plan 'paid up', which means that you stop paying premiums but your existing contributions continue to accrue benefits. If you then revert to being self-employed you can take up the policy again, though the waiver of premium option and life insurance will cost you more, relative to your age. Depending on the eventual content of the intended new legislation, however, you may simply be able to carry your own Personal Pension Plan around with you like a briefcase from job to job, whether you're self-employed or a corporate woman.

Further checkpoints

Other features to look for in a pension plan are a loanback facility (useful if you hit a crisis, though you should avoid dipping into your pension if possible) and an open market option. This is a facility whereby you can use your funds at retirement to buy a pension from any company you choose, so that you needn't be tied to the one you've been investing with if annuity rates elsewhere are more attractive.

If you're opting for a unit-linked plan you should also look for low charges, flexibility of switching between funds (one free switch a year is common) and, if possible, the option to convert to a with-profits basis when you get close to retirement. And if the potential of a unit-linked plan appeals but you're chary of attempting to be a fund-spotter, you can opt for the company's Managed Fund (as do 80 per cent of people in unit-linked pension plans).

Finally, keep an eye open for impending legislation – and not just that under current debate, but also any future legislation that could affect your financial circumstances in retirement. The tendency in the past has been for a large number of people to reach retirement with very little idea (and all too often a mistakenly inflated idea) of what they will receive in the way of pension, from whatever source.

Property

'When I say, " 'ouse", it were only a 'ole in the ground, covered by a couple of feet of torn canvas – but it were a 'ouse to *us*,' claimed John Cleese, as one of 'Four Yorkshiremen' embroidering their recollections of childhood poverty. All of us have somewhat better shelter than that. But whether we rent or buy a home, or take out a commercial lease for a business venture, we should be as canny with our brass as Yorkshire folk are popularly held to be with theirs.

Renting

Renting a place to live in has several advantages which can be summed up in one word: simplicity. You don't have to spend a long time saving for a deposit, you're not tied by the responsibilities of insuring and maintaining the building, and your outgoings are much lower than if you were paying a mortgage and other costs which are the lot of the housebuyer. If the flat is furnished you won't have to fork out for furniture, carpets and so on, and you can usually move quite quickly if you want to, so you have considerable freedom. Moreover, tenancy laws are in your favour and you're much more likely than in the past to be secure.

In all privately rented accommodation, whether furnished or unfurnished, you are protected by the Rent Act (of which there have been several; the current one dates from 1982). Local councils are exempt from the Act, but are governed by other laws; and housing associations also have their own rules. Lodgings and hostels (where at least some meals are provided) are also outside the scope of the Act.

The Act gives you security of tenure and can prevent your landlord – or landlady, come to that – charging you an exorbitant rent. As for payment in advance, it's reasonable under the Act to be asked for a deposit of up to 2 months' rent (returnable, less anything for breakages and unpaid bills, when you leave), and even something for fixtures and fittings so long as that's not exorbitant either. But a demand for 'key money' – a non-returnable fee just to get you the place – is nearly always illegal.

If you think you're up against a latter-day Rachman, contact your local Rent Officer. You should, incidentally, have a tenancy agreement signed by both you and the landlord (and contact the Rent Officer or get a solicitor to check it if you're unsure if it's fair); or, at the very least, a rent book.

The problems with renting begin where the advantages leave off. The law that protects you makes letting much less attractive to landlords, with the result that private rented accommodation is in ever-diminishing supply. (If the boot is on the other foot – that is, if you're thinking of renting your property to someone else – consult your solicitor for advice and help in drawing up a tenancy agreement, and ask your local Rent Officer to help you fix a fair rent, so you know where you stand.)

Housing associations are another source of rented accommodation, as are housing co-ops, but you may have a long wait for a place. The same applies with council tenancies – though if you are able to get a council property, hang on to it and you may be able to buy it in due course.

And buying is what you should ultimately do. The freedom offered by renting is all very well in the shorter term, but you could pay rent for ever and have nothing to show for it but a collection of rent books. And it's not the same as having a place of your own. Put that money towards your own pile of bricks and mortar and it will almost certainly make money for you in years to come.

Shared ownership

If you can't afford to make the quantum leap between renting and buying, you might consider buying through a shared ownership scheme. Shared, not in the sense of buying your house with half a dozen hard-pressed friends, but with the landlord – which may be a builder, local council, housing association or 'new town' housing corporation.

The idea is that you can become a homeowner in stages. You buy as much of the house or flat as you can afford – anything from a quarter to three-quarters. The rest is let to you by the housing association (or whatever) at a fixed fair rent which may be partly subsidized, with the government's blessing.

If you have strange visions of owning the kitchen but having only tenancy rights over the bedroom etc., rest assured – you get all the benefits of home ownership, including security, tax relief on mortgage repayments and any increase in the value of your portion should you wish to sell. And if your circumstances change and you can afford to buy a bit more – or all of it – then you can.

The scheme is still fairly new, though spreading fast, but there may not be one operating in your area: ask locally, or see the 'Useful addresses' section at the end of this chapter.

Buying

Ever since the 1930s, when home ownership began to take off on a large scale, buying a home has proved an excellent investment – especially in the early 1970s, when market values shot through the roof and 'gazumping' entered popular vocabulary. We're unlikely to see a similar escalation of prices, but a home of your own is usually a sound investment. By mid-1985, house prices had become fairly steady but saw an increase of some 11 per cent over the previous year alone. That isn't much if you're investing purely for return – you could do far better with equities – but then, you can't live in a rolled-up share certificate.

The first step in house-buying is to find your finance – and a certain percentage of it will have to come from you. Building societies and banks generally advance at least 80 per cent of the price at which they value it for mortgage purposes (which may be lower than the market price), most will go up to 90 per cent – and, depending on the mortgage market at the time you buy, you may even get a 100 per cent mortgage. But mortgage rates vary, and the people who are willing to lend the most aren't necessarily the cheapest source of finance in the long run. So do shop around – or use a professional intermediary to help you. Mortgage and insurance brokers, estate agents and even solicitors can often smooth your path to a willing lender, and some first-time buyers' schemes for newly-built properties have mortgage finance facilities already set up. Building societies also sometimes do special deals for first-timers, with the first year's repayments at a reduced rate, and free valuation, for example.

Even if you get a 100 per cent mortgage, you'll still need a fund to cover the associated costs of buying, from conveyancing fees to hiring a removal van, to say nothing of the cost of setting up home (for which we could all do with a bottomless purse). If you've been sensible and saved with a building society, that relationship will stand you in good stead should you want to get your mortgage there.

It's advisable to get a rough idea of how much you'll be able to borrow, before you start house-hunting – there's no point in looking at properties you can't afford. The usual multiple is $2\frac{1}{2} \times$ gross annual salary if you're buying alone, or $2 \times$ main salary plus $1 \times$ lesser salary if you're buying with someone else; but some lenders will advance up to three times the main salary.

Once you've found the home of your dreams, or as near to it as you can stretch, make an offer (which should always be 'subject to survey and contract', so you're not committed if a survey reveals terminal dry rot) and, assuming it's accepted, hightail it down to your building society or other lender. The society, say, will then instruct a valuer to inspect the property and submit a report (and you'll pay his fee) on its loan-worthiness. The valuation report is *not* a structural survey, and though some building societies may offer a hybrid version at a slightly higher fee, the safest way is to find a good chartered surveyor and pay for a full survey.

By law, building societies must take some extra security if the loan exceeds the society's normal maximum percentage.

Usually it takes the form of an insurance indemnity for which you pay a one-off premium.

There are two types of mortgage to choose from: repayment, and endowment. The first combines repayment of both capital and interest in each monthly repayment. In the early years the payments comprise mainly interest, but as the years go by the ratio changes until in the final years you are paying mainly capital.

Endowment loans are made in conjunction with a life insurance company, which issues an endowment policy on your life, to the amount and period of the loan. During that period you pay only interest to the society, and the insurance premium to the life company. At maturity the proceeds of the policy pay off the capital loan, and the surplus (they're designed to provide a surplus) goes to you.

Self-employed housebuyers have a further option: namely, to link the mortgage loan to a personal pension plan instead of an endowment policy. This has the advantage of attracting two lots of tax relief – on the mortgage interest, and on the pension premiums (both at your highest rate of tax). But whether it is wise to commit your pension to paying for your house is a moot point.

The ceiling for tax relief on mortgage interest is currently £30,000, but two single people buying a house together can each claim the full relief, enabling you – in theory at least – to take out a £60,000 mortgage. Married couples, alas, are treated as one. If the mortgage on your home is less than £30,000, basic rate tax relief will be granted automatically through the MIRAS (Mortgage Interest Relief At Source) system, so you just pay less. If it's more, or if you're a higher rate taxpayer, you'll need to stake your claim with the Inland Revenue.

You'll need a solicitor to handle the conveyancing (if you don't choose to do it yourself), and you'll also need money lined up for the customary 10 per cent deposit to be paid to the vendor's solicitor on exchange of contracts, when the sale becomes binding. From there to completion takes about 28 days, and your solicitor's bill will wing its way to you. Then the responsibility hits you as you fork out for buildings and contents insurance, rates, water rates, and higher heating bills because you've moved from a tiny studio flat to a two-bedroomed house with a large lounge . . . But it's worth it.

To find out more: most building societies produce booklets for intending housebuyers, and the Building Societies Association (BSA) is a helpful source of information (see 'Useful addresses').

Leasing

When you're running your own business and need premises other than your home, finding your way through the small print of a commercial lease can be a mind-boggling experience. Failing to do so could cost you your business.

Ideally, you should take advice from both a solicitor and a surveyor – the first to examine the words and the second to translate their implications in cash terms according to the state of the property. But you can do a lot of the groundwork simply by familiarizing yourself with the jargon, and you can also get free guidance from one of the many business advice centres or the Citizens' Advice Bureau.

So, you've checked out the market and found what you hope will be a suitable base for your widget repair firm. If it is a new let the landlord will offer a fresh lease and you can begin negotiating.

If it is an 'assignment', meaning you take over an unexpired lease from a previous tenant, you can negotiate only the 'premium', the price for which he will sell the lease to you. A list of what is wrong with the state of repair will be a useful bargaining point, so compile one.

Now for the rest of the jargon – or at least, some of it. There is no standard form of commercial lease, but here are some of the usual features you'll encounter.

Demise: like domain, the area for which you are responsible. Beware that being mistress of all you survey doesn't include the rotting joists supporting your upstairs neighbour's floor: check precisely who is responsible for precisely what:

Rack rent or **current market rent:** what the landlord will tell you is the going rate for such a wonderful property. Don't believe it – at least not until you've haggled, perhaps bringing in a professional negotiator from an estate agent.

Term: how long the property is legally yours. A long lease can be handy as security for a bank loan, and you can sell it when you want to leave – hopefully for bigger and better things. But if your business fails and you're forced to sell, you're still responsible for the rent meanwhile – and an assignment can take a long time to arrange.

Rent: yes, as it says. Just remember to negotiate hard if it is a new lease, and ask around locally to check on rents for comparable properties.

Rent-free period: this won't appear in the lease, but you should try to negotiate a rent-free period on the basis of what it will cost you to clean and prepare the place for use.

Rent review: the landlord's chance to raise the rent, which can happen as often as every three years. Make sure you have the right to negotiate it when the time comes.

Upward-only rent increases: are there any other kinds, you may well remark. In this case it means that if you and the landlord can't agree on the amount of the increase, an independent assessor should be called in to decide the current market rent and you are obliged to pay it – unless it's lower than your current rent, when you carry on paying that, but no less.

Insurance rent: what you pay the landlord towards insuring the building, plus cover for 'rent loss' – what he would lose in rent from you if it burnt to the ground. Any third party or contents insurance is your responsibility.

Proportion: your share of the building – and hence of any costs which the landlord can pass on. It's usually worked out in terms of the area you occupy (square feet of space, or number of floors) or the rateable value of your unit. Watch that the landlord doesn't get the chance to redistribute the burden unfairly on to you if someone else in the building moves out and their bit remains unlet.

Repairs: Do call in a surveyor to see what repairs are necessary before you sign anything, and don't touch a . . .

Full repairing lease: it means *you* are responsible for repairs both inside and out, and your landlord could get his place done up for nothing while you go rapidly bankrupt.

Internal repairing lease: say yes to this one – it means you're only responsible for the upkeep of your unit from the plaster inwards.

Internal repairing with a contribution to the external: the most common type; but again, make sure he can't charge you for more than your proportion even if you're the only tenant left in a 50-unit space.

Service charge: what you pay (again, proportionally) towards overheads like heating and lighting, decoration of common parts and the like. The landlord should be obliged, under the terms of the lease, to provide a certified statement of expenditure (which should be only on the things itemized in the lease).

Sinking fund: the pool of contributions towards external repairs, paid regularly so that you won't be hit by a sudden massive bill. You should be provided with an annual update: scrutinize to see if the landlord is creaming off interest or the 'repairs' aren't valid.

Legal costs: make sure you don't get lumbered with both your own solicitor's costs, and those of the landlord's solicitor, for the drawing up and completing of a lease – landlords are becoming increasingly fond of inserting a clause requiring you to do so.

Use: the description of what you propose to do in the property, and you should word it carefully. A broad description such as 'retail shop' will make it easier to assign the lease should you wish to, but get too specific and you could be stuck there indefinitely – which is fine if you were planning to anyway, as a narrow description lowers the value of the lease and at review time the landlord won't be able to increase the rent so much.

Planning use: somewhere in your lease there'll be a clause obliging you to abide by the planning laws, so check the official use regulations with the local authority.

Side letter: a signed and legally recognized document attached to the lease and which overrides some condition of the lease – perhaps, say, because for some reason the landlord is letting to you at a rent below market level, in which case it would be made personal to you in a side letter and not passed on in an assignment.

Even if you commit all the foregoing phrases to memory, you'll need more than your wits about you when you come to take out a lease – you'll need professional help. Don't try to cut costs by doing without: it's money well spent, for your own protection – and you can set it against tax the Inland Revenue will try to claim when your business blossoms from its carefully negotiated base.

"But does the pink Bentley come with the leopard print seats AND the gold plated phone?"

Running Your Own Business

Imagine it. You've always fancied being your own boss, and beneath your corporate or wifely exterior beats an entrepreneurial heart. Then one day you get The Idea. 'It couldn't fail,' you say to yourself. 'Nobody else in this district is running a decent bistro/computerized property shop house-to-house nappy collection and laundering service etc.' And you're off.

That last idea came from a Californian married to an Englishman, on one occasion when their small London flat was draped with nappies and she bemoaned the lack of a 'diaper service' like the ones back home. 'Were I more enterprising I'd start one myself' and 'I'd be assured of at least one customer' are the seeds from which small businesses can grow.

If you're not imaginatively inspired by nature, you could run the show in a business dreamt up by someone else, and become a franchisee. Or you could attend a day school on how to set up your own business – if you don't have a clear idea of what you want to do, such a course can often prompt ideas as well as give you the opportunity to discuss them.

Once you've got your idea – the one which all your instincts tell you is a winner – then go for it, and have faith in it. But if you want your business venture to succeed, you'll need more than gut feeling behind it. Spotting a gap in the market which you could fill is exciting, and you may feel like rushing straight into it. Don't.

Research your market

If you're serious about going into business on your own account you've got to tackle it in a businesslike manner. Not even the biggest and most successful companies put anything new on the market without first researching it, so learn from them. There are a number of ways in which you can test the viability of your business concept.

Research your market thoroughly, keeping notes of your findings (which later will form part of your business presentation, when you come to raise finance). Ask yourself as many questions as you can – and answer them. For example:

● Consider the service or product you want to offer.

Is there a demand for it?

Can you supply it at a reasonable price to the customer?

Is anyone else doing anything similar?

How successful is it?

Could you compete with it in terms of quality and price?

Would you have to compete for the same customers, or is the field open in your area?

If it's a new product or service, what makes you think people will want it?

● Study your intended location.

What are its pros and cons?

What do you need from it?

Could you cut your costs by compromising sensibly? – say, if you need plenty of exposure to the public but can't afford High Street rents, and you've found somewhere in a back street that just happens to be a popular short cut for commuters heading for the railway station.

Could you operate your business from your home?

What do you see as your catchment area (how far do you think people will travel to reach you?) and how many prospective customers does it contain? 'Lots' isn't good enough – work out a realistic estimate.

● Identify your target market.

Who do you see as your main customers? The public at large, or a specific section (women only, or children, or the elderly; commuters of any kind; people in one particular trade or profession; sporty types; arty types; etc.).

How many are there in your catchment area? There may be 1,500 people in the flats near your desired pitch, but how many of those might actually want to buy your revolutionary, automatic ironing machine?

Don't forget to ask yourself how they'll get to know about you. Through local advertising? Door-to-door leaflets? Word of mouth? Special promotions?

How regular is their custom likely to be?

● Do a few sums. Work out prospective costs, both for premises and production, and also for getting yourself known. Estimate the likely turnover. You'll do all this properly later on, but the sooner you get a rough idea of what it will mean in cash terms, the better.

Ask for advice

Small firms bureaux and enterprise agencies often offer free help, but it's also worth paying to attend their seminars on setting up a new business. They'll prompt you to do homework such as the above, if you haven't done it already, and enable you to discuss your idea with others who are more experienced and objective than yourself. You'll learn about sources of finance, how to draw up a business plan, with trading and cashflow forecasts, and how to present it to a prospective backer. You'll also receive guidance on laws that may affect you, and how to keep your business running smoothly once you're over the initial hurdles.

If your idea involves something of which you know nothing, try to get some experience of it. Make a prototype product to test out your method, or take a short-term job where you'll be offering a service similar to yours. Talk to other entrepreneurs, even if they're not in the same field: you can still pick up plenty of tips and (hopefully) learn from their mistakes.

219

Blueprint for success

Draw up a business plan which is clear, concise and easily understood by those who are new to your idea. When forecasting, err on the side of caution – your backer will be pleased if you then outdo your projected turnover, but you may lose his faith, if not his continued support, if you fall far short.

Be realistic, and don't assume everything will run smoothly: it rarely does. Plan for hassles and traumas – ask yourself how you'll cope when you/your staff are ill, or stock you've ordered doesn't turn up on time, or arrives damaged, or the loo floods, or when you have to deal with an irate customer. You needn't show every detail of this to your prospective backer, but you should have an action plan worked out for yourself anyway, and in case he asks if you've considered the potential problems.

When you come to the point where you have to look for finance, your bank will probably be your first port of call. Don't be put off if the first one says no – try another bank, or simply another branch (branch managers have considerable autonomy, and different branches may have differing amounts of money available for start-up loans).

Besides the banks, there are various venture capital organizations around – ask your local enterprise agency, which should also know if there are other sources of finance in your area, such as the local authority.

Be prepared to bargain with potential backers. They are selling money, you are buying and you both want the best deal. But try to avoid using your home as security or giving personal guarantees.

Decide your trading status

A business may trade in one of four ways:

SOLE TRADER
As a sole trader, you are the only proprietor of the business and are self-employed, so will pay personal income tax on the business's profits.

220

PARTNERSHIP
A partnership can have two or more owners, and profits are divided and taxed as the personal income of each.

LIMITED COMPANY
A limited liability company is a legal entity, separate from the person running it, who will be its employee – in other words, your company will employ *you*. You'll pay PAYE, and any additional profits will be subject to corporation tax.

CO-OPERATIVE
A co-operative may be structured as a partnership or a company, or can be legally registered as a co-operative, where it is largely owned by its workers.

Whichever you choose will be influenced by your personal tax position, so you should discuss it with your accountant.

Keep on track

Like the personal financial plan discussed on p. 00, your business plan shouldn't be used just once (to impress the bank) and then discarded. Make sure you *use* it: refer to it, review it and, if necessary, revise it. Be as tough with yourself about keeping proper accounts as you are about other aspects of the business. It may seem a chore after an exhausting day (and there'll be plenty), but you'll have greater agonies in the long run if you don't do your bookkeeping.

Finally, don't give up. Problems are opportunities in disguise so face them positively. Be persistent. Be tenacious. And be bold. A successful business isn't just a good idea whose time has come, but one whose originator has the ability and determination to put it into practice. Your own determination is your biggest asset. Use it wisely. You'll probably have to work harder than you've ever done before – but the rewards will be all yours.

Help Yourself to Manage Your Money

It is possible to manage your money quite efficiently without keeping up-to-date on the latest developments, interest rates and market prices: the best way to do so is to have so much of the stuff that you can afford to place it with professional financial managers. For most of us, though, making the best use of it will entail keeping an eye on such things ourselves (and it can be fascinating to do so), which in turn means reading the financial press.

Don't be put off by the overwhelmingly masculine aura of the financial pages in national newspapers, which is where you'll look for information on everything from what's happening in the pensions field, where there's a small business course being run, which companies are coming to the Stock Market and so on, to daily updates on share prices, the pound/dollar ratio and the gold price. Weekday editions of the quality papers feature mainly general business news articles, but the weekenders have more coverage of personal finance – my own favourite being *The Guardian's* Week-End Money section every Saturday. For the most extensive coverage, of course, there's the pink paper – and you don't have to be a financial aficionado to read the FT: it's a good investment for its arts pages alone.

For explanatory and comparative articles, charts and analysis (of the 'what are investment trusts, how do they work, how do you buy them, which companies have produced the best results over various periods?' type), turn to specialist magazines like the pioneering *Money Observer* (*The Observer*'s sister publication, available as one-off issues or on subscription through *The Observer*), *What Investment*, *Money Magazine* and so on – and watch the regular personal financial articles in *Working Woman*.

Finally, don't be hesitant about approaching the experts directly if you want information or advice – whether about insurance, unit trusts, sharebuying or whatever. Anyone who makes you feel uncomfortable about your lack of knowledge doesn't deserve your custom or your cash; the more likely risk is that you'll be showered with enough free literature to occupy your bedtime reading for months. But you can cope with that.

Useful addresses

The following addresses are head offices – they will be able to give you address and telephone number of your local office or branch (where applicable).

Association of British Insurers, Aldermary House, 10–15 Queen Street, London EC4N 1TT
Tel: 01 248 4477

British Insurance Brokers Association, BIBA House, 14 Bevis Marks, London EC3A 7NT
Tel: 01 623 9043

The Building Societies Association, 3 Savile Row, London W1X 1AF
Tel: 01 437 0655
A number of free booklets are obtainable, including hints for *Home Buyers*, *Taxation and the Building Society Borrower*, and *Building Societies and House Purchase*. Write to their Information Department enclosing a large sae (first class stamp).

Corporation of Insurance and Financial Advisers, 6–7 Leapale Road, Guildford, Surrey GU1 2HZ
Tel: 0483 39121

Insurance Ombudsman Bureau, 31 Southampton Row, London WC1
Tel: 01 242 8613

The Krugerrand Directory, PO Box 4ZP, London W1A 4ZP

The Law Society, 113 Chancery Lane, London WC2
Tel: 01 242 1222

National Federation of Housing Associations, 175 Grays Inn Road, London WC1
Tel: 01 278 6571

National Tenants Organization, 142 Falcon Court, Dudley Close, Old Trafford, Manchester M15 5QT
Tel: 061 226 9542

The Royal Institution of Chartered Surveyors, 12 Great George Street, London SW1P 3AD
Tel: 01 222 7000

Unit Trust Association, 10 Belgrave Square, London SW1X 8PH
Tel: 01 245 6027/8
Publishes a free booklet – *Unit Trusts Explained*.

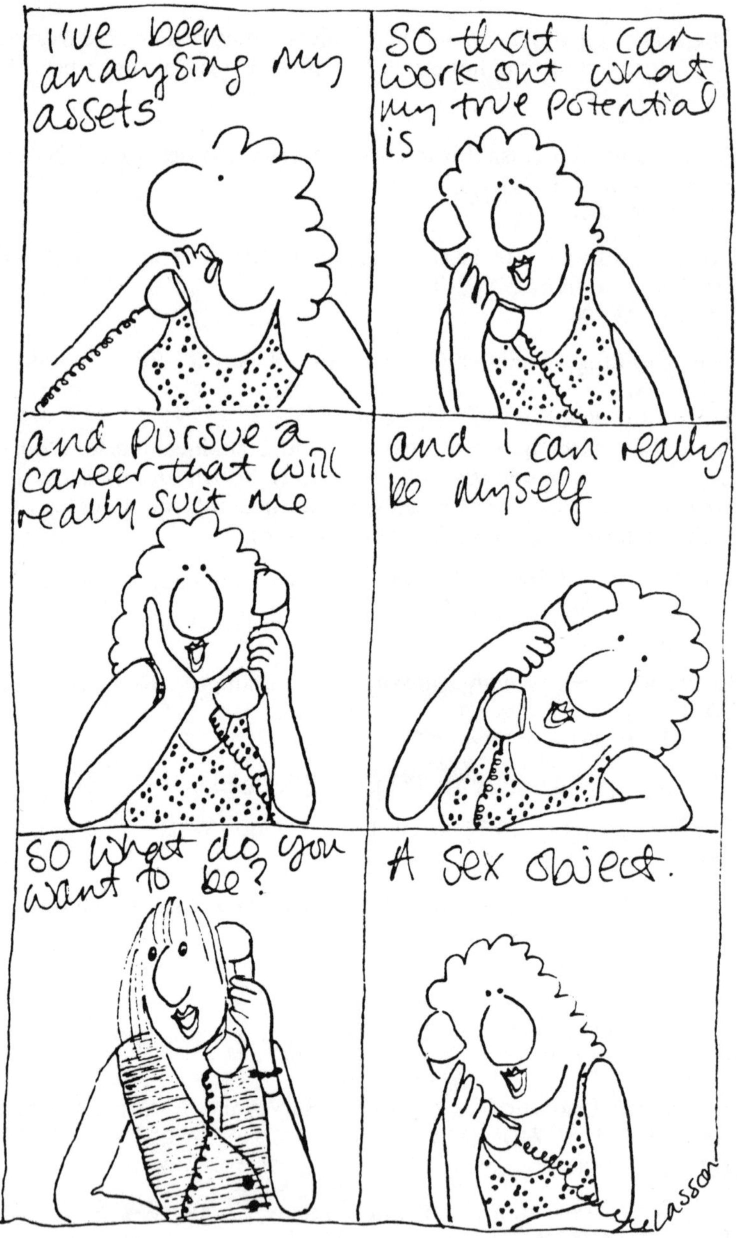
I've been analysing my assets
So that I can work out what my true potential is
and pursue a career that will really suit me
and I can really be myself
So what do you want to be?
A sex object.
Lasson

Success and Satisfaction –
Helping Yourself to Achieve
Your Aims

Deciding on a Job or Career

The lucky ones among us are those who have a strong sense of vocation or who are so interested in a particular job that they carry on with their education and training unswervingly until they've got it. But, they seem to be the minority. Most people drift into a career and sometimes inertia means there are all sorts of bored, frustrated people merely pegging away to earn a salary cheque. They never know a sense of pride or achievement or fulfilment because they don't care enough. They probably work fairly conscientiously, but their real life begins on the dot of 5.30 or whenever they leave their workplace. Since a large chunk of one's life is spent working, it seems a criminal waste of most of it to do something that has little appeal.

How do you discover the nice round hole for your smooth round peg? As you find anything else out – by research.

Seek advice

CAREER COUNSELLORS
The starting point is yourself. Some people never seem to know themselves, and they'll probably benefit from talking to a professional counsellor. They will spend the best part of a day with you, going through your likes and dislikes, the subjects you enjoyed at school, whether you are gregarious or a loner, whether you like being part of a team, like heading that team and organizing them, whether you are inventive and have the makings of an entrepreneur. They'll get you to

complete tests, write pieces and talk to them freely. At the end of the day you'll be given a 'profile' of yourself – and a large bill.

Working Woman operates a career counselling services by post, but it does require you to work hard on completing several pages of self-analysis first. We then have an industrial psychologist and career counsellor to consider your completed documents and give you postal advice. Details are published in *Working Woman* magazine.

There is also The British Psychological Society, St Andrews House, 48 Princess Road East, Leicester LE1 7DR who will send you a list of their occupational guidance advisors on receipt of a stamped addressed envelope.

Do your own research

You can do it yourself, if you have a certain amount of self-discipline and commonsense, and aren't daunted by the painstaking task of combing through relevant books and journals.

Start by listing all the subjects you enjoyed at school – including the non-academic ones like painting or the choir. Then list all the things you like doing now. Collecting perhaps? Running the local political group. Meeting new people. Reading. List everything positive, and on the opposite side of the paper the things you dislike.

After a while, a profile begins to emerge. You might find you like meeting people and organizing. Or solitary work, like research. However rough it is, you have a little idea of yourself.

The next step is to take yourself off to the local library and browse through career books. Tick all those careers that seem to appeal to you and seem to fit the qualities that you have listed. Then look at the trade or professional magazines that belong to those careers – practically every calling has one. You'll find these in another directory, also in the library with luck, called *BRAD* (*British Rate and Data*). This bible of the advertising industry lists all the publications, together with their price, advertisement rates, address. Send for those which interest you because they will give you an up-to-date and more intimate idea of your career – and more importantly

226

perhaps, there will be mention of those luminaries dominating it. It's always worth knowing a few names

Talk to those with experience

Most people who have risen in their job are quite happy to talk about it with someone toying with the idea of following in their footsteps, providing you ask politely, don't take up too much of their time, and write expressing thanks afterwards.

This is an invaluable way of gaining a first-hand insight into your chosen career, and perhaps if you're lucky, even a contact. But, if not, and you have by now decided that that is the career for you, cast around in your own circle. Look carefully through your address book – do you know someone who knows someone who is working in this field? It is amazing how fruitful this can be. Most journalists have a bulging address book, battered through long and frequent use, but it is a good idea for anyone to keep a contact book of friends and acquaintances – you will find it surprisingly useful.

However, if even after an assiduous dredging of friends and acquaintances, you draw a blank, this is the moment when you should start sending off applications and CVs to the companies mentioned in the trade and professional papers you looked at earlier.

Getting the job you want is 90 per cent effort and 10 per cent luck, and once you have a toe-hold you can convert it to a firm rung, and with enthusiasm, added skills and hard work see that ladder turn into an escalator.

How Do You Sell Yourself?

But, how do you get started in the first place?

Your curriculum vitae

The key lies first in your CV which should be good enough to get you an interview, and then in the interview itself. Both mean preparation. This is your future we're talking about and if you care enough about it you have to make sure that the faceless recipients of your first letter are flattered by what you know about the company – and them – and their interest is sufficiently aroused to see you.

Try to picture a personnel manager on the receiving end of perhaps 200 job applications on a Monday morning. You've got to help yourself by making sure you give every reason for your CV finding a place in the 'yes' pile. Remember, a carefully thought-out CV is a selling tool. A good one shows, it doesn't show-off. It mustn't inflate and make you sound as if you think the company's Chief Executive will be redundant once you join, but it has to show you at your best.

It doesn't matter if you don't have a string of qualifications, unless perhaps you're applying for a job where you would need them. But you can say how you organized a department, increased sales, introduced new techniques, produced savings, widened development, Think back over your career path and jot down the positive things you have done in each job. Start with your current job, and work back to school, not the other way around particularly as you get older. Working as a Saturday girl in Marks & Spencer shows you have initiative and know something about retailing but it can't be elevated into a major skill. Include volunteer work. If you can run a local group, have had to greet speakers, give votes of thanks, organize a programme, raise funds they are all qualities a big company would use at some time or other, so don't fail to mention them.

It is also a good idea to relate your CV to the company to wish to work for – it shows you've done your homework on them and are paying them the compliment of preparing a CV tailored to *their* needs and not an old one photocopied.

DOs and DON'Ts of a presenting good CV

DOs

Do keep your CV to one page, never more than two.

Do research the company before writing your CV, tailoring it to its needs and your qualifications.

DON'Ts

Don't include salary history unless asked. If you must, use a salary band, eg £9,500–£12,500.

Don't include age. School dates will show your approximate age. At most, date of birth only.

Do include a cover letter – a CV's complement – explaining why you want that particular job.

Do type or word process it fresh each time you send your CV out.

Do proofread your CV at least twice, so that grammar, punctuation and spelling are perfect.

Do list hobbies under the 'interests' category. Team sports, for example, are always a failsafe, as is chess (great for finance, but if you're in publishing, try Scrabble!).

Do give a contact phone number.

Do bring spare copies of your CV along to the interview, and hold it on your lap to refer to.

Do make sure every page of your CV and cover letter has your name and phone number on it.

Don't get carried away by creativity. Stick to ivory or white bond paper.

Don't make claims you can't back up, but do be positive and assertive about claims of which you are confident.

Don't include the number of children you have, if any.

Don't include referees unless you've asked their permission and unless they are relevant to the prospective job. You may want to wait, saying in your cover letter, 'Referees supplied at your request.'

Don't use long paragraphs or a letterwriting style. Break up thoughts, highlight, use UPPER CASE or lower case, <u>underlining</u> or **bold face** to help items stand out.

The interview

Your CV has achieved its object – you are called for an interview. The task now is to convert the interview into a job offer, and when you're nervous and have really set your heart on the job, that can seem an insurmountable object. Take heart, most interviewers make allowances for nerves but you have to make the adrenalin work *for* you, as actors do before going on stage. Nearly all the best admit to butterflies in the stomach, but they use this tension to heighten their performance, and you have to do the same.

Dorothy Sarnoff, who teaches self-presentation skills to top people the world over has worked out a way to help control the nerves – it's a simple matter of contracting, hard, the triangle of muscles at the base of the rib cage. This relaxes the throat muscles so that the voice doesn't squeak, and puts you back in the driver's seat. Try it before entering the room and meeting your interviewer.

Sit with a straight back, legs uncrossed, feet in front of you with weight forward on the toes. This gives you an alert, interested look, shows you're part of the interview and not a disinterested onlooker. Don't smoke, however much you're dying for a cigarette; wear appropriate clothes to show you understand the company's function. A business suit is not going to impress a design partnership whereas the wilder shores of fashion will terrify a bank or insurance company with its stiff adherence to tradition. Wear something clean, well-pressed, in which you feel comfortable, that suits the company style without making you feel you're cut out of cardboard.

Try to prepare, say, ten topics for discussion before an interview some of which are bound to come up. It's a little bit like swotting for exams. There are always a few wobblies, but that's when you show you can think on your feet. They're bound to ask you why you want the job, and if you haven't a good answer you simply haven't done your homework properly. You are also likely to be asked where you see yourself in three years' time – you need to show that the job fits in, in terms of development, with what you've been doing in the past three to five years. It should seem a reasonable, logical step so that the interviewers feel secure about you.

You should also do your homework on the company itself. Don't be wrong-footed. If the company has been in the news, perhaps because it has a new chairman, you should know about it. You should know about their successes and refer to them. If you don't do these things you're not worth an interview.

You should also do work on the company's competitors. Almost always you will be asked 'Do you have any questions?' which is the cue to say something like 'How do you plan to combat the strong competition from Company X with its new

230

keenly priced product?' Never go into an interview and expect to freewheel. If you do you're lucky if you get anywhere. If you were a ship and hadn't plotted a course, every wind would blow you in a different direction.

An interview is largely to see that the chemistry is right between the organization and the person. Companies aren't interested in what a lovely person you are, or if you're fond of animals and kind to old ladies. They want to know what you can achieve for them, if they employ you. And that's precisely what you have to put across.

Interview checklist

PRE-INTERVIEW PLANNING
Memorize all the information on your CV and letters of application, so that you present a consistent picture of yourself. Get as much information as possible about the job you are applying for. Cut out and keep the job advertisement for future reference. Ask for a job description in advance – if such a thing exists – so that you have time to study it.

THE APPLICATION FORM/CV
Have a copy of your CV/application form with you at the interview, and make sure that you have prepared answers to cover any of the weaker areas in a positive way.

THE COMPANY
Before the interview read all the company's published literature (ie, annual report, chairman's statement, product information, etc). At a second interview you can expand your background reading further to take in the company's current standing and future prospects. Newspapers or the business section at a local library can often help here.

THE SETTING
Arrive early to gather your thoughts and relax. Check the location and available transport to ensure you have enough time to get there. Be courteous to the receptionist and any secretaries who take you to the interview room. Your behaviour then adds to the total impression you create. Remember that you are never off-stage while on the com-

pany's premises: people could 'feed back' your behaviour to the interviewer.

ANSWER TECHNIQUE

Prepare adequate answers to the questions you are guaranteed to be asked. Try to remember to ask yourself whether you are selling or buying. People often make the mistake of trying to sell themselves at interviews without finding out what it is the interviewer wants to buy.

Be relevant and concise

If asked to 'tell me about yourself', provide a short list of points which will give the interviewer the opportunity to select interesting areas. It often helps to ask, 'Would you like me to enlarge on any of these areas?'

Be a winner

Emphasize successes and achievements in private and working life.

Be friendly

Convey personal details in a warm and friendly way.

Be lively

Try to make word 'pictures' of your life and career. It is easier for the interviewer to remember and more interesting to listen to. If you are not a natural raconteur, practise in front of a friend or a mirror, in advance.

Be positive

Try to make weakness seem like a strength! Give positive reasons for changing jobs. Avoid at all costs criticizing either your present or past employers.

Be enthusiastic

You'll find it's contagious.

Don't interrupt

Interviewers don't like it.

Don't try to fill the silences

This is the interviewer's job.

Don't make jokes

Keep your sense of humour under control and take your cue from the interviewer.

Don't be modest

But *don't* create a picture of yourself you can't substantiate.

Don't be thrown off balance

Don't fret over a wrong answer. Remember, it is the overall impression that will count.

Don't rush your answers
Think carefully before replying.
Don't smoke or lounge
Sit comfortably and you'll both look and feel right. Lean forwards every now and again, to show interest and keenness.
Don't be uptight
Answer any personal questions as courteously as possible. If asked questions about your young children, briefly describe your child-care arrangements. Always reply in a way that enhances your professionalism. If you let your hackles rise, you have blown it.
Handshakes
Women interviewees often get hung up on handshakes. Take your cue from the interviewer. Don't be either too limp-wristed or too hearty.
Don't fidget
Make sure you are looking at the interviewer, as the amount of eye contact is related to how much people like each other. Interviews have a lot to do with chemistry, so let your interviewer know that you are feeling favourably impressed by what you see.
Dress
A new outfit may give your self-confidence that much-needed boost – but only if you feel comfortable in it.
Look professional
Don't overdo the make-up or wear anything too fussy. Dress smartly but naturally.
First impressions
'You never get a second opportunity to make a first impression' – training slogan for American salesmen, and worth remembering by interviewees.
Take your time
Give yourself plenty of time to answer the questions or you'll kick yourself afterwards. Learn not to rush in with the first thought that comes into your head. Neither of you is in a hurry!
Be receptive
Try to forget about what you are going to say next and listen to what the interviewer is asking. Listen for cues; put up signals. 'Interviewees should think of spending 25 per cent of the time presenting themselves and 75 per cent of the time getting the right signals.'

Relax

Practise deep breathing – a well-tried Yoga technique – in the ladies' loo for a few moments before the interview.

The Trail Blazers

In the Introduction to this book we pointed out how essential it is for women, in order to believe in themselves, to see how others have achieved success. Such trail blazers are not daunted by difficulties, and most will have had problems to contend with although they may talk of them with a blithe indifference. They are all women who fix their sights on their goal and jump in the deep end. They don't see difficulties in advance. Or if they do, they dismiss them as something to be solved on the way to their goal. You never hear them saying 'what if . . .' or 'supposing that. . .'. It doesn't mean that they are ignoring possible problems, just that they regard them as trifles compared with what they want to do.

Most of us still have a short focus. A job until we get married, or until the children come along, and we think no further. In actual fact, the family with husband as bread-winner, stay-at-home-wife caring for two small children is actually our minority group – 5 per cent of the population. If we have to work, then it makes sense that we do something we enjoy, something that gives us a sense of achievement and something that is hopefully well paid.

Here are the stories of three women who have pursued success, and found it, in three vastly different areas.

Believe *anything* is possible

Caroline Marland is the Advertisement Director of the Guardian newspaper, the only woman in Fleet Street to hold such a post and a tough job even for a man in the competitive world of national newspapers. But she thrives on the challenge and the daily excitement. 'It's the best job in the world – like being let loose in a sweet shop.'

She did, in fact, start with a distinct advantage. She was the daughter of a working mother who told her twelve-year-old daughter to 'throw her hat over a windmill'. Caroline was brought up to believe that women, even mothers, *worked.*

As a child, she had a terrible lisp. It was so bad that people couldn't understand a word she said so her indomitable mother sent her off to Aida Foster's stage school. 'It was marvellous. I was there with all sorts of wonderful people – little stage moppets who dyed their hair blonde at 11, Marti Webb, and Dennis Waterman.'

All the voice and drama lessons did the trick, and she lost her lisp. She also increased in height and at 15 was 5 feet 9½ inches tall. She soon realized a stage career wasn't for her, so she left the school. Stage schools aren't renowned for their academic progress, and Caroline had to find a job where no one insisted on 'O' levels or 'A' levels. Crisply assessing her advantages, she ticked her height and her stage training as qualities needed in a model, and took herself off to the House of Lachasse. Shrewdly keeping her ambition to herself, she took the offer of a job as a tea girl and switchboard operator. Even then, she had her eye on a goal but was prepared to start small.

'I used to bring Lachasse his tea walking in backwards, or sideways or swooping over the carpet – anything as long as he noticed me.' Poor chap, he could hardly not, and before very long, the 15-year-old Caroline was appointed house model, with a wage increased to £5 a week. 'Actually it was soon £5 10s because he couldn't stand my laddered stockings, so I was given 10s a week stocking allowance.' Determination and motivation were showing up, as was making the most of an opportunity.

After 2½ years, much improved in style, Caroline thought if she was really to make it as a model, then she would have to go to Paris, the model girl's mecca. 'I was given a huge leaving party and sent off with good wishes ringing in my ears. I felt I was made.' But Dorian Leigh didn't agree. Heading the largest and most powerful model agency in Paris, she looked Caroline up and down and told her to go home. 'You're useless,' she said with a steely frankness. But Caroline couldn't go home – not after such a leaving party. Instead, she lifted her chin and knocked on other doors, including Dior. 'I supported myself for over 9 months despite Dorian Leigh,' said Caroline 'But she was right. I wasn't going to be a top model and I didn't want to be anything less.'

By this time, Britain was swinging with the sixties, Caroline's parents had moved to Yorkshire, it was a great time to be young, and Caroline did what every other teenager seemed to be doing – she opened a boutique in a disused coal depot. 'The best publicity we had was the local headmistress banning her sixth-form girls from visiting us because our miniskirts were so short she regarded us as decadent.' Business boomed, but Caroline confessed to being a rotten entrepreneur. 'I spent all the takings.'

Fortunately, Caroline's mother was a successful PR and before the boutique collapsed, Caroline went to work for her. 'It was terrible. Every time I made a mistake she'd say things like "I did that when I was six".'

Depressed, rather crestfallen, wondering where her future lay, Caroline scoured the *Yorkshire Post* for a job, and found one advertised that sounded interesting – with the *Yorkshire Post* as a telephone saleswoman. 'I didn't really know what telesales were but answering that ad was the luckiest thing I ever did. When you're selling over the telephone, you can become anything. I had lecherous motor traders believing

I was a 5ft 2in fluffy blonde, and increasing their advertising just to chat me up. Their training is superb. They believe *anything* is possible. They taught me so much, including self-discipline.'

As with anyone who enjoys a job, progress is more or less inevitable, and after three years, Caroline had made it to senior trainer.

Successful women are always planning the next step, thinking out where their career will lead, what is needed in the way of additional skills to get there, and Caroline was no exception. 'I thought at that point that if I was going to get anywhere, I would have to work on a big national – and that meant London.' So lining up three interviews, she made a day trip to London, was offered all three jobs and chose the one with *The Times*. It was a step backwards in prestige – she would have to be a junior trainer again – but she was where she wanted to be, on the most prestigious national paper.

Once more sheer slog, enthusiasm, and initiative paid off and she reached the position of Principal Trainer but, on the way, had realized that *The Times* was still stifled by chauvinism. They simply did not appoint women managers, and Caroline had her sights on a managerial role. 'They kept giving me more money, but it was the responsibility I wanted.' Like any company who can't satisfy the needs of bright people, they lose them, and Caroline left to join the *Guardian*.

'It was just brilliant. They had only three telephone sales people, including one little old lady who sat scribbling orders on bits of paper. I was only there one day and I realized it was going to explode.' Anticipating the demand, realizing the potential, Caroline rang one of her ex-colleagues and suggested she'd better come and join her. Together they organized systems, hired and trained staff, and made the *Guardian* classified advertisement pages begin to hum.

The *Guardian* management were not slow to spot a high-flyer, and in 1978 they sent her to Los Angeles to get some trans-atlantic experience. 'That's when I really learned about selling and incentives. It was very stimulating though I loathed Los Angeles.'

After that, nothing could stop her. Group Sales Director in 1980. Deputy Advertisement Director in 1981 and Advertisement Director in 1983. Still her sales are booming. She has developed the classified pages so that their recruitment advertising is second to none and she also directs the selling of all the display advertising.

'It's a terrific paper to work for – they really believe in promoting women. It was the first newspaper to have a female News Editor so I knew I had a good chance of getting on.'

But she also believes in helping and encouraging other women. Her department has more women than men, and now she heads a staff of 145, 85 per cent of whom she's hired herself. High-calibre people encouraged with incentives and good training to develop must succeed. Caroline richly deserves her substantial salary.

Has her private life suffered as a result? 'I think if you can run a job you can run a home,' Caroline replied with the same airy confidence. 'But you mustn't expect everything to be perfect.' She's married to a busy MP, has stepchildren and a young son to look after, and commutes at weekends to their Yorkshire farm. 'When I had my first substantial salary increase I used all of it to have some help on the farm. She's marvellous and I work with her running the house as I would work with my deputy running the department at work. She packs me lots of food on Sunday so we have something to eat during the week, and in town I have a lovely woman who has been with me for ages and every time I move, she just gets on her bike and cycles to the new address.'

Caroline snaps, crackles and pops like a breakfast cereal, and you wonder whether she has another horizon in view or has found her permanent niche. She laughs non-committally. 'I don't know. I can't imagine doing anything better than what I'm doing now.'

Use your eyes and ears, learn as you go along

Jeanette Borlase was all set for a career in law, with a place at Nottingham University and a respectable set of 'A' levels. Fed up with the hard slog to get them, she decided she deserved a year off before starting a new stint of study. She headed for the East Coast of America and the outer islands in the Bahamas. The glorious weather, the lazy days swimming and living off the fresh-caught fish, the sheer hedonistic pleasure of it all meant that when the time came to return to England, law had lost its charms.

'Instead, I took a course at Plymouth Polytechnic in child psychology.' Quite why she doesn't know now except that it seemed like a good idea at the time. 'But I still had my itchy feet and I couldn't contemplate staying in one place for long.' With a little persistence, she got a job as an air stewardess with British Midland Airways – only to find that a week later they were privatized and were restricted to a West Country run. Having been born in Cornwall, a daily commute by air to the west was hardly her idea of travel although, as usual, it was a lot of fun.

Fun is a word that figures in most successful women's vocabulary and perhaps it is another common denominator – they wade into everything on offer with zest and enthusiasm and get a reciprocal feedback. But despite the enjoyment, Jeanette was beginning to feel she needed to be more positive about her future. 'Like Dick Whittington, I came to London,' she grinned.

Like Caroline Marland, she wasn't sure what she was looking for so she kept an open mind and combed the papers. 'I think it was the heading "Highly paid executive required" that attracted me,' she said, believing if you're going to start anywhere it might as well be highly paid as not. 'I had an interview straight away. In fact, I was offered the job at the interview, accepted it there and then, hung up my coat in the office and waded right in.' Seizing an opportunity, giving it a go, being ready to work hard are more hallmarks of the women aiming for the top.

The work was arranging mortgages for people at the best rates, working out pension plans and investment portfolios. How did she know anything about that? 'Well, of course, they gave me some training but it's more a question of caring about your clients, being painstaking about your facts, keeping eyes and ears open, and organizing yourself so that you can put your hands on the relevant figures and work out suitable schemes.' The work obviously suited Jeanette because before very long her profits were high enough to be offered a branch of her own. Again, she started to exceed targets. 'I'm accused of being a workaholic but if you enjoy what you're doing it doesn't feel like work,' Jeanette said. In fact, her working day is quite reasonable. She starts about 9 a.m. and works through lunch because it's then she sees her own clients, and she aims to leave about 5.45 p.m. to catch her train home.

With profits still going through the ceiling, she decided to open another branch, and a bit later, yet another. The branches meant finding premises, arranging the terms of the leases, organizing the decor and recruiting and training staff. 'You learn on the job if you're keen,' she said. 'Obviously we need solicitors for the leases but the initial checks and terms are my responsibility; it isn't mysterious, just painstaking.'

She now has 60 people working for her, which means that apart from their initial training, she has to keep them motivated and committed. Her salary cheque is big enough to make the Lord Chancellor's recent and controversial salary increase look puny, but because she is a financial adviser to other people, she looks after her money herself. She's bought a couple of houses that she rents out, she's bought shares in her company, and she ploughs money back into the business so that it can go on expanding. She doesn't feel she's reached her ceiling yet.

'I've promised myself a housekeeper to make running the home easier, but it isn't too difficult. I do all the shopping on late-night openings, and I make sure the fridge and freezer are both well-stocked. Fortunately, the children are at the stage when they like baked beans on toast, and my partner and I are quite content to forgo an evening meal. We'll just have some prawns and a glass of wine perhaps, with some cheese and biscuits. But I cook at weekends.'

The children belong to her partner as she doesn't feel quite ready for her own, although she obviously enjoys family life. 'Perhaps a little later, I don't know. We're all right as we are for the moment.' Keeping a large dog means that whether she likes it or not Jeanette has to get up and run with it. 'I do that early, for about an hour and that zips me up for the day. At weekends I swim a lot and play tennis. When you work hard in an office you need to let off steam in some outdoor sport – I get rid of my bottled up energy thwacking a tennis ball.'

Jeanette believes she was a late developer, but if she was, she has made up for lost time. 'I'm a strong believer that life is not just a rehearsal,' she says firmly. 'You should do all the things you want to do, break out and ignore all the doubts and go for it.'

240

You can never say no

Vivienne Flower and Jenny Leader are the joint Managing Directors of Katie's Kitchen, which if you're not lucky enough to have an enlightened supermarket near you, is a food manufacturing business specializing in chilled pizzas and ready-made meals. It has a turnover of over £3 million and the pizzas and packed convenience foods stream out from a brand-new purpose-built factory at Harrow, heading for Sainsbury's and Safeway, Tesco and Waitrose and all stops in between.

It all started in the kitchen of a suburban semi with two bored young mothers who felt there was more to life than looking after the children and the endless round of cooking and washing-up. 'Besides, we thought earning our own cash would be nice,' said Jenny. 'In fact, I needed to earn.' They had been friends since schooldays, married and temporarily lost touch with each other, but then Jenny moved to the same area as Vivienne and the friendship was resumed. 'We felt we wanted to do something that would fit in with looking after the children. I'd tried things like Tupperware parties, but it wasn't my scene. We'd both taken a course in sociology at our local polytechnic, but we were bored and wanted to earn some money.'

Like any business person they assessed what they had going for them. Both were good cooks. They'd taken the six-week 'housewives' Cordon Bleu course and Vivienne had done a catering course after leaving school, and both were on the dinner party circuit. 'At first we thought we'd cook for dinner parties, but then we realized we'd end up selling to friends, and then if they didn't like the food they'd be afraid to tell us and it would all be ghastly.' So instead, they put their cooking skills to work baking delicious quiches and taking them to the local delicatessen where they found a ready sale – but it was hardly swelling the housekeeping. 'We decided to venture into our local department store with a good food section and asked to see the manager. To our delight, he ordered four dozen quiches right away. We were so excited that when we'd delivered them we gave ourselves a day out as a reward. When we got back about 5 p.m., the phone had been ringing all day with the poor manager trying to place his next day's orders.

We hadn't as much as an onion in the place – the four dozen quiches had cleaned us out.'

That was their first lesson. If you produce a good product you have repeat business. And the second one was, if you're serious about business, you can't say no.

They didn't. They rushed out to the shops just as they were closing and stocked up. They pressganged their children into opening tins of tomatoes. Jenny's husband was put to work on 56 lbs of potatoes, and all the neighbours were telephoned for spare oven space since their own stove couldn't cope. Of course, it wasn't just a one-day crisis. There were more orders the next day and the next, so it was clear good neighbours weren't going to remain friendly for long if they couldn't get to their own oven for Vivienne and Jenny's quiches.

Slipping out in turns from the kitchen, they scoured the neighbourhood for suitable premises to rent and luckily found an old bakery, complete with hygienic tiled walls and floors. 'Thank goodness we didn't know about food regulations then,' said Vivienne 'We might not have started.' But they did, borrowing a £100 from the bank to buy a second-hand catering oven, and again all hands set about redecorating and renovating the bakery, and installing the oven. With 800 square feet, and a proper oven, they felt really in business, and took on another partner to help. They did their own deliveries, as well as the shopping and they started to develop what Vivienne says she supposed was telesales. 'We'd ring up the customers and take orders over the phone, so that we only made to order and didn't waste food. But when we delivered we would also take samples of other lines, so we were adding to our range – cheesecakes, chocolate cake, apple pies.'

The local department store manager was very helpful. 'He said we'd never get anywhere without a catchy name, so we came up with "Katie's Kitchen". I suspect people think we're little old ladies with gingham aprons and rosy cheeks,' Jenny laughed.

In addition to developing the business, they were also improving their presentation. 'We couldn't afford proper packaging equipment, but we had a hot plate and a fan heater. We used to seal cling-film over the products on the hotplate and shrink it with the fan heater. We were always improvising. In fact, I think women are very good at improvisation on the whole.'

Pizzas were just about to become popular – like quiches the quick solution to a tasty snack, snapped up by busy working women and mothers fed up with constantly cooking for the ever open beaks of their young. 'We moved into pizzas,' said Vivienne. 'We could do pizzas much more cheaply than quiches and produce them faster.' In fact the demand became so great that they had to drop their other lines in order to concentrate on pizza production. 'What we never dropped was our quality,' said Jenny. 'We always kept the value and quality high.'

Everything was ticking over very nicely, when they had their first order from a multiple supermarket chain – Waitrose. And that was big stuff. Waitrose too were helpful to the young women entrepreneurs with limited resources. 'We couldn't have delivered to all their branches so they would accept one big batch at their central depot, and despatch the individual orders to the branches themselves. That was very helpful. They came to inspect our premises too, and suggested we all wore hairnets and overalls. By that time we had not only taken on more workers, but we were working an evening shift. It was very hard work physically.' With Waitrose, their daily orders rose hugely and it was soon obvious that even the old bakery was too small. They found more premises and baked in the bakery and put the cheeses and sauces on in the new factory. 'People were beginning to come to us; they liked our quality and the fact everything was fresh and well cooked.'

Another prerequisite for success – if you're interested in repeat sales, keep the quality high.

Once more demand outstripped production resources, and that meant another move. This time they took on 10,000 sq ft in Wembley, with another 5,000 available if they wanted it. They did. They started their own-label business. 'You grow with every stage,' said Vivienne, as if all self-employed business people are as willing to listen to advice as they were. 'You can always learn if you're ready to listen. If you don't accept advice, you don't grow.'

With all that square footage, and no sign of orders diminishing, the next step was to mechanize production. How did two housewives know about advanced machinery? 'You ask people. And you visit exhibitions. We decided to buy a particular conveyor system and just as we'd paid cash, the supplier went bust. It was a terrible blow as the receiver impounded the machine. We had to scream at him every day until he released it.'

With a machine to cut production time, they could afford to go into other lines again and chose garlic bread. Surely it was so easy to make garlic bread that there wasn't a demand for that? Wrong, it sold out as quickly as it went into the shops. 'Working women have created the demand for such things. They have gourmet tastes but haven't time to do all the trimmings – why, when you're doing a job all day should you go home and cook all evening? Once they get over the guilt – and no one's died of malnutrition eating ready-prepared meals – they soon get used to picking up their dinner party food on the way home from work.' Vivienne was realistic.

She herself, though fully-stretched during the day, has very little help in the house. She slips the shopping for the family into her daily journey to work and has a daily twice a week. The hardest part, she finds, is to go home after a hard day and get ready to go up to town and a theatre. 'It seems such a fag that we don't do it much. Instead, we have friends round or go to dinner with them. It's essential to make your home an important focus when you work hard.'

The next and final stage, of course, was their own shining new factory, built from scratch and to their own specifications. Food regulations are such that Vivienne doubts whether many people could start the way they did 14 years ago. 'But I expect they can – if they're determined enough and perhaps, like us in some respects, blithely ignorant.'

What has the cost been in personal terms. Their third partner had to give up because her husband began to resent her increasing involvement and Jenny is now divorced. 'I worked in the first instance because we needed the money, and then I worked because I needed the stimulus and variety. I think, perhaps, if my husband had been more successful himself he could have coped and would not have minded my success. Sometimes I worry a bit about the children. I asked my daughter the other day – she's now 24 – if, having seen how hard I worked and the break-up of our marriage, whether she didn't feel she'd rather be a housewife herself? Not a bit. 'No mum,' she said. 'I want to be just like you.'

Vivienne's husband is an easy-going man and hasn't resented her success. 'But it is as well to recognize that a job can cause problems,' warns Vivienne. 'If you're stimulated by your job, you don't need a husband quite as much – and that makes it difficult for them. Both my husband and I were brought up to believe the man is the breadwinner, so it is difficult to adjust to a different viewpoint. It changes the balance of a relationship and you have to make adjustments. I'm sure it will be easier for our children's generation.'

Neither woman regrets that first commercial quiche and the path it led them along. 'It's funny, we probably are professional now,' said Vivienne 'But we don't think of ourselves as professionals. I think we took a long time to get to this point – a man would probably have done it more quickly if he had been able to concentrate on it full-time, but we had to cope with our children and homes as well. On the other hand, we didn't waste money on secretaries and frills because we didn't worry about prestige as perhaps a man would. We really worked on line.'

Index